BACKSTAGE PASS

DECADES OF SEX, DRUGS, TRAGEDY
AND THE DARKER SIDE OF ROCK & ROLL

BACKSTAGE PASS

DECADES OF SEX, DRUGS, TRAGEDY
AND THE DARKER SIDE OF ROCK & ROLL

A Backstage Memoir

JD DECOSTA

STONEHOUSE
PRESS U.K.

Book cover and photo art © 2025 by Jack Brando Media LLC
Jacket design © 2025 by Stonehouse Press UK
Foreword © 2025 Kevin Estrada

STONEHOUSE
PRESS U.K.

For inquires/permissions: contact@stonehousepress.uk

First edition, 2025

Published by Stonehouse Press UK

Library of Congress Cataloging-in-Publication Data
DeCosta, JD (Musician, author)

Backstage Pass: Decades of Sex, Drugs, Tragedy, and the Darker Side of Rock & Roll : a memoir / JD DeCosta.
Description: First edition. | Stonehouse Press U.K., 2025. | Memoir / Personal narrative.

Identifiers: ISBNs: eBook **979-8-9932316-0-0** · Paperback (Amazon) **979-8-9932316-6-2** · Paperback (Ingram) **979-8-9932316-1-7** · Hardcover (Amazon) **979-8-9932316-5-5** · Hardcover (Ingram) **979-8-9932316-3-1** · (audiobook) **979-8-9932316-2-4** · (special signed edition) **979-8-9932316-4-8**

Subjects: LCSH: DeCosta, JD—Anecdotes. | Rock music—United States—Anecdotes. | Music trade—United States—Personal narratives. | United States—Social life and customs—20th century—Personal narratives. | Sunset Strip (Los Angeles, Calif.)—Social life and customs. | Hollywood (Los Angeles, Calif.)—Music.
LCGFT: Personal narratives. | Memoirs.
Classification: ML419.D46 A3 2025 (print) | DDC 787.87/166092 [B]—dc23
LC record available at https://lccn.loc.gov/2025920875

Printed in the United States of America
10 9 8 7 6 5 4 3 2 1

DISCLAIMER:

This memoir is a work of nonfiction. It reflects the author's personal experiences from 1996 to
2011 at the Roxy Theatre, Whisky a Go Go, and other venues, along with earlier insights from 1989
onward in the music industry through his roles as a production, stage, hospitality, and general
manager, and as a signed major-label artist and musician.

The events and conversations described are based on the author's recollections to the best of
his memory. Some details—including dates, timelines, and dialogue—have been reconstructed,
condensed, or paraphrased for clarity and narrative flow. While every effort has been made to
ensure accuracy, others may remember the same events differently.

This book represents the author's perspective and truth. It is not intended to defame, malign, or
harm the reputation of any person, living or deceased, or any organization or entity. Any errors
or omissions are unintentional.

Neither the author nor the publisher shall be liable for any loss, injury, or damages—commercial,
personal, incidental, consequential, or otherwise—that may result from the use of or reliance
upon the information contained herein.

To every band and artist who bled for the
holy grail of music and came up short.

To the bandmates, friends, and crew
who didn't make it out alive.

To the Lost Picassos—burning bright
in the dark where nobody gave a damn.

And to the patron saints of mediocrity,
grinding it out with broken dreams and
false hope still rattling in their bones.

I absolve you.

This book is dedicated to you…

Not every hand was fashioned for the lyre, nor every spirit summoned to greatness. Some pursue the chalice and taste only silence, yet even in defeat the burden loosens, and what is relinquished becomes its own form of peace.

—JD DeCosta

TABLE OF CONTENTS

Welcome to the Jungle...

WARNING: Not for kids. Rated "R" for reality—adult themes, filthy language, and stories that rip the curtain back on some nights too wild to make up. Enter at your own risk. Don't say I didn't warn ya.

Shhhhh...We just snuck in backstage at the world-famous Roxy

"Hey there, honey, I absolutely love your band." I felt her hand guide mine up toward her huge boobs...

That was the first time I met Anna Nicole Smith. Yes, the world-famous—or maybe I should say infamous—model. Backstage at the Roxy, right as I was coming off stage, caught in that strange no-man's-land between reality and whatever Hollywood was pretending to be. She was totally out of her mind that night, and maybe that was exactly why she pulled me into her sexual orbit.

And yeah, that's how this whole memoir kicks off.

But this isn't just her story. It's mine. Theirs. Maybe even a little of yours.

This book is a trip through decades in music's trenches. The dark corners where stars weren't just seen, they were known. Before and after the fame, in the middle of the chaos, and sometimes in the quiet moments right before future tragic endings. Artists who passed on—Chris Cornell, Amy Winehouse, Scott Weiland, Chester Bennington, and many others—are here in these pages, not as distant icons, but as flesh-and-blood people I crossed paths with, people I sometimes caught brief glimpses of destiny in. Raw. Fragile. Human.

It's also an unfiltered backstage pass into the reality of live music. The grit. The breakdowns. The wild highs and the nights that bent into dark comedy. The moments when the dream felt alive—too alive—and the crashes when it all collapsed. These are stories pulled from the shit I saw up close, but they're tied to something bigger: the chase for meaning, the survival through failure, the clawing for purpose when the ride doesn't end the way you thought it would. Maybe some of that feels like your story. Maybe it's a glimpse of your future. Only you know. Time will tell.

And yeah, it's about me too. You probably don't know my name, and maybe you don't care about the story of someone almost-famous. But trust me—things got pretty damn wild when I was juggling life behind the scenes while still chasing my own shot at the musical Holy Grail… and maybe even the Holy Grail of life itself.

ok! enough with all the intro crap. LFG!

Foreword

By Kevin Estrada

Nirvana — Roxy Theatre, 1991.
Photo by Kevin Estrada

It was in the early days when JD was playing the stages, often hot, sweaty, and chaotic, with his band **Mind Heavy Mustard**. I was a music photographer at the time, chasing moments and capturing the energy of the scene. I'd been shooting music for years by then—**Nirvana, Soundgarden, Jane's Addiction**—and just about every band that tore through Los Angeles in those days. We connected immediately, like long-lost brothers bound together by the music. Even then, I saw something in him that went beyond raw talent. There was vision, and that vision would go on to define so much of his journey.

I would go on to work in **A&R** for various record labels. That's where I got a front-row seat to the real magic behind his artistry. While many musicians are content just to play, he was different. He didn't just perform; he felt it, lived it, and shaped the soul of the music itself. Shortly after that, I tried—unsuccessfully—to sign his next band, **Hot Sauce Johnson**. Then, in 2002, I secured a record deal at **Roadrunner Records** for his next project, **Rumblefish**. It became clear there was far more to him than what you hear in the music and see on stage.

As **General Manager of The Roxy Theatre**, one of the most iconic venues on the **Sunset Strip**, he wasn't just managing a space—he was shaping moments. He knew how to think outside the box, to navigate the chaos when money couldn't fix the problem. The Roxy wasn't just a stage; it was a *living, breathing place* where artists found their roots again. For him, it became the place where he helped legends rediscover their freedom. The stories from that time, both onstage and behind the scenes, are a testament to the gritty, unseen work that keeps the wheels of the music industry turning.

He's seen the real side of some of the biggest names in music—the moments, the struggles, and the triumphs that go far beyond the glossy press releases. He knows what it's like to be in the trenches, to fight for a dream, and to help others do the same. The stories he tells are raw, brutal, and honest—there are *no sugarcoated truths here*. The names aren't changed to protect the innocent or the guilty. These are real stories of real people, and he's lived them.

What makes him truly special is the way he connects with people. Music saved his life, and in turn, he's saved others through that same power. That's something you don't often see in this business—a pure soul with both talent and heart. He isn't just a musician; he's a true musical being, and that's rare in a world that often demands conformity. A great soul who's always made room for others, no matter where life took him.

One **September night in 2008**, he took on an extra duty: smuggling a photographer and his camera through The Roxy's legendary load-in doors. It was one of the hottest, sold-out shows in Los Angeles, and that photographer was me. That night, I captured some iconic images of **Cheech and Chong's** first performance together in twenty-five years. It was more than a backstage pass—it was a moment of pure magic, and he was the one making it all happen.

Over the years, our friendship has been built on a shared love of music, respect for the hustle, and a genuine sense of camaraderie. Whether it was helping me secure the upstairs **On The Rox** for my wife's surprise birthday party, or just being the steady hand behind the scenes in an often chaotic industry, he's always been the guy you could count on.

In the world of music, where one record deal can feel like a miracle, he's done it more than once. But even more than the deals or the stage time, it's his heart and vision that set him apart. He's the *real deal*—a man who's lived a life most can only dream of—and now, he's sharing it all with you.

So buckle up and grab your drink tickets. The stories ahead will take you on a ride through the highs and lows, the magic and the madness of the music business.

This is his truth—*raw, unfiltered, and unapologetically real.*

Kevin Estrada
Photographer
@KevinEstradaPhotography

Wasn't Born to Follow...

ATTENTION!

I'll be straight with you: I personally don't like the "About Me" section. It feels like the acoustic set nobody asked for before the headliner comes on. You didn't pick up this book to hear about my childhood drama or the minor leagues of my almost-fame—though maybe you did. I'm guessing you came for the chaos. The stars. The meltdowns. The nights that went sideways. Maybe you also came for the philosophy—the bruised, unpolished truth of who famous artists sometimes really are, or who they turned out to be, especially when the lights cut out and it was just us in the backstage. Don't worry—you'll get all of it.

But my agent and a couple of author friends insisted I scribble this part down. They said people want to know *why the hell they should trust me to tell these stories.* So here it is, the necessary evil. Consider it your backstage pass to the guy who survived it and wrote it all down.

But let's be real—if you're like me and you just want to get to the wild shit? Skip this. Seriously. Go straight to Chapter 2. That's where Mike Tyson shows up at a Snoop Dogg show and things get... well, let's just say interesting. Read a few chapters, soak it in, and if it hooks you, circle back here later to figure out how the heck I ended up in the middle of all this madness.

Follow me down these steps into the musical world of legends...

Still here? Alright. Let's rewind.

I want to explain how, and why, I got seduced by the beast that is the music world—and how it kept me tangled in its grip for nearly two and a half decades. These pages became more than stories; they became therapy. My way of wrestling with the endless questions about existence, about purpose, about how the chaos of the music business stitched itself into the fabric of who so many of us were.

And somewhere in that wreckage, I stumbled across answers. Not all of them. Just fragments. But fragments of truth some people spend their whole lives chasing.

So yeah… with that, let's start at the beginning.

I was born in the '70s, adopted at birth into a Jewish–Mexican family in Malibu. My adopted dad had already lived ten lives by then. He grew up in extreme poverty, dropped out of school in the third grade to pick grapes in Texas, and watched his father get killed in a construction gunfight gone wrong. By fourteen, he'd had enough—so he hitchhiked to Hollywood with nothing but survival in his blood.

He clawed his way up from an underage busboy to a waiter, then into leasing cars—Cadillacs he was putting into the hands of Diana Ross,

Neil Diamond, Elton John, and plenty of others. Over time, they stopped being customers and started becoming friends. Eventually, he opened a dive bar in North Hollywood where Lou Adler liked to hang—yeah, *that* Lou Adler, the man behind The Roxy, the same place I'd later bleed years of my own life, and one of the main stages of this book.

My adopted mom was a Sophia Loren–looking Latina painter out of the hard streets of East L.A., poverty at her back, beauty and defiance on her face. Together they stitched a life from grit, hustle, and scraps of art. And then I got dropped right into the middle of it—Malibu kid on paper, but I also had chaos in my DNA.

By eleven, I had a neighborhood band. By twelve, I already knew I wanted to be famous.

Brentwood and Malibu in the '70s and '80s were crawling with rich kids, surfers, skaters, actors, and wannabe rock stars. At Paul Revere Junior High, I watched guys like Jay Adams, Stacy Peralta, and Tony Alva carve up the asphalt before Dogtown became legend. I used to see O.J. Simpson and Marcus Allen running on the school field after hours, and I eventually ended up hanging out and of course getting in trouble with Simpson's son, Jason. Malcolm-Jamal Warner sat next to me in class, helped me cheat on history tests, and then went on to be Theo on *The Cosby Show*[1]. My best friend's dad, Murray Lerner, had already won an Academy Award for his film From Mao to Mozart. Another best friend's dad, Mustapha Akkad, was the famed movie producer behind the Halloween horror franchise—yeah, Michael Myers. Everywhere I turned, people were either in the spotlight or destined for it. I wasn't about to sit on the sidelines.

---

1. **Sadly, Malcolm-Jamal Warner** tragically lost his life on July 20, 2025, at the age of 54 during a family vacation in Costa Rica, having drowned off Playa Cocles in Limón Province after being caught in a powerful ocean current; despite frantic rescue efforts and prolonged CPR, he was pronounced dead at the scene—a heartbreaking end to the life of a beloved actor, musician, and childhood friend.

I cut my teeth in bands I helped create, like Ku De Tah, who landed gigs at The Whisky where we had to "pay-to-play[2]". By 1990, we were leaning into *Chili Peppers* inspired funk-rock, sneering at the Aqua Net glam rockers still hanging onto the Strip like it was still 1986. At the same time, I was behind the scenes—loading gear for cash at The Roxy and The Whisky, plastering flyers at 3 a.m., and taking any gig that kept me close to the heartbeat of it all.

I wasn't just on the stage—I was in the trenches. And I believed, with every fiber, that music wasn't just a dream, it was destiny. My God-given destiny.

Ku De Tah was ahead of its time—Limp Bizkit a decade before Limp Bizkit was even a thought. We had a loyal neighborhood following, played all the right venues, and carried real momentum. We even opened for hair-rock bands like Lock Up at The Whisky, where a young guitarist named Tom Morello stood in the crowd—long before Rage Against the Machine. I always figured maybe he walked away with something from watching us.

Then came the crash. Out of nowhere, chronic fatigue syndrome knocked me flat just as labels had finally started calling. The band fizzled without me at the wheel, and that one cut deep. Looking back, it made sense—I was burning the candle at both ends, chewing through myself at 110%, eating crap, barely sleeping. Something had to give. It did.

Depression followed close behind. And I'll be straight—I almost checked out for good. One night, confined to my room for almost a year with no end in sight, I picked up my dad's chrome .38 and stared straight

---

2. **On the Sunset Strip in the late '80s and '90s**, especially at the Whisky a Go Go, "pay to play" became the dirty little industry standard. Clubs would make up-and-coming bands *buy* a set number of tickets (usually 50–100) for their own show. It didn't matter if you were a high school garage band or the next Guns N' Roses—you had to cough up the cash first. Then it was your job to hustle those tickets to friends, family, or random strangers just to break even. If you didn't sell them? Too bad. The club got paid either way.

down the barrel. In that surreal moment, I thought, *I could end this pain in a split second.* But then, through the walls, I heard some commotion—my dad talking to my ex-girlfriend, who'd shown up unannounced. As I dragged myself down the hallway, I caught him saying:

"Me and his mom are heartbroken about the rough patch he's going through… but you know, when we adopted him at just two months old—looking for that impossible mix of Hispanic and Jewish blood—we could see it right away. He was different. Special. Destined for something amazing."

My ex agreed wholeheartedly and they both started crying.

Hearing that killed any suicide thoughts instantly. No way I could let him or my mom down. Not after that. So instead of checking out, I asked him to check me in—somewhere I could get help. He drove me two hours to College Hospital in Costa Mesa, a place specializing in chronic fatigue syndrome. But before I ever made it to that program, they dropped me in the psych ward first.

Why? Because when they asked if I'd ever thought about hurting myself, I told the truth. Mistake.

Suddenly I was staring at huge locked double doors with wire mesh in the glass—straight out of *One Flew Over the Cuckoo's Nest.* As they buzzed us in, and right on cue, a teenage girl with wild red hair pressed her face against the small rectangular glass part of a thick metal door, lips cracked and dry, eyes bloodshot and glazed, softly screaming: *"Help me… please, let me out…"* It was a padded room.

As if that wasn't enough, a middle-aged woman shuffled past me muttering, *"This hotel is terrible. They don't even have a hair dryer."* That's when I realized: I wasn't just in a hospital. I was in a dark comedy mental asylum written at my expense.

Dinner that night only sealed it. I grabbed a tray, sat in the TV room on the sofa, and found myself next to a huge, towering native-American man in a hospital gown that, no joke, looked like the big indian guy "Chief" from *Cuckoo's Nest.* He turned to me and asked, "So, what are you in for?" Like we were cellmates. I told him the truth: "I'm just tired, man. Chronic fatigue. Somehow I ended up in here." He nodded, dead serious, and said the TV and aliens sometimes told him things he didn't like, but he was working on getting out. Then he stood up, turned, and took some big steps out of the room towards the hallway—hospital gown flapping in the wind while his bare ass hung out like some deranged punchline.

That's when I laughed. I had to. It hit me that my life had officially become a comedic nightmare, and someone, somewhere, maybe God or the algorithm of nature was probably entertained.

I spent two weeks in the psych ward before they moved me into the real program. Three brutal months later, doped up on antidepressants and CFS meds, I started to claw my way back. Somehow, I survived and then in the face of it all, I actually thrived when they finally let me fly free.

By '93, armed with the hard-earned skills it took just to claw my way back to health, I came out swinging with a new band: *Mind Heavy Mustard*—a grunge-drenched beast loud enough to rattle every dive in the Valley and Hollywood. We even scored track one on Nic Adler's (*yeah, Lou's son, and my future boss*) *Monster Mosh* CD[3] , shoulder to shoulder with the heaviest bands tearing up L.A. and the Sunset Strip. I wasn't dead—and I sure as hell wasn't done.

Here's one of the kickers, though: a starving young Armenian metal band called *System of a Down* begged Eddie—the Roxy's soundman and local gatekeeper—to get on that bill. Eddie shut them down cold. I went to bat for them, swore up and down they were gonna blow the fuck up.

---

3. **Even though System of a Down** didn't make the cut—they weren't quite big enough yet—other local popular bands like **Coal Chamber**, **Manhole**, **STS**, **Human Waste Project**, and **Pothole** tore it up and ended up on the live CD.

Hell, I'd already helped them land a couple of early gigs when nobody else would touch them. But nope. Eddie wasn't having it. Said they weren't ready. Big mistake. Huge.

The rest of us? We never sniffed the kind of rise they did. Closest was the band *Snot*—they had the firepower, the attitude, the songs. They were ready to break through. Then fate sucker-punched them. Their singer, Lynn, died in a car crash[4] just as their record dropped, and sadly, the whole thing collapsed overnight.

The years that followed blurred into hustle and hope. I was booking shows at Canoga Park dives and the locally infamous Cobalt Café, cramming bodies into rooms for bands like Sublime, No Doubt, Reel Big Fish, and Incubus—before the masses ever knew their names.

Mind Heavy Mustard finally signed with Noise Records, dropped an album, and flamed out.

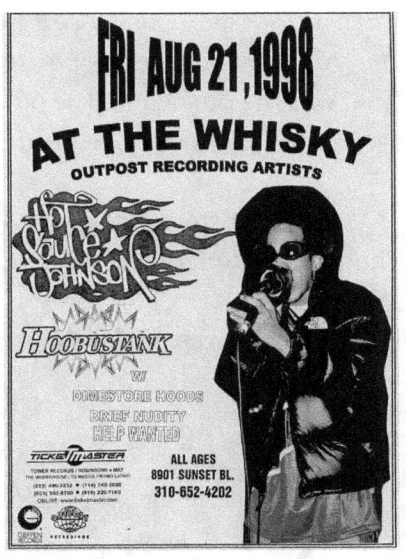

Then came *Hot Sauce Johnson*—a chaotic mash of bass, DJ scratches, and brass, fronted by Sun Sannes, this introverted Lenny Kravitz-type kid out of Central L.A. Our shows were fire. After just six gigs, we scored a deal with Outpost/Geffen, worked with the Beastie Boys' Mario C, and had the whole damn machine behind us. It felt unstoppable.

---

4. **Lynn Strait, Snot's frontman,** was killed in a car crash at just 30 years old—right as their debut *Get Some* was about to blow up. Brutal timing. To make it even crazier, Nic Adler was managing them then... and had managed my band, Mind Heavy Mustard. One band about to rocket, one band that just stayed in the trenches. You can guess which side of that equation I was on.

And then it all collapsed. The Universal/Polygram merger hit, Outpost evaporated, our record got shelved, and the dream was crushed before it even had a chance to breathe.

But I wasn't done. With my drummer and partner-in-crime, Possum, I jumped back in with *Rumblefish*, chasing the high one more time. Kevin Estrada—iconic photographer, West Coast Roadrunner A&R rep, old friend, and the guy who would later write my foreword—went to bat for us again. He had wanted to sign *Hot Sauce Johnson*, so he doubled down on me. Roadrunner/Island Def Jam signed us. Andy Wallace—the same legend who mixed *Nevermind*—mixed a few tracks. It should've been the moment.

Behind the curtain, though, the rot had already set in. Kevin pulled me aside and said the staff thought we were contrived, fake, inauthentic. Then he smirked: *"Don't take it too hard. They probably thought the same thing about Nickelback before they sold ten million fuckin' records for us."* That was the punchline. The office didn't believe. And just like that, we were focus-grouped to death, quietly shelved, erased.

That's the story: I got signed. I got shelved. I always seemed to fall short. I watched friends rise into legends, and I watched others vanish into the abyss.

Rumblefish almost reached that musical Holy Grail, 2001.

And I've been backstage with everyone—from Mötley Crüe to Adele to Snoop. I've seen the machine rocket nobodies into stardom and grind the rest down like trash. The difference? I remember it all like it was yesterday.

After *Rumblefish* crumbled, I should've known it was over. But I couldn't walk away. Not yet. I'd been pounding this road for twenty-something years, and the stage still had its claws in me. Or maybe it was just my ego refusing to die. Either way, the whisper was always there: *one more shot, this is your destiny.*

So yeah... I'll leave you hanging. Go dive into the mayhem. Read the wild-ass stories. When you're done, we'll circle back to the long, jacked-up, glorious era of chasing it under the lights and hustling in the shadows. The ending's waiting for you in the back.

For now, buckle the hell up. This is the raw inside ride where life and music collide.

And if you're tuned in close enough, maybe you'll find answers to questions you didn't even know you were asking.

And if nothing else, maybe you'll see a little of your own fight in mine—the chase, the heartbreak, the stubborn hope. Because underneath the noise, that's what this is really about: holding onto a dream long enough to see what it makes of you.

—JD

Chapter 1

ANNA NICOLE SMITH—The Holy Grail

The Roxy's backstage stairs weren't just steps—they were a portal to debauchery and redemption.

"I keep my hand right there on her giant breast...At this point, all I could think about was how massive her boobs were"

Let's start this book off with something personally wild from 1999. And yeah, I've got bona fide witnesses if you don't believe me. (You'll see their names in this story—they gave me the OK.)

I'd been playing bass in my band, Hot Sauce Johnson, while grinding behind the scenes at the Roxy and the Whisky, cranking out graphics for their flyers and LA Weekly ads. Luckily, I'd learned Photoshop before most people even knew what it was, and back then, that rare skill actually paid.

This was a couple years before I officially became the Roxy's stage manager, but I was already neck-deep in the scene through M Productions and the Whisky a Go Go.

We cut a homemade demo with our track "Jack Kerouac,[1] "a song I wrote after tearing through *On the Road* during a bout of brutal insomnia . Believe it or not, just six live shows in, we had real label heat—not just industry smoke and bullshit which was usually the norm.

We signed with Outpost/Geffen and quickly became local favorites, playing almost every venue in town: Troubadour, Viper Room... all of them. Thanks to my connections at the Roxy and Whisky, we were headlining killer nights, and bands like Hoobastank—yeah, the same guys who went on to sell millions of records—were opening for us.

It's funny, because years later I'd hear their smash hit *The Reason* everywhere—elevators, radio, grocery stores—and every time it reminded me that I'd been standing right there on the edge of that elusive

---

1. **My song Jack Kerouac** became a Kaazaa and Napster (remember those music sharing platforms?) phenomenon. Purely by accident, some college kid uploaded our song *Jack Kerouac* onto those music platforms and gave the credit to Jack Johnson (they mixed up our band name, Hot Sauce Johnson, and the song title *Jack Kerouac*). Jack Johnson was already booming on radio and all the college campuses. What ensued was pretty cool, as hundreds of thousands of people downloaded the song. There were even full-on online discussions where people were arguing about who actually wrote the song, etc. It was like a battle between people who said it was a Jack Johnson song and people who said it wasn't. Today, you can still type in *Jack Kerouac* + Jack Johnson and find blogs crediting him as the songwriter, etc.

stardom, watching band after band I personally knew leapfrog over my ass into the spotlight[2] ...definitely stung a bit.

Hoobastank opening for us on this one...

It wasn't bitterness though. It was truth. A hard, unavoidable truth: talent isn't always enough. Timing, luck, politics—they're part of the game. And the game doesn't always give a crap how hard you work.

But man, I tell ya... there was one badass show—right before our album dropped in '99—that I'll never forget. Sold-out night at the Roxy, and we felt bulletproof. We had one strict rule: no hard drinking or drugs before hitting the stage. We'd seen too many bands tank by getting sloppy, and once people start whispering you're shit live, you're screwed—it sticks like glue.

---

2. **I watched so many bands I knew that were** chasing that oh-so-elusive musical Holy Grail finally grab it—System of a Down, Linkin Park, Papa Roach, Alien Ant Farm, Korn, Static-X, Crazy Town, Incubus... the list goes on. And while they shot to the top, I was left in the dust, still grinding in the shadows.

As showtime crept closer, we headed down from the upstairs dressing room and waited in the wings. The crowd was already buzzing—smoke curling up from weed pipes, bodies packed in shoulder to shoulder, laughter and shouting bouncing off the walls.

For a rare second, as I stood there on stage behind the curtain, it felt like everything was finally breaking right for me and the band. But I had no idea how fast it was about to turn, or that a major future tragedy[3] was just lurking around the corner waiting to gut-punch us all.

Then our sound guy, Dr. Evil, got on the mic: "Please give it up! L.A.'s own... Hot Sauce Johnson!"

On tour tearing it up while opening for Kid Rock...

The place exploded. The Roxy curtain lifted and we tore into our set like a wrecking ball. One of those rare nights when everything locked in—tight, loud, electric. You could probably hear us bleeding through the walls all the way to the Rainbow Bar & Grill next door.

The energy from the crowd slammed into us like a wave. I scanned the room, half-blinded by Bolle—the Roxy's mad-scientist lighting guy, who later became a close friend before flaming out in his own tragedy, like too many others you'll meet in this book. Between the strobes and the fog choking the stage, one figure stood out. A tall, blonde Amazon in the very back, bouncing like she was front row at a Backstreet Boys concert. She towered over the sea of bodies, waving like she knew me. Maybe she did. Maybe she was just high as hell. Either way, I couldn't take my eyes off her.

---

3. **Tragically, our sensitive, talented and troubled singer,** Sun Sannes born as Doral Fields, committed suicide in 2009, by jumping off a 10-level grand central parking structure in LA. He was only 32 years old. We found out that after Hot Sauce Johnson had broken up, he had never really found any other success in music. He had gained a bunch of weight, was doing drugs, drinking and was in a tough situation concerning his daughter and her mother. It was a hard pill to swallow as we *knew* he must have been completely depressed and nowhere near the beautiful spark he once had.

I had no clue who she was—I couldn't see her face clear enough—but I was about to find out.

When our set finally ended and the roar kept going—even after the big Roxy curtain dropped—we walked off stage, filing toward the narrow doorway that led to the stairs up to the backstage rooms. I was the last one out. At the bottom of the stairs, where I could still glimpse the crowd, two of our closest road crew girls were waiting, hyping us up after the set.

One was Jill "Jillski" Augusto, who worked at Outpost/Geffen, our label. She always had our backs and hustled for us however she could. The other was Susie "Geerz" Geers, Jill's best friend, showing her love and support with that wild Janis Joplin vibe she carried everywhere.

As I finished hugging them, I suddenly heard my name being called frantically from outside the backstage entrance, where Juan Bones, the Roxy security guy, was standing. "JD! JD! Jason!" I heard the yells and decided to peek my head out from where I stood at the bottom of the backstage stairs. Then I finally saw who it was. It was a friend of mine, Tatiana, that we all called "Cha-Ching,"

Snapped this shot of the crowd at our show...

who also worked as a waitress at the Rainbow Bar next door. I said, "Hey you," and she flashed me this huge smile before blurting out excitedly, "My friend really wants to meet you".

I replied, "Awesome, bring her ass over here." I knew how important it was to connect with the crowd—build real fans who might stick with you for life. But yeah, I had other motives too. I was single, in a band, and like most guys in the scene, I was always on the lookout for whatever the night might bring. Maybe she'd be into it. Maybe she wouldn't. But she definitely had my attention.

As I stood at the bottom of the stairs with Jillski and Geerz by my side, I noticed my friend bringing over that giant Amazon woman that I couldn't see clearly from the stage earlier. As they made their way through the smoke-filled, noisy Roxy room, I started to doubt my own eyes. As the womanly silhouette got closer and closer, I found myself thinking, *"No way, no fukin' way..."* I looked over at Geerz and Jillski, and I could see their jaws drop—just like mine.

I straightened myself up and smiled, but before I could say anything, the Amazon spoke in a sweet Texas accent, "Hey there, honey, I absolutely love your band."

I wanted to respond, but for a split second, I started thinking way too hard about what to say. As I pulled myself together, trying to play it cool like any pseudo almost-famous rock star would, I finally said, "Wow, Anna Nicole Smith[4]! Ummmm, wow, I saw you dancing at the back." Scrambling to come up with something witty to impress her, I shifted into boss mode when I saw my bass tech, Shawnski, coming from the stage.

I yelled, "Shawnski, go to the merch booth and grab Anna Nicole Smith a CD and shirt, right now!"

Shawnski stood there frozen for a few seconds, then, after collecting his own jaw off the floor, said in a funny way, "Yes, sir, right now."

So there she was—Anna Nicole Smith, in all her glory—standing there with my friend, looking absolutely amazing. I finally got past my shock and turned to Cha-Ching, "Is this the friend you were talking about?" She smiled and said, "Of course... didn't you see her dancing the whole time?"

At that moment, Anna Nicole spoke again, "I just love your music, and you are so damn cute... can I give you a little hug?"

I looked over at Cha-Ching, who was nodding enthusiastically, mouthing the words SAYYY YESSS... Taking her advice, I said, "Yes, definitely!"

As Anna stepped into the backstage area with open arms, painted nails, the sweet smell of perfume, and expensive-conditioned blonde hair, I realized I was still standing on the bottom step of the stairs—which

---

4. **This was the Anna Nicole Smith** that was still somewhat in her prime—towards the end of her prime, but not the disaster she would become when she was unhealthy, overweight, and had her reality show. In this moment of 1999, she looked vibrant, happy, and healthy... She wasn't skinny by any means and was probably much heavier than when she was a young model, but man, she looked quite amazing in person.

made me a tiny bit taller than her. (I'm only 5'8" and she looked like she was wearing 3 or 4-inch heels, making her about 6'3" or something.)

I opened my arms, and as she came toward me, I welcomed the giant bear hug that practically suffocated me. At this point, all I could think about was how *massive* her boobs were and how I was somehow embracing the woman who was once one of the most famous and stunning models from back in the day. I could clearly remember us kids drooling when we saw her in those Guess Jeans ads all those years ago.

As we're almost finished hugging (which felt like a short, yet awesome eternity), I feel her hand guide mine up towards her *huge* boobs as she whispers in my ear... " I'm soooo damn horny". I'm in complete shock and go into autopilot as my left hand gently lands on her right breast. It's so big that my hand looks *engulfed*—comically small—just resting there on top of it (and I don't even have small hands, promise...lol)

But all of a sudden—and this has never happened before—I get this weird jolt of fright. A feeling like... maybe I'm not *man* enough to handle this larger-than-life and literally large legendary Amazon woman. Like she might laugh me right out of bed while saying in her cute Texas drawl, "Is that all you got honey?"

My mind starts betraying me. My usual band member confidence begins to slip, but somehow, I keep my hand right there on her giant breast... even manage to give it a very soft and tender squeeze, like some horny kid that's quite out of his league.

As our hug starts to come to an end, I look up at her face. Her eyes are closed, lips all puckered, waiting for a *kiss*—or maybe even a full-on French kiss. I know this is it... the big moment.

But I'm frozen. Damn near frozen. Afraid to fail like all those knights in *Excalibur* who came up short trying to reach that damn Holy Grail.

I just stand there stiff, not letting my lips go forward. Seconds later, she opens her eyes. She looks totally surprised, then pulls her hair back and says—loudly, for all the girls to hear—"Is this boy dumb or something?"

And that's the nail in the coffin... or should I say, a hammer blow to the ego? Yeah. You get it.

I start slinking away, my hand slowly dropping, as I glance over at the girls—who are now staring, wide-eyed, laughing at what they just saw.

Anna takes a final step away from me and says, "Oh well... I thought we could have had a fun time or something. That's too bad."

Then she turns and slowly disappears, walking back into the smoke-filled room. Cha-Ching just shrugs, scrunches up her shoulders like, *You blew it, dude,* and starts following Anna[5].

I look up, utterly defeated, and see Shawnski holding our CD and a T-shirt. He says, "Here you go, boss."

I glance up at him and say sheepishly, "Too late, man. Way too late..."

I turn around. Jilllski is still cracking up. Geerz blurts out,

"Dude, you were almost full on making out with Anna Nicole Smith, and your hand was on her friggin' boob! This is legendary*!*"

I softly reply, "Yeah..."—feeling pretty dejected. Like how I imagine the fictional Percival or Lancelot must've felt, Holy Grail within reach... and yet, like so many before them, just falling just short of the required *greatness*.

Or should I say... fell short and, in my case, went damn limp.

Legendary? Sure. Just not the way I wanted.

And after all that, I never saw Anna in person again[6].

---

5. **I found out later** that from Tatiana (Cha-Ching) that Anna Nicole was in Los Angeles for her hearing about her bankruptcy case and multi-million dollar *inheritance* claim. However, that night at the Roxy, her boyfriend at the time, was nowhere in sight.

6. **Sadly, Anna Nicole Smith died** on February 8, 2007, at age 39, from an accidental drug overdose at the Seminole Hard Rock Hotel & Casino in Hollywood, Florida. She was found unresponsive in her suite by her private nurse, Tasma Brighthaupt, and despite CPR attempts by her bodyguard and paramedics, she was pronounced dead at Memorial Regional Hospital

So You're Telling Me There's A Chance...

"Your merciful God... He destroyed His own beloved, rather than let a mediocrity share in the smallest part of His glory."
— Salieri to Father Vogler, Amadeus (1984)

Years later, I'd tell the Anna Nicole story to friends, and they'd laugh, calling it a once-in-a-lifetime, surreal backstage moment. They'd tell me not to feel bad because she probably didn't even remember it. I laughed too, but deep down I always wondered what paths might have unfolded if I hadn't lost confidence that night—or in other moments of my life. And the truth is, it wasn't the only time I couldn't deliver. It happened more than once, and the sad part? I couldn't seem to fix it.

But that night with Anna also showed me something else I couldn't ignore: my life was stacked with uncanny, intimate, up-close brushes with fame—shit most people never even get close to, but I always seemed to be right on the edge of them. I don't know if I manifested them, or if they just found me because I kept chasing my borderline-delusional dreams like gospel.

And that word—*delusional*—wasn't just some lazy insult. It was jet fuel. The bloodstream of every half-mad artist clawing their way toward the spotlight. I wasn't alone in it. Everyone I knew was drinking the same poison, living in some warped fantasy where "making it" was always just one more gig or performance away—except for the rare few who actually did. And when the letdowns piled up, when the hype went nowhere and the rooms stayed half-empty, I'd soothe my bruised ego by pointing at all the other poor bastards who couldn't even fill a small dive bar. (Meanwhile, me? Eventually four record deals deep and still wandering the desert looking for the promised land. How's that for delusion?)

I even wrote a song about it—Lost Picasso—my twisted little hymn to blind hope and straight-up self deception. It's about that seductive lie that keeps you grinding long after logic is begging, "Quit, man. Give it the fuck up already." The lyric cuts two ways: first, the stubborn dreamer whispering, "I'm not a failure—I'm brilliant. The world just hasn't caught up yet. I'm just an unknown star waiting to be discovered." And second, that same voice screaming back from the void: "Don't let me be a lost Picasso. Don't let me simmer in obscurity, thinking I'm the real deal when I'm just another fool, painting in the dark where nobody will ever see a goddamn thing."

In 1994, I was filled with delusion and hope—aka the jr. patron saint of mediocrity.

But here's the hard reality nobody likes to admit: most of us don't have it. Maybe it's talent, maybe it's drive, or maybe it's just that elusive natural-born gift you can't fake. Everyone knows someone—maybe a friend, a cousin, a hopeful bartender or waitress—who swears they're destined for greatness. Ninety-nine times out of a hundred, it's delusion dressed up like destiny.

Still, without that false belief? None of us would even step foot on that slim-chance road to stardom. That's the joke. That's the trap. The odds are microscopic, but they're still odds.

Reminds me of that Jim Carrey line from *Dumb and Dumber*: *"So you're telling me there's a chance."* That's all it takes to keep most of us going.

Some are born with brilliance — others spend their lives chasing it. (Nirvana, Roxy Theatre, 1991. Photo by Kevin Estrada.)

Most of us run on fumes and fantasy. And a rare few actually have the thing—the spark, the mojo, whatever the hell it is. They didn't stumble into it by accident. They were born wired different. And maybe, just maybe, so was I... or at least that's what I told myself to keep breathing at the time.

Here's what finally clicked for me though: the rest of us—the dreamers, the almosts, the delusional souls—we still got something real out of the struggle. The reward wasn't the fame. It was the fight. The chase. The nights that break you and the nights that keep you alive.

Nietzsche had it right: *"He who has a why to live can bear almost any how."* My *why* was the dream. The *how* was chaos, heartbreak, and bad decisions by the truckload—but it kept me moving. And maybe that's the real gift hidden in all the wreckage: if you keep chasing your own why, even broken roads can lead somewhere worth going. The dream isn't just about the final success—it's about proving to yourself that you kept trying when everything in you wanted to quit.

I'll go deeper into that later. For now, let's move to another unforgettable night on the Backstage Pass ride—years after Anna Nicole. Because not all my Sunset Strip insanity came wrapped in heels and perfume.

Sometimes, it showed up in clouds of weed smoke and the human version of Cujo…

Chapter 2

TYSON & SNOOP—Nuthin' but a 'G' Thang

"You let him backstage?" Hell yeah. What am I gonna do, tell Mike Tyson no?

Although I was hyped that one of my favorite boxing champions was coming back to the Roxy for the Snoop Dogg show, I was also a bit nervous as his volatile nature had already been exposed the last time he came through in 2004, when Jay-Z and Linkin Park performed. He was cool to our Latin tank of a front door guy, "Big Mario," slipping him a crisp $100 bill and telling him to keep an eye on his car. But later, he acted like he didn't give a shit—blocking the Roxy hallway, making everyone squeeze around while he took his sweet time talking on the phone.

I also remember seeing him after the show, stopping his car and blocking the small exit from our parking lot because he wanted to talk to some girls passing by. It was quite a funny situation because the people he happened to be blocking (and was oblivious to) were Jay-Z and his entourage. I say funny because they didn't say anything or honk their horn for a while as he took his time chatting up the girls outside his car door.

I could see Jay-Z's face—a look of impatience, yet not really knowing what to do. I guess no one messes with good ol' Iron Mike Tyson, and even the main man in Hip-Hop wasn't about to tangle with the human version of Cujo.

Eventually the cops showed up and asked him to move, but the way they said it? Soft, nervous, like some boxing fan begging forgiveness for stepping on his foot. Tyson ignored them until he was damn well ready, then finally rolled on—just as Jay-Z's guys were getting out of their cars, maybe ready to handle it themselves. That was the memory that stuck in my mind—dynamite situations that could explode at any moment. All of us at the Roxy had to be on guard and make sure not to help light any fuse.

Now, I assumed that there might be a fair number of problems with Snoop performing (unfortunately, there always seemed to be a blend of different issues with the hip hop and punk shows[1] whenever we hosted

---

1. **For some reason,** we always had trouble with most of the hip-hop or punk shows at the Roxy. There always seemed to be underage drinking, fights breaking out, clouds of weed smoke hanging over the crowd, and plenty of hard drugs getting done in the bathrooms. The bad attitudes were nonstop. It wasn't that all hip-hop or punk kids were bad, but there always seemed to be a few rotten ones who ruined it for everyone. Security had to deal with it constantly, and it was always a damn headache. I actually felt bad for them sometimes—they didn't get paid nearly enough to play Roxy jail guards. But it was what it was, and we made that clear when we hired them.

them). And since I knew Tyson was coming—along with the usual mix of wannabe hip-hop kids and a myriad of real and fake gangstas—well, I devised a backup plan. I planned to put all the waitresses in the kitchen and lock the door in case some kind of riot or gangsta stuff went down (it definitely wouldn't have been the first time[2]).

Sometimes the hip hop shows ended with graffiti etched right into our mirrors......

I went to my office and loaded up with some pepper spray to disperse the crowd… just in case.

When Snoop arrived, he had three of the biggest, ex-con, tattooed, for-ties-or-fifties-aged looking guys as his bodyguards. One guy must have been lifting weights for like 30 years or something… even our large Latin se-curity guys looked kinda small com-pared to them. They proceeded to block off the backstage area and wouldn't let anyone through as Snoop walked past.

However, I was one of the lucky few who could move freely be-cause I knew their *vato gangsta* production manager—a friend from way back—and he introduced me to the bodyguards and crew. Suddenly I was honorary crew for the night—and yeah, it felt pretty damn good…

Things still got gnarly, though, when our General Manager at the time—let's call him "Tizzle"—tried to bolt up the backstage stairs lead-ing to our offices on the second floor. He ignored the first bodyguard, running right past him, not realizing that the backstage area had been locked down for Snoop. Although he cleared the first guy, he ran directly into the second bodyguard at the top of the stairs, who grabbed him by the neck, lifted him off the ground and then carried his ass back

---

2. **There were quite a few big fights** and full-on riots that broke out when I was working at music venues—from the Reseda Country Club, Mancini's, and The Cobalt in the San Fernando Valley to the Whisky A Go Go and the Roxy in Hollywood. I used to spray pepper straight above the crowd toward the ceiling to break up riots, and it always worked like a charm as the mist rained down. Even the biggest and baddest dudes couldn't fight it—they'd all come stumbling out of the venue coughing, sneezing, and wheezing. It stopped the chaos instantly, because it's pretty damn hard to fight when you can't see and can't breathe.

down the stairs, propping him up against the bottom wall with his feet dangling at least a foot from the floor—it totally reminded me of that scene in the original 1977 *Star Wars*, when Darth Vader gets super pissed and lifts Captain Antilles off the ground by his neck and props him up against the wall. Strangely, it was actually pretty interesting to see it happen in real life—though unfortunately, at little Tizzle's expense.

For what seemed like an eternity, I kept telling the bodyguard that the small guy he was holding was our General Manager. After it finally registered—from his brain to his giant muscles—he let him down, fixed his collar, and apologized. Tizzle looked like a pale ghost in shock. I heard that it took him at a couple of weeks to recover psychologically and I'm pretty sure he got some PTSD from it.

As we got closer to showtime, luckily, everything else was going smoothly... in fact, my *vato* production buddy handed me Snoop's mic to hold by the side of the stage before he came on to perform. He told me he had just picked it up from the jeweler, and when I looked at it, I guessed it to be worth somewhere around $25-35K[3]. It was platinum or white gold, encrusted with hundreds of diamonds forming a big marijuana leaf. It was damn near heavy as a small cantaloupe.

When Snoop came down the stairs, sliding into the side of the stage where the audience couldn't see him, I said, "Hey, Snoop, I got your mic here." He took it, stared at it like it was some alien gadget, seemingly blasted on some strong indica. Hell, I was baked myself from the unintentional contact high. The damn backstage was like one giant smoke machine filled with THC.

Watching him fumble with the mic was comical. He didn't even know how to turn the thing on. He fumbled for what felt like an hour—though in my THC-soaked brain it was probably more like 20 seconds. Finally, I laughed and said, "Here, Snoop, lemme help you." I flipped the mic over and hit the tiny switch. The green light popped on. He looked at me for a second like I'd just solved a physics equation, then smirked and said, "Thanx, playa, I owe ya one." Then hit his blunt, exhaled slow, and

---

3. **Later on, I confirmed with my buddy** (Snoop's production manager) that they actually paid $30K for the custom weed mic, and it was white gold with real diamonds. Years later, after I had left the Roxy, I became the Marketing Director for my ex-wife's awesome jewelry company, *Julez Bryant*, and ended up pricing Snoop's mic from memory—we could have done it for about $10K.

strutted onto the stage yelling, "Snoop Doggy Dogg is in tha hizzle!" or something to that effect.

I was watching the show from my usual spot—right next to the stage—when I realized there was still no sign of Tyson. The audience, on the other hand, was having a hell of a time. The entire venue was hazy with smoke, thick enough to give anyone in the building a solid contact high—including our sixty-something-year-old cooks, the bar-backs, waitresses, kitchen staff, even security. (You can't stop people from lighting up at shows like this. In fact, any Reggae nights we had, were basically hotboxes with a cover charge[4].)

Audience pumped up right before Snoop hit the stage...

I figured all the weed had vacuumed out any violent, alpha-male energy that might've otherwise crept in. Everyone was just vibing—stoned, mellow, grinning like blissed-out gangsta-hippie hybrids. And I was here

---

4. **At all the reggae and hip-hop shows**, we'd try to confiscate the joints and blunts people were lighting up in the crowd, but it quickly got ridiculous. Take one person's weed or pipe, and two or three others would fire up right after. The amount of weed snuck in was insane—it felt like every single person in the room smoked. Eventually, we made it policy: confiscate for the first hour while it was still manageable, and after that, just let it ride. The Roxy would turn into one giant hotbox, and everybody got high—even the ones who didn't smoke. We told employees they didn't have to work those shows if they didn't want a contact high—no questions asked.

for it. My only thought: Hell yeah, let's keep this peace-train rolling all the way to closing time.

Just as I was debating whether to sneak outside for a breath of non-cannabis-infused oxygen, I turned my head and—boom—there he was. Iron Mike. Moving through the crowd like a slow-rolling tank, drink in one hand, a tall, model-type Russian call girl draped over the other. He had that look—like the human embodiment of *"Oh, shit... what's about to happen now?"*.

I bolted to the kitchen and barked at the crew and waitresses: "Tyson's here. No bullshit. No side-eyes or attitude—just give the man his drinks and make him feel like he's at home, okay?"

When I came back out, I spotted him at the backstage door, puffing on either a cigar or a blunt (hard to tell), talking to one of our security guys like he owned the joint. Meanwhile, all three of Snoop's bodyguards were already on stage, sweeping the crowd with that cold, all-business stare—like the kind you would get from the secret service.

In case you've never seen a hip-hop entourage up close, here's how it goes: the stage becomes a human parking lot—wives, girlfriends, dealers, childhood friends, hype men, and bodyguards all crammed up there like it's a block party. Half of them don't even belong there, but nobody dares say shit. It's a spectacle, every damn time.

I then notice our security guard letting Tyson backstage, and I run up to him and say,

"Bones, what did Mike say to you?"

He tells me that Mike said he wants to go onstage, and I was like, "You let him backstage?"

And he was like, "Hell yeah. What am I gonna do, tell Mike Tyson *no*?"

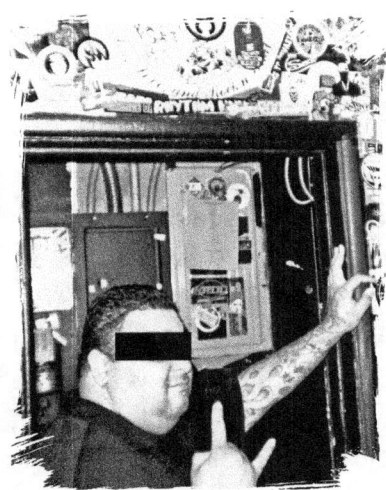

Even our big security dudes seemed small compared to Snoop's guys...

Out of the corner of my eye, I caught Mike heading for the narrow staircase that led from backstage to the main stage—where Snoop was still mid-set. I made a split-second call and stepped in front of him, like the last line of defense between him and a powder keg. Snoop's tour manager had been crystal clear: once Snoop started, no one was allowed onstage unless they were up there already. Absolutely no one. The stage was on lockdown—no exceptions.

"Hey Mike!" I said, putting on my most casual fanboy grin. "I'm JD, Production Manager for The Roxy. Huge fan, man—been following you since I was a teenager."

Before he could reply, I threw in, "How you doing tonight?"

He just stared at me. About five long, silent seconds. It felt like an hour. My brain was racing. Was he about to knock me the fuck out? bite my ass? or perhaps just walk through me like I didn't exist?

Mike wasn't tall—about my height, maybe an inch or two taller (I'm only 5'8") but he was built like a Pit Bull that mated with a short NFL linebacker. Tree-trunk legs. A massive neck that would almost be impossible to put into a choke hold. Fists that looked like hammers...

Finally, his lips moved. There was a slur in his speech, a little spit flying, and the soft, almost sweet lisp of a creature that wouldn't even hurt a fly.

"Thanks, man... I'm havin' a great time. Can I get anotha' drink?"

My heart finally exhaled. "Hell yeah, Mike," I said. "Stay right here—I'll go grab you one myself."

I head to the kitchen, grab him another drink, and as I head back—expecting to find him still backstage—I look up and see him dancing on stage, holding his empty glass in one hand and his blunt in the other.

The crowd starts cheering, but I immediately clock Snoop's face—he looks stunned. So do his bodyguards and entourage. They clearly know who Tyson is, but it's obvious none of them know him personally.

Mike starts dancing next to this insanely hot chick—either one of Snoop's girls or someone from the entourage—but it seems like Mike don't give a shit. He keeps thrusting next to her like it's a private party, and she's visibly uncomfortable. You could see it in her eyes—nervous, unsure, maybe even a little scared. She starts slowly dancing away, inching closer to the massive bodyguards stationed on the left side of the stage.

As she gets near them, I watch Mike lock eyes with both dudes and shoot them a death stare. Not the kind that says, "Back off." More like, "You want to go? You wanna be the guy who tries to stop me? Fuckin' try me."

It was a silent showdown. No words. Just hardcore energy. A ticking time bomb. And somehow, I was the only one tuned into it.

Suddenly, I see the "head" bodyguard—an older guy who looked like he'd rag-dolled his share of fools—staring right back at Tyson. Then he nudges the other bodyguard, this giant motherfucker built like Shaq, to check out what's going down.

I'm like, Oh fuck... here we go. These dudes are about to try and flex, maybe toss Mike off stage, and if that happens? Shit's gonna get ugly fast. Crowd goes nuts. Mike goes nuclear. It's a lose-lose. I grip the pepper spray in my pocket, ready to jump in like I'm gonna make a difference.

But then—plot twist—I see the bodyguards nod their heads slightly... and look away. Just like that. They broke the stare and dropped it. No words. No action. Just... surrender.

They wanted no part of Mike Tyson.

These were guys easily twice his size, but in that moment, they looked like those prideful lions on National Geographic who back down from the alpha male after a long stare-down. You could almost hear them muttering to themselves, "You know what... nah. I ain't fuckin' with that."

Man, one part of me was laughing inside, but another part was still a bit nervous. To me, Mike had just made it very clear—no one was gonna stop him from doing whatever the hell he wanted at The Roxy.

But then, almost like a switch flipped, he started to mellow out. He kept dancing, mouthing lyrics. He knew every word to "Drop It Like It's Hot" and some of the old-school bangers like "Nuthin' but a 'G' Thang." Snoop still looked a little uneasy, but he played it cool—smart move. He handed Mike the mic for a few bars, and Mike puffed away on his blunt while rubbing his pudgy extended belly.

That's when I knew we were good. No mayhem. No brawls. Just Iron Mike soaking up the moment.

Eventually, he stumbled offstage, found his Russian call girl, and slipped me a hundred-dollar bill on the way, which I later split with my security guy Juan "Bones," who just grinned at me and said, "Damn, you look stoned, bro."

I laughed, we high-fived, and then parted ways.

Tyson hanging at the Rainbow with my former boss from M Productions, and the grandson of Mario Maglieri the legendary owner of both the Rainbow and the Whisky a Go-Go, Big Mikey Jr. "Mags"

Alcohol, Drugs & Neo-Nazis—The Punk Battle of Braveheart

"That's when a huge Neo-Nazi monster appeared—a massive looking Viking dude. Covered in tattoos, thick beard, bald head, and crazy big arms."

Later, in hindsight, I realized that the nights we had with Tyson and Snoop—which felt like they might explode—actually turned out to be some of the best memories. Volatility, comedy, danger, ego… somehow, it all worked. Nights like that didn't just make for great stories—they reminded me that at The Roxy, even the most unpredictable stuff could end in a high-five, hundred-dollar handshake, and a damn good laugh. That was the magic of the place.

However, not every chaotic show ended so cleanly. Some exploded into full-on riots, violence, and mayhem—which brings me to my earlier days, when I had to deal with unruly punk rockers, delinquents, and, at times, young neo-Nazi skinheads.

Most of the shows I booked at the Cobalt were amazing, but a few turned into complete disasters…

I remember one particular night in the mid-1990s when I was the booker and sometimes front-door guy at the Cobalt Café in the San Fernando Valley. There was this presence of Nazi punks from both SFV and Antelope Valley who would show up to punk shows all over the area. That night, a small high school punk band called Government Cheese was playing a free show, and the place was packed with their family and friends—parents, grandparents, kids. The vibe was pure Green Day-style punk—fun, energetic, harmless.

To our surprise, about halfway through the set, a dozen or so Nazi punks came stomping through the front doors. Their leader, CeeCee—who Dave (the owner of the Cobalt) and I knew from previous run-ins, assured us they just wanted to mosh and there'd be no trouble. Dave, who was super tolerant but also Jewish, and knowing that I had some Jewish blood as well, weighed his options and chose not to escalate the situation. So, against our gut instincts, we let them in.

At first, they kept their word. But before long, they started moshing and throwing up Sieg Heils. Some of the elderly guests, including this one pair of grandparents, whom we found out later, had actually fled the Holocaust as kids, were horrified. Dave asked me to handle it, since I had a weirdly decent rapport with CeeCee and his crew—probably because they didn't know I was half Jewish, with my other half-Hispanic background seemingly passing their ridiculous *whiteness test,* which I guess made them think that I was just "white enough" to be tolerated.

I pulled CeeCee aside and told him the crowd was totally offended and that they needed to tone it down. He looked at me, eyes glazed, obviously high, and said, "Are they all such a bunch of lame pussies or what? …and Sieg Heil isn't even offensive, man."

I stayed calm and got him to promise to talk to his guys and get them to chill.

He agreed, and talked to them, but less than fifteen minutes later, one of the skins stood dead center on the floor, cracked open a shaken beer he'd snuck in, sprayed it everywhere, and screamed at the top of his lungs, "Heil Hitler!!!"

Luckily, the band's set ended right after that, and all of the families bailed out fast.

I stepped outside for air, only to see two SHARPs (Skinheads Against Racial Prejudice—the mortal enemies of the White Power Skinheads) walk up. One of them, a white kid and friend of mine named Junior, immediately clocked the Nazi presence and knew they were fucked.

I quickly and quietly handed him my pepper spray and told him and his buddy to take off and start running while I tried to stall the incoming shitstorm.

A second later, someone inside yelled, "Fucking SHARPs! Get them!" I grabbed at CeeCee as he and his crew came barreling out the front door. I shouted, "There are like 20 more SHARPs coming with weapons! You guys need to get out of here—now's your chance." That stalled them just long enough for Junior and his friend to get a head start. But CeeCee growled, "Fuck it. Let's go get those two we just saw and jump them before their boys show."

Right then, they all started tearing down the sidewalk, yelling in that unhinged, movie-style way that reminded me of *The Warriors*—all battle cries and craziness.

Fortunately, my friends ducked into a nearby hippie smoke shop, Lion's Lair, where the staff stashed them behind bongs and glass pipes like some punk rock witness protection program. I kept watch, then eventually signaled them back when the coast was clear. We hid them in our office.

When the Nazi skins finally returned—sweaty, amped, and pissed—I told them the SHARPs probably caught a ride with their crew and vanished. CeeCee bought it. Just barely.

The Nazi crew stuck around, spewing garbage about punk rock, Hitler, and whatever else fueled their heads, while my friends hid in the windowless Cobalt office—sweating it out for hours. When I finally cracked the door, they looked pale, hungry, and drenched. One croaked, "There's no air conditioning in here." I told him, "A little heat and hunger beats a Nazi beatdown any day." They gave weak laughs and thanked me and Dave for saving their asses.

Over time, there were plenty more incidents like this—fights, stabbings, all the usual mayhem—but somehow, no one ever ended up dead. One night, though, I did stop it from getting that far. A young Nazi skinhead wandered into the Cobalt for the wrong show wearing white shoelaces—a dead giveaway for white power punks. About thirty furious kids had him surrounded, ready to tear him apart.

I jumped in and talked them down. They listened—probably because I'd built up some street cred over the years by sticking my neck out for SHARPs when they were also outnumbered. The crowd made him strip off his suspenders and shirt, then yank the laces from his boots so he had to walk out in socks, bare-chested and shaken. Half-naked and humiliated, he bolted. I never saw him again.

Weirdly, I felt good about helping him. He even thanked me before he ran. To the mob, I guess I came off like a legit older-brother figure deep in the music scene, and that alone saved this dumb kid from what could've been a very different, very ugly ending. I always wondered if saving him that night might have sparked something in him—some realization that the path he was on only led to pain and destruction. I'm still not sure.

Now, there was this other violent and Neo-Nazi whacked mess that happened when I worked as the booking assistant at this restaurant dive bar called Mancinis in the mid-1990s. At night, the restaurant became "Club M" and before I got a job there, it was a haven for glam and hair rock. But that scene was definitely fading, and my own band Ku De Tah—had played there a few times, selling out the place with other younger, up-and-coming non-glam bands which were in the vein of alternative, grunge and punk stylings.

Eventually, the booking agent for Mancinis decided that she needed to tap into this new scene, so she asked me to be her assistant and bring all the new stuff with me. At first, it was very successful. The owner, Dennis Mancini, was happy because the new bands packed the place and the kids from this scene still drank at the bar. He was making money, so they welcomed it. I ended up decorating the whole place like I did years later at the Roxy backstage—like a 17-year-old's room, plastered with posters and memorabilia.

Things were working well. I booked bands like Incubus, Unwritten Law, The Adolescents, JFA, and many others.

But there was this one night that went completely off the rails when I booked RKL (Rich Kids on LSD), and they attracted a ton of neo-Nazis from Antelope Valley. In particular, a white power gang that called themselves the *Nazi Low Riders*. They were a weird mix—some were full-on white dudes, but plenty were Hispanic dudes covered in Nazi tattoos, sieg-heiling in the pit. It didn't quite make sense to me, but it was definitely a real thing.

I had no idea RKL had a Nazi following, and I remember being pumped about the sold out show because me and my boss Leslie got a cut of the door—that's how we got paid. When the doors opened at 8 p.m., everything seemed smooth, the opening bands played, and kids were moshing with no fights. But by 10 p.m., right before RKL's set, I felt the vibe shift. There was tension in the air. A few people were squabbling, but that was par for the course at punk shows. I didn't think too much of it.

qUIKMUD PRODUCTIONS BRINGS YOU:

sUNDAY jAN. 15th 8:00pm

U.X.A. chromosome tea - bored - eight - sinister buzz

sATURDAY jAN. 21st 7:30pm

pUNK Legends : **J.F.A.** - **CHINA WHITE**
bad samaritans - no consent - cold - chief drink alot

located at: *MANCINIS 20923 Roscoe bl. (at DeSoto)*

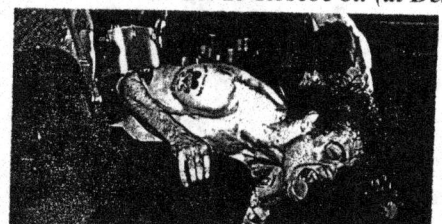

fRIDAY fEB. 3rd 7:00pm

oh yeah! ADZ a.k.a. **ADOLESCENTS** - GLUE GUN -
HARMFUL IF SWALLOWED - inhale - sixty six percent -
epsilon minus

tHURSDAY jAN. 19th 8:00pm

R.K.L. - sprung monkey - entrust

qUIKMUD productions brings you all new shows!! to get your band booked
call (818) 341-8503 or (310)358-6142

or mail demo to : 20923 Roscoe bl. canoga park. Ca. 91304 attn. jASON or lESLIE
Attn: jASON or lESLIE

I booked these bands (see the RKL show?) and made this
flyer before Photoshop... Old Skool

RKL hit the stage and that's when everything erupted.

We had security—big bouncers, a few white, a few Hispanic, and our guy T-Bone, a towering giant 40-year-old Black dude whose presence was usually enough to squash any nonsense just by standing there.

The pit went nuts, probably 150 people deep. Kids were diving off the tiny stage, bouncing off RKL's members and gear, bodies slamming into bodies. With a capacity of around 300, half the club moshing at once looked mental.

I was watching from our oversized sound booth at the back of the club, which had plexiglass shields to protect our fully analog sound-board. From there, I began to see everything break loose. The Nazi Low Riders were brawling with some of the long-haired metal kids. Shoving escalated, fists flew, and the crowd snowballed into an all-out brawl.

T-Bone jumped in to break up the first fight and got blindsided. Four Nazi punks jumped him at once. He wrestled one into a chokehold but the others kept swinging on him.

All around the floor, fights erupted. Our other bouncers were over-whelmed, tied up just trying to defend themselves. I saw T-Bone starting to wear down under the weight of the attack. I knew I had to help.

My girlfriend, my sound guy, his girlfriend, and a buddy were with me in the booth, watching it unfold. I told them I was going in. I grabbed the small can of pepper spray I kept in the booth and headed out. They yelled at me not to leave the safety of the booth. I waved them off.

The second I stepped onto the floor, a fist came out of nowhere and I ducked. The guy stumbled into another cluster of fighting bodies. That's when it hit me—I had just walked into a full-on riot, and I wasn't sure I'd even make it to T-Bone who was still swinging for his life at the front of the stage.

I kicked into overdrive, weaving and dodging as fists and bodies flew around me like some punk version of *Braveheart*. I was closing in on T-Bone when someone clipped my leg and I went down hard. My pepper spray slipped from my hand and rolled into the mayhem. I hit the sticky floor and immediately started crawling army-style through boots and bodies, trying to grab the can as it skidded away.

Just as I reached out, a boot sent the can spinning back toward me and I barely got a hold of it. At almost the same time, I felt someone yank me up by the back of my shirt. I spun around and there he was—some random skinhead dude with a huge beard cocking his fist to punch me. Instinct kicked in. I pulled up and squeezed the pepper spray right into his eyes. Direct hit. He staggered backward, screaming and clutching his face as he disappeared into the frenzy.

I looked up and saw T-Bone still battling, bent over and covering himself under a barrage of punches and kicks but refusing to be knocked to the ground. Without thinking, I pushed through the crowd and started spraying the attackers *point blank* one by one. Two of them stopped immediately, cursing and putting their hands to their faces. The other two swung blindly, coughing and gasping, but they couldn't see shit anymore.

That's when a huge Neo-Nazi monster appeared—a massive looking Viking dude. Covered in tattoos, thick beard, bald head, and crazy big arms. He locked eyes with me, pointed, and roared: "You're gonna pay, motherfucker!"

I bolted. My adrenaline spiked, and I juked and zigzagged my way through the frenzy back toward the sound booth. I dove over the little step like my life was on the line. My friends stared at me wide-eyed, realizing at the same moment that the sound booth had no door. We were trapped.

I told everyone to get low in the corner while I stood hiding by the entrance, holding my now nearly-empty spray can. The Viking Nazi charged through the crowd toward me. I waited until he was right under me, reached over the ledge, and blasted him full force. He yelled in agony, spinning around, trying to grab me through the air. He had pure rage but the pure blindness and pain shut him down.

I stepped back and realized my pepper spray was empty. No more backup. My crew stared at me like we were in big trouble.

I knew there was only one move left.

I told them, "Stay put. I'm gonna end this shit."

I jumped back onto the floor and sprinted gladiator-style toward the booking office behind the stage. I dodged punches, caught a few random glancing blows, but stayed on my feet. I burst into the office where the bar staff and waitresses were already huddled, frantically calling 911.

"What the hell is going on out there?" one of them asked.

"It's a full-on riot," I said, heading straight for my desk. I grabbed my last-resort weapon: a giant industrial bear spray canister.

They looked at me like I was totally nuts.

"Lock the door behind me," I said as I headed back into the mayhem.

The stage was trashed. RKL had bailed. I climbed up, aimed the bear spray at the ceiling, and unleashed all of it. A thick, toxic cloud spread through the room like a chemical mushroom cloud. Within seconds, the crowd turned from violent maniacs into gasping, choking fools stumbling for the exits.

People wiped at their eyes and throats, desperately trying to get out. It worked. The club emptied. I stood coughing on the stage, watching the crowd spill out the front doors into the fresh air of the parking lot.

By some miracle, no one had been critically hurt or stabbed. We had used metal detectors at the door, and I was thankful for that. I stumbled out, still wheezing and sneezing, as the last of the stragglers staggered into the street.

When I got outside, the parking lot looked like a war zone. About ten police cars, sirens screaming, floodlights blasting. A police helicopter circled overhead. The cops had twenty or so Nazi Low Riders lying face down on the asphalt, others standing with their hands laced behind their heads. Faces were bloody, hands were busted up. A few ambulances had arrived, and even a firetruck pulled up for good measure. The air was thick with leftover bear spray and pepper dust. Kids were coughing, sneezing, wailing—it was nuts.

I knew this was probably the end of any punk shows at Club M/Mancinis. Hell, I figured it was probably the end of my job too. But I was just relieved I hadn't been completely stomped out, my girlfriend and the staff were safe, and even T-Bone and the bouncers—though bloodied and bruised—were alive and standing around.

T-Bone spotted me across the parking lot, limped over, stuck out his massive hand, and shook his head in disbelief.

"Damn, man," he said. "I ain't never had a white boy save my ass before... You're fuckin' legit."

I smiled and said, "I got your back, T-Bone... and I'm only a half white boy, brother."

He laughed, we shook hands, and for a second in all the mayhem, everything felt okay.

Later I found out some of the guys arrested had active warrants. The cops had been searching for members of that Nazi Low Rider crew for assaults, robbery, even grand theft auto and they finally got them. It could've been so much worse. No one died, no one got stabbed, and I walked away knowing we got lucky as hell. I was thankful for at least that.

After these incidents, plus several more over the years, it left me thinking about that strange, ugly conundrum. Why did so many different kids—even some barely out of high school—gravitate toward violence and anger? I realized most of them were outcasts from broken homes, kids who couldn't find acceptance anywhere else. Their anger somehow twisted into a desperate need to belong to something, even if that something was completely toxic. They wanted to feel powerful, even if it meant becoming monsters. That warped psychology fascinated me and made me perplexed at the same time. I didn't like what they stood for, but I understood the emptiness and unhappiness that probably helped push them there.

That night burned a lesson into me that would repeat again and again throughout my music career: bad energy and bad choices are always lurking, ready to blow up a good thing. Alcohol, drugs, violence, ego—it's the same ugly formula.

Over the years, I noticed that same self-destructive pattern everywhere—from unknown local band kids to mega-famous headliners. The drinking and the drugs always pushed people over the edge, whether it was random Nazi punks or riot-starting crowds causing unrest at little-known clubs, or artists spiraling out of control onstage and backstage in Hollywood. Of course, as we all know, alcohol in particular seemed to be one of the main components in the destruction of so many.

However, on the flip side, there were plenty of incredible moments where alcohol served more as a social lubricant than a destructive force. Nights when nearly everyone was vibing, connecting, and living for one shared goal: to have a good time with great music.

I remember being a little kid in the 1970s, when rock concerts seemed to be happening on every corner. People got buzzed just to let loose, and the energy was nuts but somehow easygoing. Fights were rare. Sure, there were probably plenty of people battling drinking problems, but it didn't feel like a "problem" then—it was just the culture. Everyone drank. Everyone smoked. It was woven into the air, part of the atmosphere, like the smell of sweat and patchouli at a Grateful Dead show.

Even my dad carried that vibe into his daily life. He had a fully stocked bar in his office at Executive Car Leasing in West Hollywood—top-shelf booze, crystal glasses, the works. He'd pour drinks for clients and coworkers in the middle of the afternoon like it was completely normal. And back then, it was. I used to watch him, sharp suit on, glass in hand, and it felt like a movie set. Later, when I first watched Mad Men, it hit me hard—that was my dad in his prime, living that exact world. The bar, the smoke curling in the air, the confidence of closing a deal with a scotch in hand. That was the 70s: messy, glamorous, intoxicating, and just a little bit dangerous at all times.

That whole 70s and 80s "sex, drugs, and rock & roll" vibe didn't just fade—it hung in the air like cigarette smoke, waiting to be sparked again. And the Roxy brought it roaring back in the 2000s during the Camp Freddy and Metal Skool/Steel Panther residencies. Those nights weren't just shows; they were time machines.

Some nights the line between nostalgia and excess blurred, but the energy was pure magic. It wasn't always chaos or bad behavior. Sometimes it was people reconnecting with a version of themselves they'd lost... or maybe never got to be.

That's the real lesson. Sometimes we chase madness looking for mean-

The Roxy time machine...

ing, and other times we just want to dance in the firelight of the past for a little while. When the lights drop and the amps kick in, we remember what it feels like to be free.

So buckle up. Now it's time to get decadent.

Chapter 3

CAMP FREDDY & STEEL PANTHER—Bringin' Back the Days of Sex, Drugs, Porn, and Rock & Roll

The backstage wasn't nostalgia. It was resurrection. The Roxy breathing like it was 1986 again.

"Where decadence and debauchery roamed free!"

Man… this one was a blast to remember and write. Our Camp Freddy and Steel Panther nights weren't just manic—they were *fuckin' bedlam,* and every rock 'n' roll stereotype you've ever heard? *Dead-on.*

I remember it like it was yesterday: the Suicide Girls turning the dressing room into a full-on porno shoot, Steve-O from *Jackass* going all-in rock-and-roll style, and Dave Navarro lighting up onstage just so he could flip me off with a wink—just a few of the damn great stories in this chapter.

Every one of those nights was pure ego, excess, and insanity, all topped with a heavy dose of nostalgia. A head-on collision of Sunset Strip rock and raw Hollywood grit. But it wasn't madness for madness' sake. Somewhere in that blur of sex, smoke, and noise, I started to understand something deeper. *People didn't come just to be entertained. They came to forget.*

Of course, strip away the havoc and the guest stars and you'd see the truth—it was all just a well-oiled hustle. In reality, both bands were just highly decorated cover acts, but they sold out every damn time. *My band—Sound of the Struggle—regularly opened for one of them…* the debaucherous '80s tribute act known at first as *Metal Skool,* later reborn as the now-legendary *Steel Panther.* Their shows were pure carnage in the craziest way—drinks spilling, white lines cut in the shadows, the whole place buzzing like the Strip in its sleaziest, yesteryear prime.

The other residency, *Camp Freddy,* was a rotating supergroup: Dave Navarro of *Jane's Addiction,* Matt Sorum of *Guns N' Roses,* Billy Duffy of *The Cult,* and surprise guests like Ozzy, Slash, Chester from *Linkin Park,* ZZ Top, Fred Durst—hell, you never knew who'd walk onstage.

The energy was electric, the crowd unhinged: old- and new-school rockers chasing one more high, kids diving in for their first taste of it all.

I'll admit it—when I was younger, I never understood the obsession with '80s glam rock. I straight-up hated it. All that Aqua Net and spandex felt fake as hell to me: plastic, overproduced, more about image than authenticity. I was all about the rawness and emotional depth that came in with grunge. *Nirvana, Pearl Jam*—that was real to me. That was pain. That was truth.

What I missed back then was that '80s music wasn't supposed to be about truth. It was about escaping it. About fun. Feeling good. Dodging the heaviness of real life.

In contrast, the '90s made you sit with your pain. Feel it. Own it. Almost romanticize it. And when I look back now—knowing how many of those '90s legends died by their own hands or from overdoses—*Kurt Cobain, Chris Cornell, Bradley Nowell, Scott Weiland, Layne Staley*—I can't help but think: maybe there was something to the surface-level joy of glam rock. Maybe it wasn't so shallow after all. Maybe that kind of fun was a form of survival, too.

The '90s gave us emotional honesty, sure—but it also handed us darkness, burnout, and a whole generation of rock stars who couldn't make it to 40. The '80s? Messy and ridiculous, yeah—but it had laughter, color, and pure fun. Somewhere along the way, I started craving that more and more. I just wanted to feel good at the shows I worked on—escape the outside pain of reality. Not through big-time drinking or reckless drugs, but by reaching back to that era of good and simple surface-level times.

One artist I always found talented but hard to read was *Dave Navarro* from *Jane's Addiction.* He played guitar in *Camp Freddy,* and I'd seen him around for years. Something about him always felt... off. Arrogant, narcissistic, but actually kinda cool at the same time. His ex, *Carmen Electra,* had performed at *The Roxy* in the early 2000s with the original *Pussycat Dolls,* before they blew up. That's actually where I first met her. She was stunning, yeah—but also surprisingly sweet and down-to-earth. I'll admit it, I had a crush. Who didn't?

In 2009, Carmen came back to perform with *The Chelsea Girls,* an all-female cover band—basically the female version of *Camp Freddy.* They tore through rock and metal with killer musicianship and serious stage presence. Their singer, *Jill Janus,* was a friend of mine. We met when she was DJing topless in Hollywood under the alias *Penelope Tuesdae.* Tragically, she later took her own life while fronting her metal band *Huntress.*

Even after she was gone, I thought about her sometimes. She had the looks, the talent, and that untouchable aura of a star, but she'd struggled with mental health since she was young. It broke me that she never fully blossomed into the superstar she seemed destined to be. *Damn.*

Back to Carmen. She'd sometimes jump onstage with *The Chelsea Girls* to do burlesque. One night, she seemed like she might've been on something—not out of control, just amped up. But honestly, I never saw her party backstage. She always carried herself cool. That night, though, something shifted.

We were side-stage, watching the band, when she stepped closer. Out of nowhere, she slid her hand into mine. I was married at the time—wedding ring on my finger—so it caught me off guard. She leaned in, like she was about to kiss me or whisper something. I held up my ring hand, gave her a half-grin, and mouthed, *"Damn, I'm married."*

She smiled, nodded, and said, "I understand." Then she stood there quietly, watching the band, getting ready to step out under the lights.

In my head I was thinking, *"Seriously? This is how the algorithm of the universe works?"* One of the most beautiful women on the planet is about to kiss me—or at least get close—and I'm already taken. Why couldn't this have happened five years earlier? Lol. Damn algorithm.

See the wedding ring...

The funny part is, unlike *Anna Nicole Smith* in my Chapter One story—towering, Amazonian, intimidating—Carmen was tiny. Five-two tiny. I could've handled that. But life had other plans.

Now back to Navarro.

There was one time when my bias against Dave Navarro came out full force. Lemmy from *Motörhead* was scheduled to guest with Camp Freddy. He rolled in straight from the *Rainbow Bar & Grill*, already puffing on a cigarette. While his bass was getting set up, I got a call from the office: Nic (Adler) said Lemmy couldn't smoke inside *The Roxy*. I was like, "Okay… let me talk to him."

I waved over my assistant, Caveman, and we walked up to Lemmy. "Hey Lemmy, glad to have you here. One thing though—we just got word you can't smoke inside." He took a long drag, exhaled the smoke in our faces, and said, calm as hell: "Look, I'm a 62-year-old man who's been smoking my whole fucking life. I'll be damned if anyone tells me I can't smoke anywhere I want."

I looked at Caveman—we laughed, nodded, and said, "Sounds good to us. We'll let the office know."

Upstairs, Nic asked, "What did Lemmy say?" I told him, "Basically, fuck off. He's not putting it out." Nic shook his head. "You gotta try again. Tell him he has to stop." I stared right back: "Then you go tell him. Lemmy's not listening to me, and I'm not getting into a showdown with a metal legend over a cigarette." Nic threw up his arms, realizing I wasn't budging.

Right then I looked over the balcony and saw Navarro lighting up. I pointed it out. "That's where we draw the line," Nic said. "Go tell Dave he can't smoke inside."

This time I didn't hesitate. "No problem."

I grabbed Caveman and headed to Navarro. "Hey man, you can't smoke in here," I said. He motioned toward Lemmy. "But Lemmy's smoking!" "Yeah, well... you ain't Lemmy. That's how it works." Caveman backed me up.

Navarro shook his head. "That's totally fucked up."

I told him, "Then go talk to the boss. If he green-lights it, fine."

Navarro stomped upstairs, came back down with his cigarette out—and it stayed out. Caveman and I laughed our asses off.

Weirdly, it felt good to stand firm with Navarro but still let Lemmy bend the rules. Most people might've wrestled with a moral dilemma, but by then I was numb to the business. The bending, breaking, and rewriting of rules depending on who you were wasn't a conundrum—it was the culture just like politics. A system I'd been indoctrinated into without even realizing it.

And sure enough, Navarro got the last laugh. Later he lit up on-stage, knowing there was nothing we could do. He even looked right at me, winked, and I thought: *Touché, you little prick bastard. Touché.*

Touché...

Juliette Lewis was another regular. I'd talked with her plenty backstage—unfiltered, reckless, real. The night she hit the stage with *Camp Freddy* she was fire—like a polished Janis Joplin, raspy and magnetic.

After her set, sweaty and glowing, she nearly collapsed into my arms, laughing: "Sometimes I love music more than acting... too bad I couldn't make a living at it."

I told her, "You'd have been a modern-day Janis. You could've made it."

She smiled, kissed me on the cheek, and went backstage to hang with the band. Juliette always brought good energy—kind, present, grounded—It was always a breath of fresh air for sure.

Fights were rare at these shows, but not unheard of. One night a drunk guy slipped backstage while my security guy Bones was stopping a kid from stage-diving.

This wasted dude made it up the stairs, wandering without a wristband, high-fiving strangers. I knew he didn't belong when he staggered up to Billy Idol and slurred, *"Holy shit, Billy Idol!"* before half-singing, *"It's a nice day to… start again,"* fist pumping like an idiot.

I grabbed my cousin Jared and walked up. "Hey man, you snuck in. You're not supposed to be back here."

He glared. "Who the fuck are you?"

"I'm the boss. So you gotta go."

As I guided him to the stairs, he drew back his fist like he was gonna swing. Instinct took over—I cracked him with an elbow to the jaw. He dropped backward into a cluster of guests. One of them was Naveen Andrews from the show *LOST*, whose drink went flying, splashing a bunch of the *Camp Freddy* dance crew girls…they actually got pretty pissed as they were about to hit the stage now smelling like cheap beer.

The guy was dazed—lucky for me, because he was 6'0", 190 easy. Jared and I grabbed him, and by then Bones had circled back. Together, we tossed him out the side door of *The Roxy* onto the street.

That moment took me back to my days in the 90s, working in the San Fernando Valley at the *Cobalt Café* where I told you in my Neo-Nazi story that brawls weren't uncommon. I remember another one of those nights clearly—Aaron Embry and his actor brother, Ethan, came to my rescue during a full-on fight with some tank-sized kid who tried to sneak in without paying.

Aaron was working the register, and he was already known in the Valley as one of the most gifted musicians in the scene. His brother Ethan, already a well known actor in cult movies and later known as Coyote Bergstein on *Grace and Frankie*, was always hanging out at the shows—a totally down-to-earth and outgoing dude.

The *Cobalt* was packed with *ska* kids that night—around 350 in a room that wasn't really built for it. I was working the door, collecting money and stamping hands. I caught this big guy slipping past without a stamp.

"Yo," I said. "Where's your stamp?"

He ignored me. "I already paid."

"You didn't. You need to pay."

He tried to push past me again, and I grabbed his shirt. That's when he drew back, but I beat him to the punch and popped him—straight right to the jaw. He grabbed me while falling back and we both went down hard—I was still gripping the fat wad of cash in one hand.

He got on top of me quick. "I'm a fuckin' wrestler you idiot. I'm gonna choke your ass out."

And yeah, he was way friggin' strong. I was trying to keep that cash in hand while fending him off like some underground cage match with paper money about to fly everywhere. I was losing steam fast. He was starting to get his arm around my neck, and I knew I'd have to fully let go of the money if I had any chance of not getting choked out.

But then I heard Aaron's voice yelling: "Jason, I got you man!"

He jumped over me and tried to pull the guy off, but slipped and fell back on the concrete and then began grappling with the dude too. Suddenly, out of nowhere, his brother Ethan *leapt* over all of us and did something I'll never forget—he jabbed his two fingers into the dude's nostrils and yanked him backwards off me.

The guy let go of my neck, roaring in pain. Ethan pulled him off, but the guy bucked backward hard, slamming Ethan's head against a parking meter almost knocking him out.

Luckily though, the dude had had enough as he stumbled to get up and then just ran away down the street.

I sat there, still holding the cash, completely stunned. If Aaron and Ethan hadn't stepped in, I would've been out cold—or worse.

To this day, I still think about that moment. Those guys didn't have to jump in like that—but they did. And I'll always be grateful. What still blows my mind is how they were both mild-mannered, non-aggressive dudes on the surface, yet when shit hit the fan, they flipped without hesitation—authentic, raw, and ready to throw down if that's what it took. They risked their health, maybe even their careers, just to back me up. That kind of loyalty is rare in this world. It was more than just an act of friendship—it was a testament to who they really were. A reminder that sometimes the quietest ones are the ones you want next to you in the fire.

But getting back to *Camp Freddy*—most of their shows went off without a hitch. Tight sets, packed crowds, the kind of nights where everything just clicked and you thought, *Yeah, this is why we do it.*

But then came the night Courtney Love decided to crash the party.

She jumped onstage barefoot, unannounced, and dove headfirst into a few of her songs with the band scrambling to keep up. It was chaotic, jagged, and sloppy—but also charged with that wild, unpredictable energy only Courtney could bring. Whether it was brilliance or bedlam, the crowd soaked it up. That was her gift: even when things unraveled, people couldn't look away.

Luckily, Paris Hilton wasn't in the building this time, or it could've spiraled into a full-blown meltdown like the one I write about later in this book. (And trust me—you'll get to that crazy story soon enough.)

Now *Steel Panther*... that was a whole different beast. They were a time machine straight back to the most outrageous, spandex-soaked corners of the '80s. Yeah, it was a parody, but it was also dead-on—like stepping into a strip-club fever dream circa 1986.

The band crushed it every time, the singer was pure fire, and the crowd treated every week like New Year's Eve on the Sunset Strip. It blew up so big, I couldn't even get some of my own friends or family in through the front door anymore. So I'd sneak them in through the side when I could, or a bouncer would slip them past if they tossed him a twenty.

The 1980s mayhem returned with Steel Panther...

The *Roxy's* official capacity was 450. We hit 600 without breaking a sweat. And when it pushed past 650? Forget it—wall-to-wall bodies, the air so hot and thick it felt like breathing through a wet towel. Shoulder-to-shoulder, sweat dripping from the ceiling, the kind of nights where the building itself felt alive. But somehow—whether it was the miracle of rock & roll, blind luck, or maybe just someone somewhere getting "a little incentive" to look the other way—we never got busted by the city.

Guest appearances weren't uncommon, but it was mostly about the music. Full-on hair metal. *Poison, Winger, Ratt, Mötley Crüe* covers.

One night, *Poison's* guitarist CC DeVille showed up to jam *"Unskinny Bop."* The band launched into it, the crowd went nuts, and CC crushed it—until the song ended and he just... stayed.

He kept playing through the next two songs like he was part of the band. *Steel Panther* tried to roll with it, staying in character, but I could tell they were starting to get pissed. Satchel, the guitarist, turned to us and mouthed, "Get him off the fucking stage!"

We all exchanged looks, and I asked their tour manager, "Are we seriously about to kick CC DeVille off the stage?"

He shrugged. "Yeah, the guys are over it."

After the band finished the song *"Sister Christian,"* I walked out and tapped CC on the shoulder. He turned, red-eyed, clearly wasted.

"What's goin' on?"

I said, "CC, we gotta make room for another guest. Time to wrap it up." (Total lie.)

He slurred, "Man, I'm just jamming. They want me up here... I'm CC Deville, fukin' *Poison* man!"

I turned to Satchel, and he gave his singer a *look*. His frontman then leaned into the mic and said, "Alright guys, let's give it up for CC DeVille! Thanks for jamming with us tonight!"

The crowd roared, and we gently pulled him offstage. He stumbled down the small backstage stage stairs, tripping and stumbling to the ground with his guitar still strapped on. I unhooked the guitar, helped him up, and *Steel Panther's* manager gave him the "you killed it" routine.

I handed CC some drink tickets and said, "You were awesome, man. The real deal."

He smiled like a kid who'd just won something, and eventually, after a few drinks, made his way back to the *Rainbow* to party the rest of the night away. Total classic.

There was another night when a pack of women showed up—eight of them, dressed like they had either just walked out of a strip club or were fully committing to the fantasy. Either way, they were already tipsy and having an amazing time. They were cheering, flashing the band, showing their tattoos, and just going all out.

I had to run up to the office to grab something, and while I was up there, I heard them laughing and heading down the hallway. I figured they had wristbands—maybe they were friends of the band or girlfriends or something. But when I came out of the office, I heard moaning coming from the hallway bathroom. Over the noise of *Steel Panther* downstairs, it was loud enough to make me check it out.

That bathroom and I had seen some things—*Ron Jeremy dressed as Santa getting a blowjob, Paris Hilton dancing and pointing at herself in the mirror*—but this night added another entry to the list. The stall door was shut, but I looked down and saw four feet and two skirts around some ankles. I laughed. Another lesbian bathroom hookup at the *Roxy*. Typical.

But the moaning from the main dressing room? That was something else. I opened the door slowly and was hit with a full-blown girl-on-girl orgy. Three women on the couch, three more on the floor—all of them almost completely naked, two going down on one, and the others making out with them. I half-expected a camera crew in the corner.

No camera. Just pure live porno.

I stood there for a beat, laughed and then said, "Hey ladies! Looks like you're having a great time... but are you with the band?"
One of them looked up and said, "We're hoping to hang out with them."
"Do you have wristbands?"
Nope. They said security let them in. Then I looked closer—two of them looked familiar.
"Wait, aren't you guys from the *Suicide Girls?*"
They lit up. "Yeah, we all are!"

Turns out they were from the goth alt-nude site called *Suicide Girls,* that had teamed up with *PETA* one time for that *"I'd Rather Go Naked Than Wear Fur"* event we'd hosted prior at the *Roxy.*

It was one of those nights you couldn't make up. *Steve-O* from *Jackass* was the "special guest," stumbling onstage drunk, trying to rap over a couple of songs while the girls danced behind him. Total decadence, pure strip-club energy disguised as rock & roll. By the time he wrapped up, he somehow wound up backstage... completely naked.

When I went to check the area after the show, there he was—flat-out on our grimy backstage couch, surrounded by four *Suicide Girls* who were literally licking him from head to toe. I just cracked up on the spot. *Steve-O* looked up, grinning like a lunatic, and says in his signature voice, "Dude, the world is cruel and unusual... but this is bliss, man."

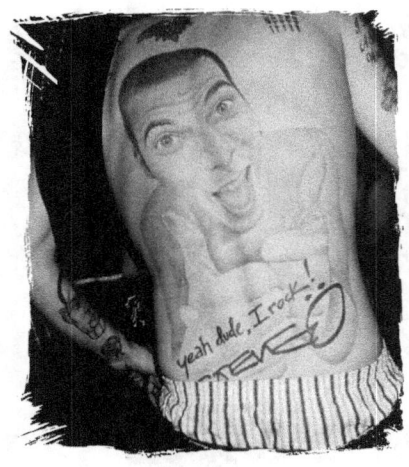

Then he adds, dead serious, slurring his words, "If anyone's looking for me, I don't care…I'm not available." I told him no problem — just lock the door so no one barges in like I did. "Thanx, dude… I swear I'm going sober after this." And the nutty thing is, he meant it. Not long after, he actually did get sober — and I think he stayed that way.

Side note: my cousin even dated one of those *Suicide Girls* for a couple of months. She was like a bisexual Tasmanian Devil, spinning through his life at full speed. It didn't last. She freaked him out when she went full-on stalker and then had his name tattooed near her breast. That was the deal-breaker. He smartly bailed out fast.

Now, Getting back to the other *Suicide Girls* I'd just stumbled in on mid-orgy… I told them flat out they had twenty minutes. "You're not on the list. You can hang a bit longer, but once the band wraps, you're out of here."

One of the girls said, "This was our dream—to get dirty backstage at the Roxy. We just wanted to be part of that history."

I laughed. "Well, congrats. First all-girl orgy I've ever walked in on back here. That's a Roxy first."

Ten minutes later, I see Mark McGrath from *Sugar Ray* coming up the stairs.

"Hey man, what's up?" he said.

I grinned. "Main dressing room. Go see for yourself."

His eyes widened, and he headed down the hall. I watched from the far end as he opened the door.

"Hot damn! Will you look at that?" he said in that signature animated voice—and then walked right in.

I laughed my ass off and headed back to the stage.

Eventually the girls came down, looking sweaty and slightly smeared, and thanked me before heading back into the crowd. My security guy at the back door, Big Al, waved at them.

"How'd they get past you?" I asked. "They snuck into the backstage and turned it into a damn porn movie."

Al grinned. "They said they'd text me nudes if I let them in. And they actually did. Besides, it was a throwback vibe tonight. Figured I'd honor the Sunset Strip."

I laughed. "Yeah, I probably would've done the same."

Some of the Suicide Girls looked like bonafide models!

There were quite a few adult film actresses who would come out to *Steel Panther* shows to party and spread the love. I knew a lot of them, and they always seemed to be chasing a good time. One of them was my friend Brandi, who became pretty famous under the name *Brittney Skye*. She called me to get on the guest list and said she was bringing a few friends. I'd known Brandi before she got into the porn world—back when we were both working for *M Production's* street team called *Sickness,* which was started by Clown from *Slipknot*.

She was super cute and young—maybe 21—and trying to make her way in the music business. About a year after working together, I remember her pulling me aside in the office one day and saying she wanted to show me something. She handed me a couple Polaroids, and my eyes nearly popped out. There she was, fully naked in a bunch of provocative poses.

I laughed, surprised. "Whoa, I didn't expect this... What are these?"

She told me they were sample shots for a casting tryout—she was about to start doing adult films. Her first movie, she said, was going to be called *Barely Legal* and then she was slated to film *Deep Oral Ladies* after. I asked how it all came about, and she said she met a producer at a concert who told her she had the look and could make serious money.

Honestly, it tracked. Brandi had always been flirty and super sexual. I remembered this one time before she started in porn, after my band *Rumblefish* played the *Key Club*—she came backstage, told me I looked hot up there, and asked if I wanted to come over to her place after I was done packing up. I said sure. I drove up to her place in Valencia—took about an hour—but by the time I got there I was so tired, nothing ended up happening and I fell asleep on her bed.

The weirdest part? In the morning, her little boy walked into the room. I didn't even know she had a kid. He casually said, "Hi mommy," like it was totally normal I was there. That's when I realized this was probably routine for her—different guys showing up after shows. She wasn't looking for anything serious. We never hooked up, but some of my friends did, and they told similar stories. It was always Brandi initiating. I guess she was *built* for the porn scene.

She showed up to the Roxy that night with a few other girls. Gave me a big hug and kiss, introduced me to her friends—one of them I already knew: Jennifer aka *Chloe Dior*. Another cute one. They were pumped to be there, and I gave them some drink tickets to offset the overpriced booze. During the show, they partied hard, even flashed the crowd a few times. People went nuts.

Toward the end of the set, they came over begging to go backstage. I knew it was going to be packed, but they were harmless and fun, so I let it slide. They kissed and hugged me and my security guy, and made their way back. You could hear them laughing and screaming from the backstage area.

Steel Panther wrapped their set, and I let their manager know there were some enthusiastic porn girl guests backstage. He was cool with it, said the band wouldn't mind since there would be a ton of hanger-ons backstage—especially on a night like this.

Then the real backstage crowd hit—tons of industry folks and band friends with wristbands, flooding the backstage like a madhouse. I'd already let my cousins and their friends back there, and I saw a few familiar faces, including my buddy Stick.

About half an hour later, Stick comes out grinning like a kid who just got away with something. "Dude," he says. "Thanks for letting Brandi and her friends back. You won't believe what happened. I was in the bathroom, and she pushed me into the stall—didn't even say hi. Undid my belt, unzipped me, actually kinda violently hit it a few times with her fist, just to get it going, then just started sucking it."

I couldn't stop laughing. "No way. For real?"

"Totally. Then, like 30 seconds in, she stops, smacks it with her hand again and says, 'Okay, that's it for now. I got more people to meet.' Left me standing there with my dick out."

"Did she come back?"

"Nope. But her friend Taylor*(Rain)* did. Pushed me against the wall and finished the job."

I just shook my head. "Welcome to the *Roxy*, man. Anything's possible."

After that night, I couldn't help thinking back to the mid-'80s. Sex, drugs, and rock and roll ruled the scene. It reminded me of that scene in *The Wrestler*, where Mickey Rourke's character, Ram, says to Marisa Tomei, *The '80s fuckin' ruled, man. Then that Cobain pussy had to come around and ruin it all.*

Damn, I thought to myself... he couldn't have been more right!

And at that moment, I finally got it. The music I didn't really vibe with as a teenager—hair metal, glam, all that stuff—that was the very essence of what the *Roxy*, the *Whisky*, the *Rainbow*, and the Strip were all about for so many people.

It wasn't about authenticity or deep lyrics. It was a weird kind of freedom. It was a place where people could party hard, feel young, and live for a few hours like the world wasn't closing in on them.

These things got me thinking about the song; *Time to Pretend* by *MGMT* — a killer young band back in 2008. It's about pretending to dive headfirst into the reckless, hedonistic rock star life — poking fun at all the clichés: drugs, models, excess — while still secretly wanting to live it. But there's a sting in there too: a nod to the emptiness and loss that comes with chasing that dream. It's a striking contradiction, naked and real. The first time I heard it, it hit me hard. I instantly loved it.

I can't list the exact lyrics here (go check them out for sure), but I can put them in my own words — from their point of view:

They're young, reckless, and in the prime of their lives. They want to make music, stack cash, and end up with beautiful wives. Maybe they'll run off to Paris, flirt with danger, and hang with the stars. They'll keep the island stocked with white powder and fast cars.

They've decided to burn bright and burn out. They see exactly where it leads, so why not live it anyway? The thought of trading it all for office jobs and morning commutes feels like slow death.

And in chasing it, they know they'll lose pieces of themselves. They'll drift from their families, from the innocence of childhood, from pets, homes, and even the kind of boredom that once felt like freedom. Love will be temporary, life will keep restarting, marriages will crumble, and the cycle will repeat.

In the end, it'll all crash in tragedy like a pre-legendary rock star choking on his own vomit— but deep down, they've always known they were fated for that role.

Would that spirit of true rock and roll ever fully come back and take over a big part of culture again? Hard to say.

But if you wanted to have a small fleeting taste of it, all you had to do was step into the *Roxy* or through the *Rainbow's* front door. In seconds, you were transported back.

It wasn't always pretty, but it was a real escape. And for some people, that was everything.

Burden and Brilliance...

Looking back, I loved the bubble of *Camp Freddy* and *Steel Panther* while it lasted at the *Roxy*. It was like watching a music scene mutate into its own jacked-up little universe. The late nights, the excess, the unfiltered joy—it wasn't a slogan, it was a simulation of the past, pulsing through that building every damn week.

But it wasn't all reckless abandon. Sometimes it was people stepping into a version of themselves they couldn't be at home or chained behind a desk. These shows gave them permission to be louder, wilder, more alive than anywhere else. And for a few hours, that was enough. Maybe that's all it ever really is.

Still, there's always a price—even for artists. The same stage that lifts you up can hollow you out. You can stand in the spotlight with everything you thought you wanted and still feel something gnawing at your chest. If you don't face it, that emptiness spreads. I saw it again and again. When the lights went dark and the crowd disappeared, too many were left chasing a high that, by definition, was never meant to last.

Like the blues taught long before rock & roll—some artists don't bargain with the devil at the crossroads. They just bleed themselves dry night after night until there's nothing left.

The next story is about someone who carried both the brilliance and the burden. She came to the *Roxy* already burning hot. You know her name. I watched her genius and her destiny collide, backstage, nursing a big bottle of Jack like her fragile life depended on it...

Chapter 4

AMY WINEHOUSE—The Destiny of Destruction

"Well, what I really want is a mixer and perhaps someone to join me for a few drinks in the backstage room...Do you want to join me?"

I remember back in 2007 when the *Roxy* booking office told me we had a "hot" new act from the UK coming in. They said there was serious industry buzz, and this would be her first U.S. show.

I didn't think much of it. The *Roxy* booked "buzzworthy" performers all the time. Some were cool and down-to-earth; others acted like they were already *Elton John* or *Janis Joplin*. Plenty flamed out before they even got going, but a lucky few went on to real fame—with the *Roxy* as their launchpad.

What I didn't realize was that this one—*Amy Winehouse*—was different. She was rare. A once-in-a-generation talent on a slow-motion collision course with disaster. And I'd get to watch it unfold, up close, on one hell of a night at the *Roxy*.

The show was mostly industry invites: *Island / Def Jam* execs lining up to see their "hyped-up" artist live for the first time. Only a handful of public tickets went on sale, and they were gone in a blink.

A few of my friends started hitting me up. I loved having them there; it made the night more fun, more unpredictable. I'd stick them on the guest list, throw them some drink tickets, and maybe sneak them backstage to stir up a little trouble. I was definitely the resident prankster at the *Roxy*… but that's a story for another time.

That day, my buddy Noah Newman—who played tennis for UCLA and gave me lessons in exchange for passes to the good shows—called and said, "Jay… a few of the guys and I want to come to the Winehouse show… she's fuckin' amazing."

I hadn't really heard much about her, probably because I was buried in work, but I trusted Noah's taste. If he said she was amazing, I figured she was worth paying attention to.

I rolled into the *Roxy* around 1 p.m., and my sound and light crew were already there. I had them in early because I knew this crowd would be crawling with industry people, and we had to be dialed in. I wanted everything locked before Amy and her crew showed up—because if something could go wrong in this business, it usually did.

I always tried (and sometimes failed) to head off the storm before it started. Nights like this, with the artist's agent, label reps, and assorted industry sharks in the room, could make or break reputations.

If the night went to shit, or if it blew people's minds, it would be remembered. And *Nic Adler* and his dad *Lou* treated the *Roxy's* rep like it was holy. The music industry's like the mafia: you deliver, or you get a bad rap (can happen even if you are a world-famous and legendary club).

I also decided to grab the backstage artist rider myself, since there was a ton of alcohol requested and my assistant wasn't old enough to buy some of the stuff we didn't already have in-house.

For anyone who's never worked in live music, the "artist rider" is basically the rock-star shopping list—the contract attachment that spells out exactly what the performer expects in their backstage setup. Food, booze, towels, lighting specs, furniture—you name it. Some riders are simple; some are straight-up diva manifestos.

This one? Pretty normal for a full band.

Amy had backup singers and a full band, so I didn't think much of the two bottles of Jack Daniels, the cabernet, vodka, case of beer, and mixers on the list.

As I was driving back from the market around 2 p.m., I figured I had time to spare. Soundcheck wasn't until 3:30 p.m. But when I pulled into the parking lot, I saw a van with equipment already being loaded through our stage roll-up door.

I parked fast and saw my crew helping unload. Luckily, my guys had shown up early, because Amy's crew had too. And even though it wouldn't have been my fault if they'd beaten us there, I knew damn well I'd never hear the end of it.

Production is a constant guessing game with zero room for error and endless ways to screw yourself.

I didn't know what *Amy Winehouse* even looked like, but I didn't see any woman near the stage or floor, so I figured she'd roll in later, once the setup was done. About forty minutes later, the band and singers were just about ready to soundcheck. I headed upstairs to my office to grab the schedules and post them around the venue.

My office was just down the hall from the main backstage room, and as I reached the top of the stairs, this scraggly, small figure suddenly emerged from the backstage door and started walking toward me.

Amy came walking down the backstage hallway...

Since I had no idea what Amy looked like, I was caught off guard when this girl stuck out her hand and said, in a thick English accent, *"Hi, I'm Amy!"*

Her hand was tiny and bony, nails painted black but chipped. Her hair looked like a rat's nest—an old hair-extension bun perched on top of frayed, frazzled real hair. She barely wore any makeup and looked nothing like the polished TV image I'd see later once she blew up. Her skin was pale, like she hadn't slept in days. She was rail-thin—long, gangly legs like a baby bird—and dressed head-to-toe in black thrift-store goth: worn, torn, and hanging loose off her frame.

The first thing that really caught my attention, though, was the bottle in her hand—a big-ass Jack Daniels she must've brought in herself. And it wasn't just open—it was half-empty.

I thought, *No way could this barely 100-pound girl knock back half a bottle of Jack by herself.* But before I could wrap my head around that image, my focus went back to her face.

In this soft, feminine, and kind of sexy tone, she asked, *"Do you guys have any mixer to go with this Jack?"*

"Yeah, definitely! You want Red Bull, Coke, Diet Coke, or something else?" I said.

She looked straight into my eyes and, without blinking, said, *"Well, what I really want is a good mixer... and perhaps someone to join me for a few drinks in the backstage room. Do you want to join me?"*

I froze for a second, wondering if this was an invite to get buzzed and messy in the dressing room—with one drink turning into a few bad decisions, which had definitely happened backstage before—or if she was just another lonely artist who'd been on the road too long, looking for a drinking buddy to kill some time with.

While that thought rolled around, I gave her another once-over. She was kinda cute, but not my type. I've never been into chicken legs on women, and I definitely couldn't picture myself running my hands through that tangled hair-extension bun while unbuttoning her shirt.

But honestly, that wasn't the real reason I was about to pass. The truth was, I wasn't much of a drinker, had never day-drank with an artist, and there was no way in hell I could run an important show like this if I wasn't sober.

So I smiled and said, *"Aww, thanks. I wish I could, but I'm the production manager, and I've gotta get your soundcheck going so you can kill it tonight... But I'll run downstairs and grab you some mixers, pronto."*

As I walked away and headed toward the kitchen, I heard her mutter under her breath—just loud enough for me to catch—*"I don't even need a mixer. Straight Jack is fine."*

I came back from the kitchen with a Diet Coke and a regular Coke, heading toward the main backstage room.

Not sure where she'd wandered off to, but when I walked in, the place looked like a thrift store had exploded—raggedy clothes tossed across the couch, bottles scattered on the table. A few of them were already cracked open, a couple sips gone.

Her band and backup singers were downstairs handling soundcheck like pros, so I figured this was just how Amy rolled. Still, I couldn't shake the thought: *How the hell is she going to pull off a show tonight if she's already halfway through a bottle of Jack—and it's only 3:45 in the afternoon?*

I could smell disaster brewing. The kind that creeps up slow and then blows up right in front of a sold-out crowd.

For some reason, Amy never did soundcheck. Her band and singers nailed theirs, though—tight, professional, zero drama. By 6 p.m., I was guessing she'd passed out on that backstage couch, marinating in Jack Daniels. I didn't say a word to my crew or hers, but in my head I was already bracing for the train wreck: her stumbling onstage, slurring lyrics, blowing notes, maybe even losing her temper when the crowd didn't cheer her drunken act.

I thought, *Here we go again—another potential superstar drowning their shot in booze.*

When doors opened at 8, the line was already snaking down the street. She wasn't on for a while, but by 8:30 the place was wall-to-wall. The VIP section[1] was stacked with important faces. The buzz in the room was insane—people leaning in, eyes darting, everyone ready to see this *"next big thing."*

I still hadn't heard a single song of hers. All I knew was that she had a doo-wop, '50s–'60s throwback vibe with a soul punch. White girls who could channel that deep, rich sound—the kind the great Black women singers of the past had mastered—were having a serious moment.

Maybe Amy was a modern-day Janis Joplin… or maybe she'd end up like a drunken Jim Morrison, plastered, off-beat, half out of tune. In my head it was a coin flip… okay, more like 90/10 that she was about to crash and burn.

As showtime crept closer, my phone buzzed. My assistant was telling me they needed another bottle of Jack backstage.

I figured it was for the band and backup singers holed up in the smaller backstage room. Since I was the only one allowed to grab booze from the kitchen, I headed down, pulled a fresh bottle of Jack from the shelf, and started down the hallway toward that room.

---

1. Our VIP section was legendary. A security guard always stood at the two little stairs behind the red velvet rope, making sure nobody got through without that prized VIP wristband. I used to crack up watching how sloppy people got up there—dancing on seats, climbing on tables, making total idiots of themselves. Since our alcohol was often marked up 10x or more (one of the only ways the Roxy kept its doors open—we never really made money off ticket sales), people would get obliterated and rack up $2,000–$3,000 tabs without blinking. It was a cash cow, plain and simple, and the waitresses loved it—bigger tabs meant bigger tips.

The smaller backstage space didn't even have a door, so I just stepped right in. And there they were: Amy's band, crammed shoulder-to-shoulder, about eight guys total.

They looked like they'd stepped straight out of a Motown time capsule: slick suits, polished shoes, the whole Temptations-meets-classic-soul vibe. Sharp as hell, ready to hit the stage like pros.

"Hey guys, here's that bottle of Jack," I said.

They all laughed at the same time, and one of them said, in this half-joking, deadpan way, *"That ain't for us—that's for Amy in the other room."*

I was like, *"Wait a second... she already has a bottle?"*

They just nodded, shaking their heads side to side, and without saying another word, their faces told me everything: *Yep. Amy does what Amy does. Ain't no one gonna stop her. She's her own boss.*

So I headed to the main backstage room and knocked. A few seconds later, the door creaked open.

To my surprise, there was Amy, now all made up, dressed in a cute little outfit that looked nothing like the thrift-store goth mess I'd met earlier. *Damn,* I thought, *she cleans up nice.*

She reached out, took the bottle from me, and said, slurring just enough for me to catch it, *"Thank you, love... you guys are great here."*

I made my way back to the front-of-house soundboard to make sure everything was squared away with my pain-in-the-ass sound guy, Frankie Fingers. Amy and her crew were now onstage, tucked behind the big Roxy curtain, doing last-minute prep.

As usual once a band hit the stage, I did my lap through the backstage area—making sure no one had passed out, no mirrors had been punched, and no sinks were leaking.

The hallway bathroom was fine. The small room where the band had been hanging out? Clothes and personal crap scattered everywhere, but no major damage.

Then I walked into Amy's main dressing room—and it was a war zone. Makeup, clothes, and random crap were everywhere.

My eyes locked on the first bottle of Jack from earlier, completely drained. Then I spotted the second bottle, the one I'd just brought her not even a full hour ago, and it was already a quarter gone.

I just stood there, shaking my head. I'd seen plenty of big-time drinking backstage, but never someone who barely hit triple digits on the scale putting away booze like that... and still walking, let alone about to perform in front of a packed house.

Damn... this is insane. Full-on rock 'n' roll, baby, I thought, laughing to myself.

I stepped out toward the floor and spotted my buddies posted up near the VIP section. My buddy Noah was there. I leaned in and said, *"Man... Amy is kinda crazy. I've got a lot to tell you later."*

I headed back to my spot by the side of the stage and saw Amy standing there in her slick little dress, ready to roll.

My monitor guy gave me the nod that we were good to go. I shot the signal up to Bolle in the lighting booth, then threw a thumbs-up to Frankie at the front-of-house soundboard.

The curtain started to rise, and the place exploded. The crowd roared, clapping and screaming like they were about to witness the second coming of rock 'n' roll.

The band kicked in tight, smooth as hell, while the backup singers launched into this full-on doo-wop routine: sync'd moves, flawless harmonies, the whole classic soul package.

Amy just stood there, head down, not moving, swaying ever so slightly like she couldn't quite find her balance.

I thought, *Oh man... here comes the shit-show.*

Then, out of nowhere, the band switched gears and slammed into *"Addicted."*

And just like that, Amy lit up. No sign of stumbling, no drunken haze. She started grooving, swaying with this magnetic, old-school sexiness, moving side to side like the stage was hers alone.

Song after song, she rolled through the set like it was second nature. Then, near the end, she hit that line—clear as a bell—*"They tried to make me go to rehab, but I said, no, no, no."*

She was dead-on in tune, swaggering with this raw, untouchable confidence I'd only seen in a handful of artists in my life.

And just like that, Amy lit up. No sign of stumbling, no drunken haze. She started grooving, swaying with this magnetic, old-school sexiness, moving side to side like the stage was hers alone.

Song after song, she rolled through the set like it was second nature. Then, near the end, she hit that line—clear as a bell—"They tried to make me go to rehab, but I said, no, no, no."

I couldn't believe it. She was everything the industry hype machine had promised, and more. The real deal. And she was doing it with enough alcohol in her system to put most people face-down on the floor.

Her voice was a reincarnation of classic Black soul divas, with a streak of Janis Joplin and a little goth shadow around the edges. It was *fucking mesmerizing.*

Right there in front of me, I was watching the rise of the next big star.

She finished *"Rehab,"* and the place erupted—people on their feet, clapping, screaming for more.

I stepped away from my spot and waded through the crowd to check on my friends.

"So… what do you think?" I asked.

Noah didn't even pause. "Dude, she's fucking incredible. Totally off the hook."

I grinned, but it wasn't just pride. It was that weird mix of awe and unease you get when you know you've just witnessed something rare… and maybe doomed. *You have no idea how truly amazing she is,* I told him. *And when I tell you the rest, you might not believe half of it.*

Walking back toward the stage, the applause still rattling the walls, it hit me: some people are just born to blaze like a goddamn supernova—brilliant, untouchable, and gone way too fast. You can drag them to rehab, throw them lifelines, beg them to change, but in the end, they're the only ones steering that ship.

Could Amy have sobered up and rewritten her story? Absolutely[2]. But maybe for certain tortured souls, tragedy is the only chapter that feels like an ending. Maybe it's the one thing that finally gives them peace.

That night, I knew I was watching both the rise of something extraordinary and the first signs of its collapse. And I can only hope that wherever she is now, in whatever comes next, she's finally found the happiness that always slipped through her fingers here on Earth.

---

2. **Sadly,** Amy seemed like she was never able to find happiness through fame or money. She definitely burned bright and fast. She passed away from alcohol poisoning and a mix of pills on July 23rd 2011 at the age of 27.

Whispers from a Different Realm...

After working with Amy and other artists cut from the same cloth, I began to realize something about certain voices. Some singers don't just entertain you; they grab you by the soul and shake something loose inside you that you didn't even know was there. *Amy had that.* Her voice burned fast and bright, a fire that could stop you in your tracks, leave you haunted, and make you feel like she was singing straight through you.

But genius doesn't always roar like that. Sometimes it whispers. Sometimes it hides inside a fragile shell, cracked but still glowing. *Amy's flame was jagged and raw,* but there are legends whose gift lives in another realm entirely: slower, quieter, more delicate, yet no less powerful.

A year after Amy's night at the *Roxy,* I found myself in the presence of one of those legends. This time, the energy wasn't wild release. It was silence. Reverence. A weight that carried decades of history, family, tragedy, and radiance—all wrapped in one tender, complicated human being.

It reminded me of something he once put into a song—the idea of shutting the door, shutting the world out, and finding a room where your fears can't reach you. That lyric always felt like his life in miniature: *music as sanctuary,* even when his own mind was anything but. His gift shaped an entire generation, yet he carried his demons right alongside the harmonies.

This show wasn't a party. It wasn't excess. It was intimate, and it left a mark on me that cut deeper than I expected. Because what I saw in him, I also saw reflected in my own family, in my father, and in my fears about how the mind can both elevate and betray us.

And now, let's talk about the recently passed legend himself. *Mr. Brian Wilson...* I had a pretty haunting interaction with him too.

Chapter 5

BRIAN WILSON–The Fragile Genius

"I've been signing poor Brian's autograph for him for decades"

I was damn excited when I heard we'd booked the Beach Boys' legend himself—and that Al Jardine would be joining him for the Carl Wilson Foundation benefit. It was 2008, the 10-year anniversary of the benefit concert, and the lineup was stacked: Dick Dale, Wendy and Carnie Wilson, and more.

Brian had played a solo concert at the Roxy once before—way back in 2000—for a live album he released called *Brian Wilson – Live at the Roxy Theatre.* I was off tour with my own band at the time, and whenever I was home, I picked up street promotion work for the Roxy and Whisky[1]. That night, Brian gave a killer performance, and fans actually flew in from all over Europe just to be there. I even scored a signed poster from the show—though it later got destroyed when my storage flooded.

Flash forward to 2008—Brian was about to perform again at the *Roxy.* I had mixed feelings about how it might go. Even in 2000, he'd seemed a bit mentally checked out, and now, in his late sixties, I figured he might be even more out of it. I wasn't sure if he could still pull off those *Beach Boys* classics—or even keep himself on track. The last thing I wanted was for it to turn into some cringe-worthy moment for a legend. I scraped together a budget to rent extra monitors and gear so at least the sound would hold up... even if everything else didn't.

I'd heard from the booking office that Brian would have one of the local Hollywood bands backing him for the gig, and that he'd be bringing

---

1. **I'd been doing street promotion** since I formed my first real band, Ku De Tah, back in 1989. And I was damn good at it—not just because I had to be, but because I actually enjoyed it. There was nothing like plastering flyers and slapping up stickers everywhere, getting people curious about this new band on the rise. There was a real rush in it. No better way to make noise, short of getting into a magazine—which was damn near impossible unless you had some serious connections or cash. Remember, this was before bands could lean on the internet for promotion. Back then, guerrilla marketing wasn't just the norm—it was the only way. And it was free, if you were willing to put in the time and hustle. And trust me, I was all in. When social media first started creeping onto the scene—Friendster, MySpace—I jumped on it like a starving man at a buffet. Free promotion? Hell yes. I was spamming message boards, blasting out messages to kids all over the world, building little "street teams" of fans who'd pass out flyers, spread the word, and get people hyped. I used the internet like a scalpel, carving out awareness for my bands in places we'd never even set foot. That grind? That raw, DIY hustle? It paid off. It's a big reason I got signed—not once, but at least twice—out of the four record deals I landed over the years with different bands. Street promotion wasn't just a side hustle; it was part of my DNA. It was survival in a world where only the loudest voices got heard.

his own keyboard for a short soundcheck. I figured he'd probably stick to the classics and keep it loose—surrounded by family, friends, and plenty of support.

As we got closer to soundcheck, I saw Brian come in through the side roll-up door with another guy, who I assumed was his "handler" or manager. I knew I wanted him to sign the old *Roxy* poster from the 2000 gig—the one from his live album. I told my assistant at the time, a guy we called *Caveman,* to keep an eye out for Brian when he came backstage, and to make sure he signed the poster if I wasn't around.

I was wrapping up a few things in my office when I realized it had been 45 minutes and the soundcheck still hadn't started. That usually meant something was off—tech issues, delays, whatever. I stepped out into the backstage hallway and was surprised to see Brian just wandering around, looking lost and completely disoriented. He was staring at the framed pictures and posters I'd hung all over the Roxy's backstage walls, but not really seeing them—like he didn't even know where he was.

I walked over and asked, "Brian, you alright? Are you looking for the backstage rooms?"

He turned slowly, looked right at me, and said, "Oh hi, I don't really know what room I'm supposed to be in."

His voice, the way he said it—it had that confused, fragile tone. Like early dementia.

I knew that voice. My dad had it.

My dad suffered from something called *Korsakoff Syndrome*—alcohol-induced dementia. He spent the last ten years of his life in a convalescent care facility, and somehow, he remembered me right up until that last year. I'll never forget coming off tour one time, going to visit him after many months, and seeing him down the hall, walking slow, looking all confused.

I tapped him on the shoulder and said, "Hey Dad, how's it going?"

He turned to me, eyes vacant, and said, "Oh hi, ummm, do I know you?"

It was one of the strangest, saddest feelings I've ever had. I hugged him, led him to his room, trying to play it cool. When we sat down, he looked at me again and said, "I don't know why, but your face looks so familiar. I don't understand, but for some reason, I feel like crying."

That hit me like a dagger to the heart. I could feel the tears coming, so I excused myself to the bathroom. Staring at myself in the mirror, I knew then—it was over. The man I called Dad was gone. I couldn't lean on him anymore. It was a shift, a turning point. I no longer had a "dad," but I still had love for him, and I would stay with him until the end.

Now, as I stood there looking into Brian's eyes, I saw that same look—the same hollow, lost confusion. A tear welled up, but I bit my lip and shook it off. Standing face to face with a living legend, a musical genius, I was pulled back to reality by voices yelling from downstairs, "Where's Brian? Anyone seen where he wandered off to?"

I yelled back down that he was in the hallway and on his way.

I turned to Brian and said, "Your band's ready—they're waiting for you to soundcheck."

He smiled and said, "Sometimes I get a bit lost, but everyone always lets me know where I need to be."

I pointed him toward the stairs. He gripped the railing, steadying himself, and made his way down to the stage.

The soundcheck was something we were all looking forward to. My whole crew was curious to see and hear Brian run through a few songs. As soon as he started, the office staff came out too. Some watched from the upstairs DJ booth balcony, while others gathered on the floor.

Brian eased into a few *Beach Boys* classics. His voice was a little shaky, but honestly, he sounded pretty damn good. His hands trembled on the keys, but the music still came through clean, and his backing band was tight.

We wrapped the soundcheck without any issues. I turned to Caveman and said, "We've got to get Brian's autograph on the Roxy 2000 live performance poster, and on the big Roxy wall poster with all the famous signatures."

As showtime crept closer, my wife at the time showed up. She was from eastern Europe where they loved anything that was considered rock music[2] and thus, a huge *Beach Boys* fan. Since this was a private event for the *Carl Wilson Foundation,* the guest list was tight, and I could only bring in a few people. Family always came first, then maybe a couple of close friends if there was room.

When she arrived, she headed straight for the backstage area to meet me.

As she walked up the stairs, I spotted Brian coming out of his dressing room, wandering alone again. Caveman and I were at the top of the stairs, and when she reached us, I pointed down the hallway. "There's Brian," I said. "Let's go get his autograph."

The three of us walked toward him. Brian was standing there, staring at the old posters and pictures lining the walls, looking like he was lost in thought—or just lost again. Caveman spoke up: "Hey Brian, would you mind signing some stuff for the Roxy?"

Brian turned to us and said, "Sure… ummm, where do you want me to sign?"

Brian's small scraggly autograph that Al Jardine shook his head a t...

I stood there watching and thinking, *This ain't exactly a John Hancock moment… anyone who sees this is gonna think it's a fake.* But at least I had proof.

I snapped a photo of Brian signing it with Caveman standing next to him, then a bunch more of him posing with my wife, who proudly held up the signed poster. I figured those pictures would come in handy one day to back up the authenticity.

Just before showtime, she and I moved to the side of the stage to catch the performance and hopefully see the magic come alive.

---

2. **The only real vacation I ever took** while working a decade at the Roxy was a two-week trip to visit my ex-wife's family in the Czech Republic. It felt like another planet compared to the States. Her dad was a cop and investigator—but the kind who cranked rock and metal nonstop.

The curtain went up, and there he was: Brian Wilson, seated at his keyboard in the center of the stage, the band surrounding him. But instead of launching into a song, he just sat there smiling, scanning the room like a kid seeing something for the first time.

The crowd cheered and called his name, but he didn't budge. After a couple of minutes, his manager, standing just offstage, started whispering: "*God Only Knows… God Only Knows, Brian… time to start the show.*"

Finally, Brian started playing the intro to *God Only Knows,* and the band joined in. But it was too fast for him. About twenty seconds in, he stopped everything.

"Let's try that again, this time on my beat," he said into the mic.

He raised his hand, counted out the rhythm with his fingers—"*1 & 2 & 3 & boom!*"—and they kicked back in, this time following his lead.

I'd never seen a big-name act stop a song dead and start over like that, not in the middle of a packed house. It felt more like a rehearsal than a show.

Even though Brian seemed scattered, he managed to get through the first few songs. His hands shook on the keys, but the sound was clear and captivating. His voice wasn't perfect, but it was in tune, and he started to settle in.

The last half of the set was pure gold. He tore through *California Girls, I Get Around, Good Vibrations,* and then brought out Al Jardine, who crushed *Help Me, Rhonda.* Dick Dale and the rest joined him for a killer encore.

Wendy and Carney Wilson smiling for me before they went onstage...

It was a special show, no doubt. The intimate crowd proved it with the standing ovation they roared at the end. You could feel that kind of energy. It wasn't fake.

As I headed backstage with my wife, I told Bolle, my lighting guy, to keep an eye on the stage while the crew started corralling gear out through the side roll-up door. The band was still up there, breaking down their stuff. I was watching from the backstage DJ balcony when I spotted Al Jardine coming up the stairs.

I rushed to grab the poster from my office. I wasn't gonna miss the chance to get Jardine's autograph too.

As he reached the top, I met him with my wife by my side and said, "Al, man, great job out there… awesome! Would you mind signing this poster?"

He glanced at it and asked, "Did you get Brian to sign it yet?"

I pointed to the small, scraggly signature at the bottom. "Yeah, he signed it right there."

Jardine laughed, shook his head, and muttered, "Oh Brian, man, you still don't know how to sign a proper autograph." Then he grinned, grabbed the marker, and said, "Let me sign his name properly."

He wrote *Brian Wilson* in big, bold letters right smack in the middle of the poster—exactly where we figured Brian would've signed in the first place.

"Don't worry," Jardine added, "I've been signing Brian's autograph for him for decades."

At that moment, Caveman came up the stairs and caught it too. We looked at each other like, *Holy shit, Al Jardine has been signing Brian's autograph forever… do fans even know this?*

After he finished signing Brian's name, Jardine signed his own, smiling, happy to pose for photos with us and answer a few questions.

I'll never forget asking him why he thought Brian had ended up so mentally unwell, even when he was young. Jardine didn't even pause.

"Well," he said, "two things—being a genius, and having a bad father."

With that, someone called him from down the hall to head to the backstage room. We shook his hand, thanked him, and let him go.

I made my way back down to the stage. Brian's keyboard was still there, and his setlist was taped to the top of it. I carefully peeled it off, took it back to my office, and later framed it.

It hung on my wall for years, all the way until I left the Roxy for the next chapter in my life.

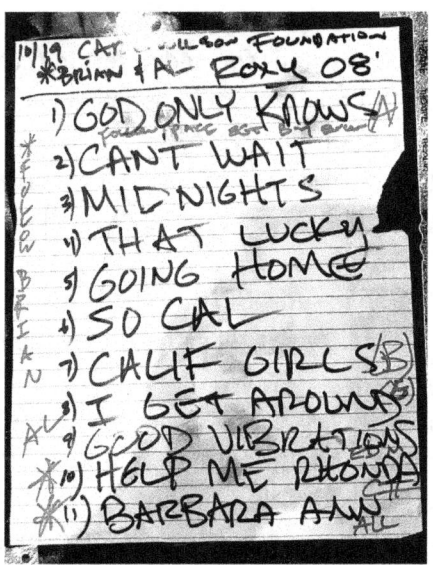

*Took this setlist from Brian's key-
board after the performance...*

That poster and setlist ended up with one of my family members, a massive Brian Wilson fan. I've never been the type to chase money, but I know damn well that set could've pulled a solid price on eBay—especially now, after Brian's passing.

He passed in early 2025 at eighty-two, after decades of wrestling with mental-health struggles and the scars of a brutal childhood. The news hit me harder than I expected. It wasn't just losing a legend. It was losing that tender, luminous presence I'd stood face to face with—the one that mirrored pieces of my dad.

But here's the truth: some things are worth more than money. That setlist and that strange, double-signed poster aren't just artifacts. They're anchors. Proof that I was there for one of the last truly intimate nights of a genius who, for all his flaws and fragility, still gave the world a soundtrack to dream by.

Al Jardine's better version of Brian Wilson's autograph, the way he's had to do it for him for years…

Born Broke: Destroyer of Biker Gangs

There was something mesmerizing about that night with Brian Wilson and Al Jardine. Not just the music, but the weight behind it—history, survival, quiet resilience.

For me, it cut even deeper. My dad went through his own mental decline in his later years, like I shared in the Wilson story. Watching someone you love slowly lose pieces of themselves leaves a scar that never fades. And when I saw Brian up there—present, unsteady, but still standing—it felt personal. Like I was staring at a parallel version of my own life, playing out under the stage lights. It was heavy. It was real.

That night taught me something: sometimes just showing up is its own act of courage. Survival—quiet, imperfect, messy—can be more powerful than any comeback or chart-topping single. Maybe that's why it burned so deep into me.

However, not every night at the Roxy was about chasing young blood or betting on the next big thing. Sometimes it was about honoring the long haul—where we'd been, what we'd endured. Brian reminded me that sticking it out to the end has its own kind of heroism.

That idea of courage hit home hard for me.

Remember back in the intro—if you've read it yet (and if not, no sweat)—when I told you about my adopted dad and his gritty climb as a poor, first-generation Mexican-American? Dropping out of third grade to pick grapes and help feed his fatherless family? Years later, when I was a pre-teen, he laid out the full story.

At fourteen, he got on a bus alone from Riverside to Hollywood to find work. Any work. Just to escape the harsh Latin style ghetto his family had always existed in. He landed an under-the-table busboy job and worked his ass off from there. Something deep inside him refused to accept a lifetime of picking crops. Poverty, no education, skin color, his Mexican and Jewish roots—none of it was going to chain him down.

He told his mom and brothers he was leaving to carve out a better life, and he'd die trying if he had to. They let him go. Maybe they thought he'd come crawling back because he was just a kid. He never did.

Then he told me something that stuck. As his bus rolled into Hollywood, a luxury car pulled up alongside—family inside, pointing and laughing at him. This skinny, dark-skinned kid in worn-out clothes. Right then and there, my dad vowed he'd never be laughed at again. He swore he'd claw his way out of poverty, break into the mainstream, and become someone people respected.

And damn if he didn't do it. He had the inner fire, the mojo, and he kept every promise he ever made to himself.

One time in particular, I saw it all in action—my dad's courage, his grit—and it burned into me just how much I'd come to see him as my personal hero and mentor. The guy who always backed me in my music journey.

It happened after he remarried a woman with two kids, and we were at a supermarket in Santa Monica.

My dad loved the non-macho, metro style of European men, especially the French. He wore it proudly: softer look, sleek clothes—the kind of style some people back then would stereotype as "gay." As a twelve-year-old, I wasn't exactly a fan. I was already embarrassed enough, but what really killed me was his European-style men's purse—the kind with a snapping clasp, like a woman's coin purse.

Mom, my metro dad, and me — 1975.

This was 1982. Preppy style was in, but it wasn't necessarily labeled *gay*. Still, if you weren't rocking preppy, you were probably leaning into the rugged, masculine thing pushed by guys like Charles Bronson and Clint Eastwood. My dad's look was a mash-up of metro and preppy—long before *metro* was even a word—and he stood out. Big time. That style was just starting to creep into the new wave scene, but my dad was one of the first to fully embrace it. The term *metrosexual* wouldn't even exist until the mid-'90s.

So we're in line at the supermarket, and this pack of bikers rolls in behind us. Big dudes. Loud, brash, hairy, stinking of sweat and beer. Jeans, cut-off flannels, wallets on chains. My stomach sank. I started praying my stepmom would pay, just so we could get out of there before anything happened.

No such luck. My dad calmly reached into his shoulder bag (which I also hated) and pulled out the damn coin purse. I stared at the floor, bracing myself. And right on cue, the bikers started snickering, pointing, cracking jokes.

I peeked up at my dad, mortified. But he never flinched. Pulled out the cash, smiled at the checker, took the receipt. Cool as hell, like nothing happened. I was dying inside… until he turned, locked eyes with the bikers, and said:

"You guys can bark and howl like dogs all you want, but it'll never help you understand a man who's earned every ounce of resilience like me. And that's okay. I can accept your shortcomings and insecurities. I forgive you."

The bikers went dead quiet, looking almost puzzled. I don't think they understood a damn word he'd just said—and neither did I. As they stood there, my stepmom—who, no joke, looked like Farrah Fawcett—started laughing right in their direction.

We walked out of that market like nothing happened. As the doors swung shut behind us, I could still hear them muttering: *"What the fuck was he talking about?"* followed by more confused insults, as we climbed into my dad's new luxury Jensen Interceptor and rolled off toward our place in Marina del Rey.

For years, I had no clue what my dad's words really meant. I'd hear him throw out some version of that same speech anytime someone tried to mess with him, and it always left me wondering.

It wasn't until I hit my forties that it clicked.

My dad's strength wasn't about fists or aggression. It was stronger than the fake, loud-mouthed "power" those bikers thought they had. He lived life on his own terms, no matter the era, no matter the crowd—ridicule or not. He stood out, and he never apologized for it.

That natural defiance, that quiet bravery, is what took him from a third-grade-educated, fatherless, dark-skinned immigrant kid to a successful, respected man. When the deck was stacked against him, he always bet on himself, and he never lost till the very end.

He was a rebel against anything that tried to keep him down. An unknown hero who refused the life that was *supposed* to be his.

And yeah, I guess that's why I—and a lot of others—are drawn to rebellion. To refuse the beaten path. To chase your dreams even when the odds are a joke.

It's the journey that matters. Always. And sometimes, to chase your dream, you've got to flat-out reject what everyone else calls "normal" or "acceptable."

In music, I carved my own path—no doubt. I always admired bands who did the same. Early on, I knew the Sex Pistols—and later, the Red Hot Chili Peppers, among others—weren't just bands. They were one in a million to make it as far as they did... and their road? It was anything but easy. It wasn't safe. And I respected the hell out of that.

In fact, Flea did something in my next story that I'll never forget. It completely restored my faith that some rock stars were still grounded—and still rebellious as hell in their own way.

Chapter 6

BLOOD SUGAR SEX &
Backstage MAGIK...

"The OG Red Hot Chili Peppers literally wanted to party on your pussy!"

I first heard about the *Red Hot Chili Peppers* when I was a teenager at Paul Revere Junior High in Brentwood, California. It was late '84, and my punk buddy from school had a sister named Michele—she was dating Flea.

The first time I heard their music was in her room. She had their album blasting, telling us about her thing with Flea. There was a *Peppers* poster on her wall—they looked funky and weird, but cool as hell. The music felt different, unrefined, and somehow… intoxicating to my young, fragile, eggshelled mind.

My buddy Mike, Michele's little brother, and our friend Brady even ended up in their *Catholic School Girls Rule* video because of her. I remember watching, thinking how surreal it was to see them up there—dressed as choirboys, mouthing the words to that raw funk-punk track while Anthony Kiedis and the rest of the band flanked them.

A few years later, in '87, everything went to hell. Michele was in a car with three others when it plunged off a cliff on Pacific Coast Highway. Everyone was killed. That shit stuck with me. I always wondered how Flea dealt with losing her… decades later, I'd find out firsthand.

Even though my first brush with the *Peppers* was back in '84, I didn't become a full-blown fan until '87, when *The Uplift Mofo Party Plan* dropped—and then I was all in.

Back in the '80s, I used to hit Westwood near UCLA all the time. The place was booming—kids packed into movie theaters, blasting through arcade games, fighting, flirting, and just roaming the streets looking for trouble. Punks, jocks, nerds, stoners—didn't matter. Everyone mixed together on those Westwood streets, raising hell and having fun.

There were a few record stores in the area, but one in particular had me hooked. On the wall, they had this massive *Chili Peppers* poster—Kiedis, Flea, original guitarist Hillel Slovak (before he passed), and drummer Jack Irons—standing there in all their naked glory with nothing but socks on their schlongs. It was hilarious, bold, and punk as fuck. I bought *The Uplift Mofo Party Plan* on the spot, and that was it—I was locked in as a fan for life.

By '89, the world was drowning in hair metal, glam rock, and R&B pop. None of that shit spoke to me. So, the band I started with my buddies, called *Ku De Tah*, was 100% modeled after the *Peppers'* style. When *Mother's Milk* dropped that same year, I was stoked. It was a gritty, funky alternative to the overblown MTV bands like Winger, Poison, and Cinderella among so many others.

Our first show at the Whisky A Go Go...

With *Ku De Tah*, we took the *Peppers'* vibe and mashed it with more rap—kind of like *Walk This Way* meets *Run-DMC.* We ended up sounding like a broke-ass mix of the *Chili Peppers*, *Beastie Boys*, and *Faith No More*—and honestly, I loved it.

Then in late '91, it all came crashing down for me. I got nailed with Chronic Fatigue Syndrome and had to drop out of the band. It took over a year to crawl back to normal. By the time I was well again, my band had morphed into something completely different—new singer, new songwriting, and a sound that was basically rapcore decades before anyone knew what that was. But it had zero funk, zero melody—just blunt rap and metal.

Maybe they were too far ahead of their time... or maybe the songs just weren't catchy enough. Either way, nothing big ever came of them as *Ku De Tah*. A few years later, they changed their name to *Sullen,* and the band I'd created ended up in the same graveyard as a thousand other hopefuls—just another almost in the long line of *what could've been.*

Fast-forward to 2006. By now, I'd seen the *Peppers* live more times than I could count. They were beyond world-famous—monster hits, massive tours, platinum records. But since I'd started working at *The Roxy,* they hadn't set foot on that stage. I always hoped they'd do some kind of secret fan show there, like so many other legends had.

Then one day, it happened. I got the internal email: the *Peppers* were doing a secret show at *The Roxy*—for the launch of the *Zune* player. Yeah… the *Zune*. Microsoft's weak-ass attempt to compete with the iPod and iTunes. But they had deep pockets, so why not throw down with one of the coolest, most iconic bands in the world?

We had an internal production meeting to figure out how the hell we were going to accommodate them—our monitor and sound systems were limited, and our backstage was… let's just say, not exactly stadium-level. We had two modest dressing rooms, and I knew damn well they wouldn't cut it for a band that was now used to playing arenas with sprawling backstage compounds.

Luckily, I'd gotten an email weeks earlier saying their production team would handle our "crappy logistics" and make it work. Fine by me.

When we finally met with their crew, they dropped a bomb—they wanted to send their own backstage team in the day before the show to renovate our dressing rooms and tailor them to *RHCP's* standards. At the time, I wasn't even sure what the hell that meant.

I tried to explain that our rooms had character—grit—covered in framed, signed posters, walls littered with stickers and graffiti from years of bands. The vibe was pure *Roxy*—kind of like a West Coast cousin to *CBGB's* in New York. But they didn't give a shit. They politely nodded, then shut me down fast.

Our main backstage room was crappy but it had vibe...

They were clear: their set-up, their standards, period. And here's the thing—this was a first. We'd had everyone through those rooms—*Sting, Prince, Ozzy, Korn, Foo Fighters, Linkin Park, Rage Against the Machine… even John Paul Jones from Zeppelin*—you name it. Not one of them had ever demanded a complete dressing room takeover.

Then their production team hit us with another one—they wanted exclusive use of the east side of *The Roxy* parking lot so each band member's personal chef could set up a tent and prepare individualized meals. Yeah... each guy with his own damn chef. I couldn't help but laugh out loud right there on the call.

Nic Adler, my boss, shot me a look that could've burned through steel. I covered my mouth and raised my eyebrows like a busted kid. (I was always getting in trouble at *The Roxy* for one thing or another, but I was good at my job, so Nic usually gave me a long leash and just the occasional slap on the wrist.)

Still, we complied. My job was to make it all happen, and I did. But inside, I was shaking my head. I couldn't believe how far they'd come from the band I first knew—the scrappy, rebellious outcasts from humble beginnings. Somewhere along the way, the gritty funk-punk street kids with socks on their dicks had turned into a corporate machine with all the bougie perks that came with it.

I'd always thought they were different from the arrogant rock-star types I couldn't stand—but here they were, living the exact same playbook. The band that once dropped songs like *Catholic School Girls Rule* and *Special Secret Song Inside*—a track literally about wanting to party on some girl's pussy[1] — now had chefs in tents in our parking lot.

The next day, after we'd locked in everything with their production team (they were bringing in extra monitors and other sound upgrades to make sure it was at their level), I got called into the main office to sign a *Non-Disclosure Agreement.*

I'd never been asked to sign anything like this before, so when I walked into the upstairs *Roxy* office and someone tossed me an 11-page stapled NDA, I was like, "What the hell is this?" They just shrugged and said, "You gotta sign this or you can't work the show."

Apparently, all those pages basically said I couldn't leak who the "surprise" band was or reveal how much they were getting paid—at least not for a year after the show.

---

1. **The Peppers tucked a track onto *The Uplift Mofo Party Plan*** (1987) called **"Special Secret Song Inside."** Fans know the real title: *"Party on Your Pussy."* Straight-up dirty funk about oral sex, no mystery there. The fake name was just a smokescreen so Warner Bros. could get away with printing it without a record store meltdown in the Reagan era. Even then, the label buried it as a hidden bonus track, not something they wanted blasted next to the singles.

Then I skimmed through and hit the number. *$350,000.* For *35 minutes* of music. I read it again just to make sure my eyes weren't screwing with me. Yep—*$350K for 35 minutes.* That's $10,000 a fucking minute.

My brain short-circuited for a second. These guys had reached some other level—floating somewhere near *Rolling Stones* territory. I thought back to 1984, when I first heard of them—they were probably lucky to make $500 a gig, if that. Now they had personal chefs, drivers, and entire teams assigned to each member.

Was this still rock 'n' roll? I wasn't sure. But it was definitely capitalism at its finest. And yeah... I guess they really had hit that *Higher Ground* after all.

As I walked out of the office after signing the NDA, they told me the Peppers' wardrobe and backstage crew would be rolling in later that afternoon to start setting up for the show the next day. I still couldn't wrap my head around what they were going to do that was so different from our usual setup—what, maybe a little cleanup?

Because here's the truth—our backstage rooms were never deep cleaned. The couch? That thing hadn't been cleaned in years. And I don't mean "a little dusty." I'm talking stains, food, booze, and... other fluids... soaked into it over god-knows-how-long. Every couple months I'd toss a new cover on it, but if anyone saw what was underneath—especially a germaphobe—they'd lose their shit.

In the daytime, the rooms were nasty. Actually, the whole *Roxy* was. If you saw it under the sun, it looked like some beat-up, past-its-prime dump that had seen better days. But at night? When the house lights went down and the colored lights hit—boom—she transformed into something special.

I was always fascinated by that difference between day and night. The same thing happened with people—every girl you swore was drop-dead gorgeous in the dark of *The Roxy* could instantly morph into just "average" once those bright white lights flipped on at the end of a show. Same went for famous artists, band members, their gear, and yeah—especially the backstage rooms.

Nighttime was magic. Daytime was the hangover.

NOTE: There were parts of *The Roxy* most people never even knew existed—hidden spots I'd poke around in for years just because I liked exploring. The attic was one of them. Up there, I found decades-old dust, dirt, scraps, and piles of forgotten memorabilia.

One year, I hit the jackpot. Management told me to clear out everything from those hidden spaces—the attic, random closets, and the *Roxy* storage down the street. That storage was its own goldmine—treasures from decades of shows. I was supposed to destroy all of it.

So yeah... I did as I was told. Mostly. I tossed the true garbage, but anything cool or worth hanging onto? I kept it. And I still have most of it today. One of the treasures I kept was a few giant drink tab books with all the tabs written down that were owed from legendary stars like *Jack Nicholson, Robert De Niro, John Belushi,* and even *John Lennon.* I'm not friggin' kidding. They would sign off on the tabs, as it was an accounting per month of what they owed for drinking at *On the Rox.* There was just no way I could destroy those books!

The day before the Zune launch, I got a call from the office letting me know the Peppers' backstage and wardrobe crew had arrived. I let them in through the side door, greeted them, and told them they could do whatever the hell they wanted with the rooms—just don't touch the framed stuff on the walls. Everything else? *Carte blanche.*

They were actually cool—mostly women from wardrobe and production. I walked them back so they could see what they were working with. First thing out of their mouths: "Wow... these are really small, but we'll try to make them into something amazing." I laughed and told them to give it their best shot, apologizing for the rooms' daytime ugliness and lack of square footage.

Then the truck doors opened. Out came thick, plush Middle Eastern carpets, followed by gorgeous lamps and accessories that looked like they'd been swiped from a Beverly Hills mansion. I asked if they needed my crew, but they waved me off—they had it handled. Fine by me. I told my guys to chill. They'd still get paid to "supervise," which they loved. (Didn't matter if the band needed them or not—my rule was no booze or drugs until after the show. Period.)

From my upstairs office, I could hear them hauling and arranging all this stuff, debating the best way to cram luxury into our cramped little rooms. I just shook my head and chuckled, figuring it was all a giant waste of time—because honestly, I didn't think the Peppers would even end up using our backstage.

About four hours later, I could tell they were wrapping up. Curiosity got the better of me, so the second they left, I headed down to see what kind of magic they'd worked.

Half the hallway leading to the rooms was now draped in rich-looking tapestries, with these hip, boho-style chandeliers hanging overhead. When I opened the door to the main room, my jaw dropped. Somehow, they'd turned our *Hard Rock Cafe*-looking gritty-ass space into something straight out of the *Taj Mahal*—or maybe one of *Saddam Hussein's* palaces.

The floors were covered in thick rugs, the walls draped in hardcore tapestries. Exotic lamps and Middle Eastern-style furniture were scattered everywhere. Even the bathroom looked like a Turkish den. The second room got the same treatment, and I just stood there, grinning like an idiot.

"Hell yeah," I thought, "I hope they leave it like this." I was already imagining moving the framed posters they'd covered into the hallway or the other bathroom, then putting special autographed ones—*Guns N' Roses, Linkin Park, Sublime, Deftones, Incubus*—over the tapestries. It would've been this insane Middle Eastern palace-meets-*Hard Rock Cafe* vibe.

Of course, that dream got crushed the next day after the show, when the Peppers' crew came back, packed it all up, and left the rooms exactly as they'd found them. Damn.

The next day, I had my crew ready to load in the Peppers' gear. We'd already reserved the entire east side of the *Roxy* parking lot for their chefs and whoever else needed tent space to start cooking.

A few big trucks rolled up, and the crew started unloading through our side roll-up door that led straight to the stage. Everything was smooth—fast, professional, zero drama. My guys just stood by as paid backup in case anyone needed help.

They had a lot of gear for a club show. Good thing *The Roxy* stage is huge compared to places like *The Whisky, Viper Room,* or *Troubadour. John Frusciante* had three Marshall double stacks, and *Flea* had three of his own. *Chad's* drum kit was big but thankfully not some sprawling *Neil Peart* monstrosity. They even brought in a digital FOH board and their own monitor rig—which was fine by me, because I knew our system wasn't exactly stadium-ready.

Setup went off without a hitch, so I wandered outside to check out the tent situation. It looked like a mini-festival out there—except each tent had this full-on *Benihana* vibe. Chefs in crisp white uniforms were prepping fresh food, one tent per band member, personalized menus and all.

I couldn't help laughing. Between the *Taj Mahal* backstage makeover and this chef army in our grimy-ass parking lot, it was strange. For a second, it felt like *Hell's Kitchen* had set up shop behind *The Roxy*, with *Emeril Lagasse* running the show.

And that's when it really hit me—how massive the Chili Peppers had become. Never in a million years would I have guessed that these rebellious, former drug-using, possible ADHD maniacs would keep it together for decades... but damn, they did—and then some.

As I was still processing the whole chef-and-*Taj Mahal*-backstage thing, a black *Escalade*-type SUV rolled right up next to the tents. Out of the backseat popped *Anthony Kiedis.* I started to introduce myself, but before I could get more than a "Hey—" out, a few more cars pulled in. *Flea, Frusciante,* and *Chad Smith* all jumped out of separate rides and headed straight for the roll-up door ramp like they owned the place.

They clearly knew the drill, so I ditched the official intro and just followed them inside. Their techs were already on stage, locked and loaded. With their gear eating up most of the stage space, I stepped back to give them room.

Then they kicked into soundcheck—running through classics like *Give It Away, Higher Ground,* and a few others. And man... they still sounded tight as hell. *Kiedis,* 44 years old at the time, was still bouncing around with insane energy. *Frusciante*—back in the band since '98—was locked in, playing like it was a sold-out arena instead of a secret gig.

When they wrapped soundcheck, they scattered—*Flea* headed backstage, *Kiedis* straight into his waiting car, and *Chad* and *Frusciante* vanished somewhere I couldn't track. I decided to make my move and see if I could get *Flea* to sign my neon yellow custom-built electric guitar—the one with the old Chili Peppers sticker slapped on it.

Backstage was surprisingly empty; most of the crew was still hanging outside by the chef tents. As I walked down the hallway, I spotted *Flea* checking out the posters and framed photos I'd plastered everywhere. The whole hallway looked like a 17-year-old skater's bedroom—unruly, colorful, and crammed with music history. It took me two years to get it the way I wanted, and I loved seeing big-name artists stop and take it in like they were wandering through the *Hard Rock Cafe.*

Flea was loving the backstage...

I called out, *"Flea!"* He turned and, with a smirk, said, "That's me." As I got closer, I noticed the lines on his face—deep creases that made him look ten years older than he was—pale skin, weathered but still sharp. He was shorter than me, maybe 5'5" or 5'6", but in great shape—zero body fat—and there was a real warmth in his eyes.

I stuck out my hand, and he shook it as I introduced myself. Half-joking, I said, "Damn, you guys are getting $350K to play 12 songs for 35 minutes... that's like $10K a minute!" He grinned and laughed.

I told him I'd first heard about the *Peppers* back in 1984 because my buddy's sister, Michelle, had been dating him then. His face shifted—he remembered. He said it was so tragic when he heard about Michelle dying in that car accident with a few others. He said it was a big loss, and that it hit him with the same kind of horrible shock as when original *Peppers* guitarist *Hillel Slovak* died.

"Shocking. Just shocking. Over the years, it sometimes pops out of nowhere into my dreams," he said quietly. I nodded. Then I pivoted and asked if he'd sign the guitar I'd brought just for the *Zune* launch, telling him I planned to hang it with the rest of the memorabilia I'd collected over the years. "No problem, for sure," he said.

I darted to my office, grabbed my neon yellow custom-built electric, and came back with a silver marker. He signed it with a smile, then looked up and asked, "Do you want *Anthony* and the others' signatures too?" I laughed and said, "Hell yeah—I'll wait until they come back here."

He told me the other three probably wouldn't even come back-stage—the only reason he had was to check out the posters and see the rooms. He planned to leave right after and come back just before the show. My first thought was, *Oh, damn... guess I'm not getting their autographs on the guitar if they're not even hanging back here.*

Then he surprised the hell out of me. "Check it out," he said, "give me the guitar and I'll get them to sign it." I was stunned—this bass-playing legend was offering to go get the rest of the *Chili Peppers'* autographs for me. Hell yes. "Take it!" I told him.

I asked if he needed anything—water, food, whatever—but he waved me off. "I'm all good," he said, pulling on his *Lakers* jersey before heading out, guitar in hand.

I was buzzing. Maybe I'd been wrong about them being a full-blown bourgeois pop machine. *Flea* was easily one of the most genuine, down-to-earth musicians I'd met—right up there with *John Paul Jones* from *Led Zeppelin*, who I'd had a great backstage conversation with years earlier.

For a minute, my faith in artists was restored. I even caught myself thinking, *If I ever make it big, I hope I'm like Flea or John Paul Jones.* But the truth was, I hadn't climbed that mountain. Not even close. I was starting to believe I was destined to just stay in the gutter—a working stiff grinding away in the music biz till the end. *The Roxy* felt like my ceiling, the top of the climb. I hated admitting it, but with every passing day, it felt more like the truth pressing down on me.

As showtime crept closer, the kids outside were buzzing. The doors opened, and they poured in—racing for the front of the stage. No bar-riers, and our stage barely four feet high, so the crowd would be within arm's reach of the *Peppers*. They could literally touch the band.

The *Peppers* tore through their setlist—classic favorites mixed with newer hits off their latest album. The crowd was on fire, dancing, jump-ing, and belting out every lyric. Thirty-five minutes blew by in what felt like seconds, and just like that, the show was over.

The band was drenched in sweat, the crowd was drenched in sweat, and for almost the first time, everything went off without a single hitch. No disasters, no last-minute crises—one of those rare unicorn nights in live music.

Before the stage crew could clear everything, I snagged two setlists—one for me, one for the *Roxy* backstage wall.

Then I headed to the dressing rooms... and nothing. The place was untouched. Not a single bottle opened, not a chair moved. All that time, money, and effort transforming the space into a Middle Eastern palace—and they never even set foot in it. Drinks, snacks, everything... untouched.

I'd never seen anything like it—except for *Dolly Parton*, who once played the *Roxy*, finished her set in 40 minutes, and then bolted immediately out the roll-up door to her waiting Escalade.

I headed back to the stage to check on the load-out. Out in the lot, the chef tents were already coming down. Their tour manager walked up and asked if my crew and security were hungry—apparently, there was a ton of cooked food left over.

I blinked. "Wait... none of the band ate any of it?" He confirmed. "Happens all the time," he said. "They just don't like to waste food, so you guys can have it."

I stood there thinking and then asked, *Then why the hell did you set up all those backstage rooms and the cooking tents if the band wasn't even going to use them?* He shrugged and explained it was all part of the production requirements—it didn't matter if the band touched any of it.

While he's telling me this, it suddenly hits me—I never got my guitar back from *Flea*. *Shit. Maybe he forgot... or maybe he's already gone.* I asked if the band was still around. Nope—they'd split. My brain instantly went to, *Damn... did Flea just steal my guitar?*

I started laughing, already imagining the story I'd tell about the day *Flea* stole my *Chili Peppers* guitar. I was picturing the looks on people's faces, the laughs I'd get… when suddenly, I see my lighting guy *Bolle* walking toward me with the neon yellow guitar in hand.

"JD," he said, "*Flea* told me to give this to you."

"Damn, that's fuckin' amazing," I said, taking it from him.

I looked down—every *Chili Pepper's* signature was on it. I felt like a stoked teenager as I carried it back to my office. I hung it on my wall, and a few years later—in 2010—I had *Josh Klinghoffer* sign it with a silver marker when he came to a show at the *Roxy*.

That's when it hit me—this might be the only guitar in the world signed by *Flea, Kiedis, Chad, Frusciante,* and *Klinghoffer. Damn.* I'd come full circle from first hearing them back in 1984 to this moment.

And yeah… that guitar is still hanging in my home office today.

Rebel with a Cause...

"It takes vision to see the future, and some people are too scared,
or too average, to ever see it..."

I've gotta admit, after the Chili Peppers show my ego always got a little kick when a big-name artist like Flea showed genuine interest in the backstage I'd transformed. People would ask me all the time how I single-handedly turned it from a plain, soulless space into something with actual vibe and swagger.

What they didn't see was the ridiculous red tape and politics I had to hack through just to make anything happen at *The Roxy*, let alone overhaul an entire part of it. Even when the idea was clearly going to make the place better for everyone, getting people to agree on a vision was like pulling teeth from a pissed-off pit bull. And yeah... jealousy crept in too, even when they knew damn well the idea was solid.

I usually got around that Roxy status quo because I've always been a rebel at heart, thanks to my dad and others. I did shit my way: act first, apologize later. That wasn't just a strategy—it became muscle memory. People couldn't see my vision until I shoved it right in front of them, where they had no choice but to notice.

By my early twenties, I made a call. No more waiting for permission. Done asking. I'd just start, finish—or at least get it close—and then drop it in their laps. Nine times out of ten, that saved me from the endless debates, the bullshit naysaying, and the kind of overthinking that kills anything *outside the box*. Sure, it didn't always work. But when it did? Pure magic.

This time, it worked like a charm.

In my first years at *The Roxy*, I decided the backstage needed a complete makeover. Not some half-assed paint job. I wanted full rock-and-roll teenage-bedroom vibes, star-studded and dripping attitude. Since 1973, it had been stuck in a time warp: busted-ass wood paneling, cheap laminate floors straight out of a shitty '70s rec room, the kind with a broken ping-pong table shoved in the corner. It was actually depressing.

I'd already turned other backstage rooms in the Valley into poster-covered hideouts—walls packed with framed shots of iconic bands—but *The Roxy* needed more. The whole damn thing needed love: hallways, bathrooms, DJ balcony, ceilings, everything.

So, in my usual rebel-with-a-cause style, I came in one Sunday when *The Roxy* was dark and just went for it. Seven straight hours. I tore into the wall next to the stairway that led from backstage to the stage, covered it completely, and when I finally stepped back, sweaty, beat, and grinning, it looked fucking amazing. At least to me.

I didn't get paid for it. Didn't expect to. I did it because I gave a damn about the place. It was about honoring all the legends—and yeah, even myself—who'd played there. It was about keeping the spirit alive. I did it out of pride, out of love. Money never really motivated me to do stuff like that. Maybe to my own detriment.

Then Monday came.

I get a call from the Roxy office, and suddenly I'm getting blasted with outrage from the desk-jockey brigade. These easily offended trippers were acting like I'd set the building on fire. I was stunned. Here I am trying to elevate the place, and they're losing their minds because it didn't go through their sacred chain of command. It was one of those moments where you realize just how insane people can get when they don't approve something ahead of time.

But then the twist.

Nic Adler—who normally sided with the office—comes in that morning. They drag him over, expecting him to tear me a new one. But it backfires. He just stands there, staring at the wall, mouth hanging open. Then out comes:

"This is fucking awesome."

Game over.

Suddenly, the same crew that wanted to crucify me is patting me on the back, gushing about my "vision." I felt like blasting them with a firehose, but I kept my cool. I just smiled and said, *"It takes vision to see the future, and some people are too scared, or too average, to ever see it. I'm glad you guys don't fall into that latter category…"* Then I walked out before they could process the jab.

The next week, Nic gave me the green light. Carte blanche. *"Do whatever you want backstage,"* he told me.

So I did.

Over the next two years, I turned that backstage into a full-blown juggernaut. And when it was finally time to crown it with something special, I knew exactly what it had to be: a huge autographed poster from a band that lit the fuse before most of us at the Roxy ever touched a stage.

Time to talk about the legendary Sex Pistols...

For 30+ years, the Roxy backstage was bland until I got my hands on it...

Chapter 7

NEVER MIND THE ROXY...
HERE'S THE SEX PISTOLS

Me and the legend himself...

"Can you believe this...I'm bloody world famous and completely broke"

"Hell yeah." That's exactly what I said when I heard from our in-house booking office that the legendary *Sex Pistols* were going to play *The Roxy* for their only U.S. tune-up gig. This wasn't just any random show—this was in preparation for a big UK tour, and they'd decided our little corner of Sunset was the place to light the fuse.

Booking also told me the Pistols' lineup would be Johnny Rotten (Lydon), Steve Jones, Paul Cook, and original bassist Glen Matlock. That was fucking cool news to me. Back when I was around fourteen, *Never Mind the Bollocks* was my holy grail. Under its influence, I morphed into a junior high pseudo-punk rocker—one of the few "punkers" to emerge from a sea of surfers, nerds, and jocks at Paul Revere JHS, in the super-wealthy enclave of Brentwood, California. For whatever reason, punk rock—and that blunt, rebellious middle finger it carried—just spoke my language.

When I got the band's rider and a promo photo, I decided to blow the photo up to poster size. My plan? Get all their autographs and hang it backstage, right above the stairway in full view of anyone walking in. Since I didn't come from the glam rock scene that had ruled the Strip in the '80s, this would be my own personal middle finger to the past—a symbol that *The Roxy* had evolved. That we'd embraced other styles. That we were still just as rebellious now as we were in the hairspray-and-spandex days.

A week before the show, booking called again—John Lydon, a.k.a. Rotten, wanted to meet with *The Roxy's* lighting and sound crew to go over everything. We set the meeting for the *Rainbow Bar & Grill* next door.

I rolled in with my lighting guy Bolle—plus my stage manager and our sound/monitor guys. We were mid-conversation when we suddenly heard a loud English accent joking with the waitress:

"John here, a true star to see some poor blokes about me Roxy gig."

She pointed toward our table. Lydon glanced over and went:

"Ahhh, alrighty then, let's get going."

Mr. Rotten was exactly what you'd expect—sharp, unpredictable, and a total character. As he walked up, he let out a loud burp and deadpanned:

"Oh, excuse me lads—pardon me French."

We all cracked up and welcomed him to sit. We had a list of questions ready, and he was completely laid-back, answering everything without any rock-star bullshit. He even started telling stories about how the Pistols got back together, and about his other post-breakup projects—like his band *PIL.*

He was hilarious and sharp—not the unhinged persona from back in the day, but someone logical, smart, and disarmingly thoughtful. I thought to myself, *Here sits a bona fide professor of punk wisdom, lurking beneath all the English bravado.*

After about forty minutes, we got down to business—talking lights, sound, and logistics. He didn't even blink when we mentioned our limited gear and tech. He just said,

"As long as the energy's there, we don't need no bougie sound system or light show—save that shite for the bands that can't play."

The meeting wrapped, we shook hands, and as we were walking out, I made him crack up when I said, *"John, you still have that genuine punk vibe—but what the hell is going on with Glen Matlock's* haircut [1] *in your promo picture?"*

It was good to see that John Lydon, a.k.a. Johnny Rotten, was the real deal. Even older, he still had that rebellious, razor-sharp spark. It wasn't an act. It was who he was. I felt honored to have met him—and now to be working with him.

Soundcheck went smooth, and as they wrapped up I caught myself thinking, *Damn, these guys can still play.* Steve Jones was hammering those chunky riffs with the same power-chord heaviness that made *Never Mind the Bollocks* iconic. Paul Cook was locked in tight, driving the groove with the kind of snap and energy that made him seem 25 again. And Glen Matlock—his bass tone had that seasoned studio-musician polish. (Sid Vicious might've been the poster boy of punk chaos, but let's be real—Matlock left him in the dust as a player.)

They tore through three songs: *"Holidays in the Sun," "God Save the Queen,"* and *"Bodies."* Each one landed like a gut punch. Standing there,

---

1. **I had blown their promo picture up** into a giant poster to hang backstage, and in it, Glen looked all clean-cut—almost preppie—with a neatly styled haircut that made him stick out like a sore thumb next to the rest of the Pistols. The other three looked like they'd just crawled out of a gutter after a street fight, and here was Glen looking like he was on his way to a yacht club mixer.

I couldn't shake the thought: *these so-called old legends still had plenty of fight left in the tank.*

Earlier that day, we prepped the backstage rooms. The Pistols were in the main room, their crew stashed in the smaller one. I had one mission in mind: get that giant promo poster signed. I'd already blown it up and plastered it over every other poster I'd decorated the walls with. Then I handed silver markers to my assistants—Caveman and TJ—and told them, *"Whenever one of the Pistols walks down this hallway, you stop him. You get a signature. Be ready."*

TJ was the real deal. Nic Adler's half-brother—his mom was Britt Ekland, the Bond girl from *The Man with the Golden Gun,* and his dad was Slim Jim Phantom from the *Stray Cats.* Like his old man, TJ played drums, but what stood out was his vibe. Sixteen years old, technically there because he was "family," but he proved himself fast. Levelheaded, hard-working, and eventually a good friend.

We clicked. Both of us loved pulling pranks and stirring shit up, especially when it came to rattling the thin-skinned office staff. For me, TJ wasn't just a kid running errands—he was a partner in crime who made the grind behind the scenes a hell of a lot more fun.

Three hours before doors, the line already stretched nearly two blocks—almost all the way to the *Whisky.* Over 500 people camped outside, turning the Sunset Strip into a full-blown street festival. Punkers, skaters, hipsters, alt-kids, industry douchebags, local band hacks, every misfit under the neon sky—everyone was there, waiting for *The Roxy* to crack open.

Our official capacity was 450, but on nights like this, it felt like 800 bodies were jammed inside. Wall to wall, shoulder to shoulder, sweat dripping from the ceiling. Definitely pushing the limits... but somehow, we never got busted. In fact, sometimes a firetruck would roll up and park right out front on Sunset, and the firemen would stroll inside like VIPs. They'd lean against the stage wall, ironically blocking the exact area that technically counted as a fire hazard.

Dr. Evil—the *Roxy* sound guy who practically birthed the new metal scene by booking and mixing half the bands that mattered—swore one of the old-school owners used to slip the fire chief a brown bag of cash. Said he saw it with his own eyes. I could never tell if he was bullshitting me or not, but judging by how blind the fire department seemed, I wouldn't rule it out.

Whenever the firemen showed up, I'd bring them water and offer them beer. They always declined, never mentioned the insane overcapacity. They just stood there in their fireman pants, nodding their heads to the music like everyone else. It cracked me up. I figured we were safe—as long as the chief himself didn't show up. And on the rare times he did? He still didn't say a word. We were packed way over the limit, and he just walked right past it.

As showtime crept closer, I stayed backstage with my crew and we scored Steve, Paul, and Glen's autographs on the poster. All three of them were surprisingly cool—friendly, easy, even joking around with us. The vibe was loose, and their crew matched it. Everyone seemed dialed in but relaxed, almost celebratory.

It was a relief, honestly. Too many artists came through *The Roxy* acting like royalty, stiff and self-important, but not these guys. These English legends carried themselves with a kind of punk humility—soaking up the attention with grins instead of ego trips.

Finally, we spotted Lydon coming out of the main dressing room. He strolled down the hallway and asked if he could see the stage from the DJ balcony. I spoke up and said, *"Sure thing, but first—can you sign this poster?"*

He grinned and said, *"I'd be most delighted to sign that poster. And let me tell ya—we ain't famous, we're bloody infamous."*

We all cracked up, and then he grabbed the silver Sharpie and wrote:
"Johnny Rotten, A true star Was here $"

We laughed even harder when he drew the "W" in *Was* as a pair of boobs.

As I led him to the balcony, he looked out over the sea of people and said, "Bloody hell, it's so damn packed... looks like a bunch of sardines." I said, "Yeah—not only is it packed and way over capacity, but the fire department is here too, and there are still like 300 people stuck outside."

He asked, *"Are we gonna get shut down for this cage bin or what?"*

I shot back, *"Don't worry, John. We already paid them off... two brown bags full o' money."*

He let out a big laugh, turned around, and headed back to the main room.

The Roxy was as packed as it could possibly get. I'm talking 800-plus people crammed in, with eight fire department guys posted up on the side by the kitchen. Their fire truck was parked dead center in the middle of Sunset, right in front of *The Roxy* like it was part of the show.

I glanced at the set list—every classic was on there. They were opening with *"Holidays in the Sun,"* and I figured the crowd would go absolutely ballistic. Fifteen minutes to showtime, and all four Pistols were huddled at the top of the backstage stairs that led to the stage. They were laughing, talking shit, and winding each other up.

Steve Jones looked over at Lydon and said, "Hey John, are you sure you did all those cardio workouts I told you about? From the looks of it—well, old chap—it doesn't look like it."

Lydon fired back without missing a beat: "Well, looky who's callin' the kettle black," *jabbing a finger into Steve's big belly.*

After that bit of ribbing, their crew gave the signal—it was go time. The *Roxy* curtain was down, Bolle started turning off the house lights, and the crowd's roar was building like a damn freight train. I gave the hand signal to start, and in all the chaos, Bolle somehow forgot to kill the bright stage lights.

The curtain began to rise. I started flashing my flashlight and yelling to get his attention, but the place was deafening—no one could hear or see a thing.

Halfway up, Lydon yelled out, "Bloody hell!" and they ripped straight into the opening chords of *"Holidays in the Sun."*

Like a volcano blowing its top, the crowd went completely unglued—singing so loud you could barely hear Lydon's mic. Right at that instant, Bolle realized the white lights were still blaring. In one motion, he killed them and fired up the colored light show.

The effect was actually perfect—bright white glare to total darkness, then an explosion of flashing reds just as Lydon started snarling:

"A cheap holiday in other people's misery… I don't wanna holiday in the sun, I wanna go to the new Belsen…"

Yeah, he forgot a few lyrics, but nobody gave a damn. For most of that room—and definitely for me—this was the first time seeing the *Sex Pistols* live. I didn't know a single person in the music business who'd ever seen them before they broke up in '78. They only played a handful of shows and did a short-lived, completely disastrous U.S. tour in '77, so for a lot of us, this night was history.

The crowd was throwing drinks, and I got splashed a few times standing at my spot next to the stage. It was unreal.

Lydon bantered with the audience—sometimes insulting them, sometimes dropping sharp, witty takes on life, politics, and whatever else popped into his head. He was on a magic carpet ride, and this felt like his full-throttle comeback to the world.

As they tore through the set with songs like *"No Feelings," "Pretty Vacant," "Submission,"* and others, Lydon suddenly blurted something off-the-cuff about Paris Hilton that made the crowd roar.

I started laughing because—for some reason—a ton of people really hated Paris (even though she was always super nice whenever she came to the *Roxy*)… but there it was. Even Johnny Rotten was dissing her.

When they were halfway through the set, I went to check on everything and make sure it was all still in order. As I headed to the front box office to check in with the girls, I could see all the people outside, packed onto the sidewalk and street, hanging around the fire truck and basically having a giant party.

It reminded me of the first time I ever went to the Sunset Strip back in the '80s—*Guns N' Roses* was playing the *Roxy,* and the outside was more packed than the inside. Same vibe outside in '91 when *Nirvana* played the *Roxy,* and I was just a twenty-year-old kid handing out flyers for my band.

I walked outside, and when *"God Save the Queen"* came on, all the outside people started singing it at the top of their lungs. I knew I should've recorded it, but I was too busy worrying about keeping the show running smooth till the very end. I was always watching for the cracks—things that could go wrong—since we hardly ever had a "perfect" show.

As they finished the song *"EMI,"* Lydon said, "We'll be back in a minute—well, might be more than a minute… it's fuckin' hotter than hell up here." I laughed along with the audience, because it totally was hotter than hell. Anytime we had 700 people or more inside, the old *Roxy* air conditioner would get completely overpowered[2]. That thing was a dinosaur—and once the room hit a certain heat level, it didn't matter if you cranked it to Arctic. You were in a sauna until the crowd left.

I proceeded to scurry up the backstage stairs so the band could have some room to stand where I'd been perched. The audience couldn't see them, but from the top of the stairs, I had a perfect view. They were

---

2. **We had the same monstrous** central air conditioner for years. Since the Roxy didn't quite have enough money to replace it, we always had to patch it together—just like our monitors and soundboard. If anyone forgot to turn the A/C on the night before a big show, we were screwed. Trying to cool it down during the day was nearly impossible (and yes, this happened more than once). When we hit capacity, it often felt like there was no air conditioning at all. Occasionally, artists would comment on how "burning hot" it was—though some actually enjoyed the sweat and heat. Either way, once the show started, there was nothing we could do about it.

drenched in sweat, and Lydon muttered, "I can't friggin' go on... It's too hot, I'm gonna have a heart attack or somethin'."

Steve chimed in, "Does anyone in this bloody place have a fan or something?"

I yelled down, "Gimmie a second, I'll get a fan for you."

I ran to my office, grabbed my personal fan, and came back down. As I looked at them, it was obvious the adrenaline had worn off. They didn't look like the punk rock icons who had kicked the show off with insane energy an hour earlier—they looked human again. Mortal.

Steve Jones desperately trying to revive Johnny Rotten with my office fan after our air conditioner got overwhelmed...

Steve and Glen were fanning Lydon with their shirts while he sat slumped on the bottom stair, looking like he'd just crawled out of the Arabian desert. We plugged in the fan, and Steve held it right up to John's face.

"John, we still have 'Bodies,' 'Anarchy,' and 'Roadrunner' to play... we can't end the show like this," Steve said.

As Lydon started cooling down, he muttered, "Alright, bloody hell... let's do 'Anarchy' then. That's all I've got left, and I'm not even sure I can pull that off... What the hell is wrong with the air cooling in here?"

I yelled down to him, "John, our air conditioner gets overwhelmed when we pack so many bodies in here... I'm sorry, you just have too many fans in here—and there are hundreds more outside!"

Lydon shot back, "This is my life... bloody hell."

And then, all four of them got back on stage to a roar from the crowd, tearing into *Anarchy in the UK* like their lives depended on it.

The show ended, and Roxy security started kicking everyone out. Now there were 800-plus people out on the street, and nobody was going home. It had turned into a full-blown punk rock block party.

I talked to Lydon's crew, and they asked if I could escort him to his waiting car—and if there was any way to sneak him out through the side or roll-up door to avoid the mob.

"Yeah," I said, "I got the secret door on the side of the Roxy. Tell him to follow me."

Lydon followed me downstairs to the side door by the big bar near the front. We stepped outside, and I spotted a car waiting for him, double-parked across the street.

As we started walking toward it, someone yelled, "Johnny Rotten... heyyyyy!"

Within seconds, hundreds of people rushed over, shoving posters, records, and hands in his face. I tried to block some of them as he swung open the back door of the car.

He looked at me one last time and said something like, "Can you believe all this? All of this fame... I'm bloody world famous—and still broke."

I shook his hand as he thanked me and the crowd, then shut the door for him. I stood there watching the car disappear down Sunset Blvd.

Damn... I guess it's better to be a broke, world-famous punk legend than just another broke asshole stuck in the shadows, still chasing the ever-elusive road to stardom.

And with that thought, it hit me... *maybe I wasn't just talking about him. Maybe I was also talking about me.*

The Pistols hanging in glory backstage...

The 1980s Lord of the Flies

Lord of the Flies...

"You sticking up for Fags now?"

Being up close and personal with a character like Johnny Rotten (Lydon) only confirmed what I already knew: most artists are playing a part. They invent a persona, wear it like armor, and the world buys it. I'd seen it with countless artists and bands I worked with. Hell, I'd done it myself. But every now and then, you meet someone who isn't acting at all.

Lydon was one of those people. Johnny Rotten wasn't a costume. He was Johnny Rotten, unfiltered, unapologetic, all the time.

It reminded me of something from my early teens, back when the 1980s were their own weird animal. Bullying was just "life," hazing was normal, and school fights were daily entertainment. New Wave was blowing the doors open—pastel jackets, eyeliner, Flock of Seagulls hair—but even with all that neon flash, the world could still be savage.

Enter Erik. He wasn't openly gay, but everyone knew. He had style: flowing shirts, flowing pants, hair sprayed to the heavens, eyeliner that would make Duran Duran jealous. Always surrounded by girls. And because of that, everyone, surfers, punks, jocks, even the kids bused in from the inner city, treated him like target practice

The morning it got ugly, we were at Paul Revere JHS. He strutted through the gates with Culture Club blasting from his Walkman, looking like a junior Boy George. No teachers around. One surfer ripped off his headphones. Another yanked down his linen pants. Then they shoved him to the ground, circled him, and spit insults. They didn't punch him. They didn't need to. They just held him down, humiliating him in front of everyone.

I froze. I was 13, 5'7", athletic. Nobody messed with me. But these were my friends. And back then, sticking up for a *fag* was a bit of social suicide.

Then one of them spit on him.

That was it. I shoved through the circle, barked, *That's enough!* and yanked him to his feet. His eyes were wet. After he pulled up his pants, I told him, *Get out of here.* He bolted.

One of the surfers, Bucky, a wiry little tough guy, got in my face. "What the fuck, man? You sticking up for fags now?" I grabbed his collar, slammed him to the ground. *No, Bucky. I'm saying no one deserves to be spit on. And he never did shit to you in the first place. Knock it the fuck off.*

When I let him up, he muttered, "Whatever, dude," and walked. The others followed. I shouted after them, *Leave him alone!* And somehow... they did. Eventually it all faded, like it never happened.

Looking back, I think I might've been the only guy who ever stood up for Erik during our time in junior high besides the New Wave girls.

Much later, in therapy, I realized something deeper. Maybe I saw something real in him that I respected. He wasn't just flamboyant. He was fearless enough to show up as himself in a junior-high *Lord of the Flies* reality, knowing exactly what was waiting, and still walking through those gates.

Golding wrote in *Lord of the Flies*: "*The mask was a thing on its own, behind which Jack hid, liberated from shame and self-consciousness.*" Erik didn't wear a mask. He had no armor. That was his rebellion. And maybe that's what lit me up inside.

I knew there were probably dozens of other kids back then in the closet, too scared to come out, terrified of what would happen if they did. Erik didn't care, or at least he didn't hide. That kind of nerve, I respected. Maybe that's why I, and so many others, gravitated toward early punk. It wasn't just music. It was rebellion. Defiance of the status quo.

I think I had to protect him that day because deep down, I knew he just might be braver than me. Truth is, I never saw him again after junior high. I tried finding him on social media, but nothing. Part of me hopes he made it, but inside I know the odds. He might've been swallowed by drugs, or maybe the weight was too much and he ended it himself. If by some miracle I did find him, even now, I'd look him in the eye and say: I'm sorry, man. Sorry nobody else stuck up for you. Sorry I didn't do more back then. You deserved better[1].

That's why, whenever I came across someone truly real—someone like Johnny Rotten—it shook me. People like that were rare. They didn't polish themselves up to make the world comfortable. They made the world uncomfortable just by existing. Erik did it in junior high. Rotten did it on stage. Sid Vicious snarled it into the mic with *"I Did It My Way."* And even if doing it his way killed him at twenty-seven, at least it was honest.

Or maybe that honesty was a mask of its own. Maybe Rotten's *no filter* was the filter, and Erik's flamboyance was its own armor. Maybe all of us are hiding, even when we swear we're not.

Still, I've always believed this: whether it's a mask or not, the courage to live without apology is the closest thing to truth we'll ever get.

Now, back to the Pistols. I figured it might be a while before anything that wild would hit us again.

I was wrong. Really wrong.

Because a few months later, Courtney Love walked into the Roxy... and so did Paris Hilton. *Let's roll.*

---

1. **Just before wrapping this memoir,** I finally found what I'd been dreading. Erik Christides—the kid I once stood up for in junior high—didn't make it. He went on to become a musician and artist, a close collaborator of Goth-rock legend, Rozz Williams from Christian Death and Shadow Project. They created together, bled together, even carved pieces of their chaos into The Whorse's Mouth, Rozz's raw ode to heroin addiction. Erik's name still lingers in underground projects like 1334 and Bloodflag if you dig deep enough. But on Thanksgiving Day, November 27, 1997, at just 27 years old, Erik died of a heroin overdose. Five months later, Rozz followed, taking his own life. I always had a feeling tragedy claimed him. Turns out my instinct was right. Heavy doesn't even begin to cover it. Damn man.

Chapter 8

COURTNEY LOVE & PARIS HILTON—The Toilet Paper Dragon

"Get that Fuckin' Bitch out of here, I'm not playing till she's gone!"

I remember the exact moment I first saw the *Smells Like Teen Spirit* video on MTV in 1991. It was on *120 Minutes,* late at night, when raw music still slipped through the cracks. I yelled out to my girlfriend at the time—

Oh my God... this is it! This is fuckin' it!!

Nirvana wasn't just another band. They were the real fucking deal—authentic, hard-edged, and somehow both underground and on the verge of exploding into the mainstream. They lit up like a Molotov cocktail in a sea of bland pop R&B crooners, boy bands, and cookie-cutter glam-rock goofs.

I didn't even know what *Grunge* really was yet, but I knew they were it. I'd already seen them live—at the Palladium in 1990, then again at the Roxy in 1991[1] —and my gut told me they weren't just a band, they were a tidal wave. They were going to bulldoze everything in their path, whether they liked it or not. It felt like destiny. And my gut instincts, which I half-jokingly called *DeCostradamus*, were almost never wrong.

That night, watching *Smells Like Teen Spirit* blast across the TV, it all crystallized. The world was finally ready for them.

By 1992, I was a full-blown Nirvana disciple. Then I heard Kurt had married Courtney Love, frontwoman of a scrappy little band called Hole. I'd seen Hole at the Whisky a Go Go not long before the world gave a damn about them, and I'm almost positive I spotted Kurt lurking around too.

---

1. **I'd been going to those venues since '87**, and by '91 I was already part of an early, unofficial street team—handing out flyers up and down the Sunset Strip for Roxy and Whisky shows. I still remember passing out flyers for Nirvana's 1991 show, which I was lucky enough to catch with some friends. Here's the cool part: my future good friend Kevin Estrada was there too, taking official photos of that same show. He later became an A&R rep for Roadrunner/Island Def Jam and ended up signing my band, Rumblefish, in 2001. And this one stings—just two days after that Roxy gig, Nirvana shot the *Smells Like Teen Spirit* video in Culver City. I actually had the flyer for the shoot, even scribbled "Gotta go to this" on it... but my lazy ass didn't go. Kevin did. And he's all over the video, standing right next to Kurt. Legendary. Meanwhile, I missed it. Small world, but damn—that was my chance to be part of history, and I blew it.

And honestly? They were terrible. Courtney looked spun out, strung tight like a bad wire, barking at the audience for not losing their minds over her sloppy set. Her attitude was pure nastiness. Her guitar playing? Sloppy as hell.

Still, it made a twisted kind of sense. Kurt was this tortured genius—brilliant, broken—and sometimes people like that gravitate toward turmoil like it's oxygen. Some of my friends who actually knew her said the same thing: controlling, messy, destructive. Maybe he thought he needed that storm in his life. Maybe he thought that kind of poison kept the art alive. You hear it in *Heart-Shaped Box.* Love described like a sickness you feed on, even as it eats you alive.

It only really clicked years later, after he was gone, that whatever drew him to her was part of the same weight that eventually crushed him.

Fast forward many years. Long after Cobain was gone, I heard from our Roxy booking department that Courtney Love was coming to play a show. It was 2007, and by then she was a star in her own right, with a handful of hit songs under her belt.

Thinking about Courtney, and all the other famous artists who came through the Roxy, hit me with a realization: I had a pretty badass job. I got to see, up close, artists who could easily pack out 10,000- or 20,000-seat arenas still wanting to come back and tear up the tiny 500-capacity Roxy. That was the power of the place. The Roxy wasn't just a venue. It was a rite of passage. Legends were born there, and legends returned there.

But this particular show? I wasn't exactly pumped. I knew the pressure was on. We had to deliver a near-flawless night because Courtney had a reputation for being unpredictable, volatile, and exhausting.

My band, Rumblefish, shared a business manager with her—a badass woman named Vicki who also repped Tool, Everclear, and a bunch of others. I was close with one of her staffers, and she used to play me Courtney's voicemails. Picture it: long, drunken, rambling messages. Sometimes sobbing. Sometimes spitting bitterness. Always meltdown mode.

Courtney was still tangled up in lawsuits over Kurt's estate and seemed to be hemorrhaging money on extravagant bills that, from what I was told, she couldn't actually cover. Out of all of Vicki's clients, Courtney was the one the office dreaded most. Which meant if shit went sideways on this show, it would land directly on me. Nic Adler, my boss, would get roasted by his dad Lou, the Roxy's owner. Then I'd be next in line for the whipping post. Trust me, that wasn't something you walked away from quickly.

I knew we were in trouble the second Courtney skipped soundcheck. That's always a red flag. In live music, even if you've got everything perfectly dialed in, at least one thing always goes wrong. Skipping soundcheck is basically an open invitation for Murphy's Law to kick you in the ass. So I said a little prayer, told my crew to stay sharp, and gave the golden rule for the night: no drinking or drugs until after the show.

By late afternoon, we'd finished soundchecks for the other bands. I checked off Courtney's backstage rider myself. Most of it was standard diva fare, but four bottles of *Ensure?* Yeah, the meal-replacement drink you buy for old people at CVS. That threw me off. Maybe the band needed a boost, maybe Courtney was living on that stuff—I didn't know. But it was on the list, so it was in the room. She also asked for her own private dressing room, with her band stuck in another. Totally on brand.

As showtime got closer, Courtney finally strolled into the Roxy through the alley door across from the Rainbow Bar & Grill. To my surprise, she looked a bit wrecked—pale, rail-thin, almost like some road-worn, female Ichabod Crane in a vintage dress and heels. Definitely not healthy, but very rock star. I pointed her and her tour manager to her room. She gave me a quick thanks, then bolted up the stairs.

And honestly, I couldn't help but think again: *what the hell did Kurt see in her?* Sure, she had that *I get whatever I want* energy, but underneath it, she radiated pure volatility. Publicly bad, maybe privately worse. In my head, Kurt should've stayed at least 100 feet away—at all times.

About thirty minutes before showtime, I got a call from the upstairs office: Paris Hilton was on her way in and wanted a VIP table for her crew.

I scrambled to get it ready, and as soon as she pulled up, my security guy Dirty Don Vito escorted her to the spot I picked out. Everything looked smooth… until the box office paged me:

JD, you need to get upstairs to Courtney's room. Now.

I sprinted up, knocked, and the door flew open. Her tour manager looked like he'd just walked out of a war zone. Before he could even open his mouth, I heard Courtney shrieking behind him:

Get that fuckin' bitch out of here! I'm not playing till she's gone!

Her tour manager basically repeated the same thing, but in a calmer, apologetic tone.

I actually laughed. *Okay, that's a weird one, but I'll see what I can do.*

But I knew damn well there was no way I could toss Paris Hilton out of the Roxy. She actually came to quite a few shows every year, and she had ties to the Adler family, who owned the Roxy (she had dated Lou Adler's other son, Cisco, before she became mega-famous).

Now I was stuck in one of my peculiar conundrums: the headliner was flat-out refusing to play if Paris didn't leave, but at the same time, there was no way I could have security eject Paris Hilton from the Roxy over nothing more than one of Courtney's tantrums. I had to think fast.

I went downstairs and texted Nic about the situation. His response was simple: no chance in hell we were kicking Paris out. He told me to talk to Tizzle, the other GM, to figure out a solution. Problem was, Tizzle and I didn't exactly see eye to eye. He wasn't my biggest fan, and the feeling was mutual. Luckily for me, Nic would never fire me—even though, honestly, I probably deserved it a few times. But since I was basically doing three jobs for the price of one, firing me would've been a stupid business move—especially with the Roxy barely keeping the lights on some weeks. In the end, like that show *Survivor,* I outlasted Tizzle and wound up the main GM myself.

So yeah… I knew I'd have to handle this Paris situation solo.

I thought it through for a second, then marched back upstairs to Courtney's dressing room. I told her tour manager that Paris was actually a guest of the Adler family—and, in fact, she'd said she was there as Courtney's friend. (Nic had confirmed they were friends, so I figured they'd gotten into some kind of feud that week or something.) The manager shut the door on me and I immediately heard the storm erupt inside—screaming, objects crashing against walls, Courtney spitting out:

I hate that bitch! and *She's a piece of shit!*

After a few minutes of mayhem, the tour manager reappeared looking wrecked but speaking in a calm, practiced tone.

Okay, Courtney agreed to play. But under no circumstances does she want Paris at the front of the stage or anywhere near backstage.

I let out a massive sigh of relief, put my hands together in mock prayer, and said, *Your wish is my command... tell Courtney thanks.*

Crisis defused—at least that one. But another grenade was waiting: the sound system. The Roxy didn't exactly have stellar monitors. Sure, the room itself had magic—the tight acoustics, the way a packed crowd soaked up high frequencies—it gave the place a warm analog feel you couldn't fake. But with Courtney blowing off soundcheck? *I knew we were in for it.* There was no way our setup was going to match her standards.

When Courtney finally walked onstage, the audience couldn't see her yet—we had a giant automatic curtain controlled by my lighting guy from the booth at the back of the room. I'd give him the *ready* sign with a flashlight, he'd hit the switch, and voilà: the curtain would rise slow and dramatic, the crowd would erupt, and the artist would be revealed. It was always a killer effect.

As Courtney began testing her vocals on the mic to see if the monitors were dialed in, *I knew we were doomed.* My monitor guy for the night, Dustin "Big Balls," couldn't get the exact level she wanted, and a few cracks and pops started spitting out of the monitors—annoying the hell out of her. The truth was our mic and monitor cables were beat to death after 300+ shows a year. We squeezed every ounce of life out of them, but with barely any budget, they were on their last leg. Add to that, Big Balls was living up to his name in the worst way—he was massively dropping the ball. His nerves were shot from the moment Courtney started complaining and cursing, and he just unraveled from there.

Our FOH sound rig crushed in the 1980s... by 2008, not so much.

I wanted to tell her, *See, Courtney, this is what happens when you skip soundcheck and act like you're play-ing in a stadium with a million-dol-lar rig,* but—thankfully—I kept my mouth shut.

As the trainwreck dragged on, my sound guy "Frankie Fingers" head-ed to the stage with my light guy to help Big Balls troubleshoot. Then came a loud thud—I looked up and saw Courtney take off her guitar and let it crash straight to the floor. She was so frustrated she just laid down on the side of the Roxy stage—on the filthy floor—with her legs sprawled out, blocking the backstage entrance. She started moaning about how nothing ever goes right and how everyone was an idiot.

By now, we were forty minutes behind, and the crowd was getting restless. *I couldn't help but laugh inside:* my crew was scrambling like headless chickens, my stage manager looked like he was on the *Titanic,* and Courtney was putting on the ultimate diva meltdown, lying on the dirty stage floor like a whiny, crying rock star.

While the shit-show unfolded, I tried to get her tour manager to calm her down and explain that the Roxy was never perfect—and that all of this could've been avoided if she'd bothered with soundcheck. That only pissed her off more. *I knew the buck stopped with me,* and even though it wasn't all my fault or my crew's fault, I'd still be dragged into the office later to explain how the night went to hell. *And I had about five minutes left to figure out how to dodge that dreaded vocal beatdown that would echo for weeks.*

Just when I was about to give up all hope, Big Balls and Frankie yell, "We fuckin' got it, we got it, man, monitors are good to go!" Courtney exhaled a huge sigh, pulled herself off the floor, grabbed her guitar, and stood ready at the mic—brushing the dust and whatever else off her dress. *I finally breathed out,* gave the flashlight signal to Bolle, and he hit that damn curtain switch.

The audience of teens, hipsters, music executives, and VIP people erupted—cheering and screaming like maniacs. *I thought we were home free.* But little did I know, there was way more shit about to go down.

The spot where I usually posted up was this little cubby hole in the back of the stage. It had a stool where I could sit and see the performance from behind, but I also had a clear view of the dressing room stairs to my right and the crowd out front. From there, I caught Paris Hilton down in the VIP section, glued to her cell phone, not even bothering to watch the show. Courtney's up there tearing it up, feeding the crowd with hardcore energy, and Paris couldn't care less.

About five or six songs in, I noticed her get up from her table and saunter over to our VIP security guy, "Dark Chocolate." She whispered something to him, and then he started escorting her straight toward the backstage entrance—where my trusty guy "Juan Bones" and I were holding down the fort.

Dark Chocolate tells us Paris wants to use the backstage bathroom instead of the regular Roxy one out by the audience. As he's explaining this, I glance at the stage—Courtney's fully locked into her songs and doesn't notice Paris slipping off to the side, trying to make her way in. *I make a split-second call:* "Hey Paris… okay, let me escort you real quick to the bathroom."

I led her upstairs to the backstage hallway bathroom. Nobody's around—just us. I open the door, and she slips past me with a mouthed *thank you* and a smile. Up close, Paris Hilton's got this unique, pretty face—exactly like she looks in pictures and on TV. Definitely not the case with most celebrities I've seen in person over the years.

I head back to the top of the stairs and wait while she's in there. After twenty minutes, *I start to worry.* Courtney could finish her set any second, and the idea of her storming backstage only to find Paris there? *Fuck.* I could see it in my head—Courtney losing it, screaming, maybe swinging, me trying to peel her off Paris, and the whole thing turning into a total shitshow. *The thought alone had me sweating.*

I give Paris two more minutes, but when those are up, *I'm like, What the hell? What the hell is she doing in there?*

I walk back down the hallway, knock on the door, but the music's blasting too loud—she can't hear a thing. Then I remember the old damage on the door handle. Over time it had slipped, leaving this tiny crack, almost like a peep hole. *So I lean in.*

The Roxy hallway bathroom had seen so much...

I bend down, peek inside—and there she is. Paris Hilton, gloriously dancing and pointing at herself in the mirror while mouthing the words to Courtney's song blasting from the stage. She's got her little purse in one hand, applying lipstick with the other, then blowing kisses to her reflection. *I'm thinking, damn, this takes the cake.* I've seen plenty of narcissistic artists roll through the Roxy, but never one literally blowing kisses at themselves in the mirror. She looked like some kind of Greek goddess of narcissism, worshipping herself for twenty straight minutes.

I decide to let her keep being her own biggest fan, but then I hear the opening notes of *"Malibu."* That's Courtney's big one. Which means about five to ten minutes before she wraps. *Do or die—I know I gotta get Paris outta there.*

By the grace of the music gods, she finally emerges before the set ends. She flashes me a glowing-toothed smile and, in this cute yet sexy voice, says, "Ok, I'm ready to go back to my table."

I let her lead the way. As we walk down the backstage stairs, I notice something flapping. *I do a double take—and holy shit.* There's a strip of toilet paper trailing from under her skirt, stuck right between her cheeks, waving like a dragon tail in the wind. On top of that, one side of her skirt is hiked up, fully exposing her right butt cheek. And let me tell you—despite being rail thin, it wasn't toned. *It looked un-toned, like she'd never done a squat or played a sport in her life.* Skinny-fat, plain and simple.

I followed behind her, staring in disbelief.

Halfway down the stairs, she stops, gazing out at the sea of people. *That's when I realize I've got a choice to make.*

Now remember—this is peak Paris Hilton fame. Everyone in the place knows her, and half of them are waiting for her to screw up in some way. *Part of me thinks, wouldn't it be hilarious to let her strut out into VIP like this? Toilet paper tail, flabby butt cheek out, paparazzi snapping away.* TMZ headline by tomorrow morning:

"Paris Hilton Shows Off Toilet Paper Dragon Tail at Courtney Love's Roxy Show."

If you look closely, up towards the right corner, you can see me smiling as I contemplate pulling out that toilet paper tail...

Or... do I play the good guy? Tap her on the shoulder, save her from total humiliation, and tell her what's hanging out?

In a split-second move, I go for the moral high ground. I reach out to tap her shoulder—too late. She steps forward, out of range. *Shit.* So I switch gears, lunge for the tail itself, and barely grab it with two fingers. One quick yank, and I've got it. In the same motion, I tug down the hiked-up skirt and cover her ass.

As this is happening, Paris takes her final step out into the audience. The second she does, people start cheering, flashes go off, and the phones come up. *I think to myself—man, she'll never know it was my quick reflexes that just saved her from a lifetime of memes that would've lived online forever*[2].

There's this strange mix in the crowd—some cheering like they'd just seen royalty, others groaning in annoyance at her grand entrance. But, by the grace of the music gods once again, Courtney's too busy belting out her set to notice a damn thing.

---

2. **The next day,** a picture emerged of Paris Hilton coming out of the backstage with my face behind her smiling (It was the moment right before I pulled the toilet paper out of her butt). It was taken by the awesome and crazy blogger known as *"Perez Hilton"* and he seemed to know all about how Courtney Love despised Paris as that was what his article was all about.

Truth be told, Courtney's voice actually sounded pretty good that night. But her guitar playing? Still bad. She never really sharpened those skills since the first time I saw her at the Whisky all those years ago.

Toward the end of any show, when the set's wrapping or the encore's happening, I make my rounds backstage. Standard procedure. I'd hand over a copy of the dressing room key to the artist or their tour manager, but I always kept one for myself. After all, somebody had to check for damage—clogged toilets, busted furniture, trashed walls. I'd also make sure the basics were stocked—beer, water, whatever else was supposed to be there.

When I went into Courtney's room that night, the evidence was scattered all over the floor. All four of those *Ensure* drinks she'd requested earlier? Empty and tossed around. I figured they were either hurled at her tour manager in a rage or slammed against the wall when she found out we weren't booting Paris. Later I learned the *Ensures* weren't some weird diva request—they were doctor-ordered, part of her effort to get back to a healthy weight.

Courtney ended the show strong, though. The audience roared their approval, satisfied, and for once she actually looked lighter coming off-stage—like she'd finally blown off enough steam. Good thing too, since she was hosting her after-party at our exclusive upstairs club, *On The Rox.*

*Put a giant carboard cut-out of Paris in my office as
a tribute to the Courtney Love show...*

On The Rox was its own beast. Hangers-on, label guys, Hollywood scenesters, lucky fans—it would be wall-to-wall until 2 a.m. Easy. Drinks flowing, people dancing, plenty of lines being racked up in corners. This was peak music-vampire culture in Hollywood. The kind of scene people romanticize—until they've seen it up close or been in it too long.

For nights like this, with someone like Courtney, I always had a few friends swing by. It was one of the rare perks of working at the Roxy. They sure as hell didn't pay me more than peanuts, but at least I could get a couple names on the VIP list. My friends would have the time of their lives, and when the spectacle was over, they'd hang with me while I came down from the craziness.

My one good friend, Paul *"Shug"* Shugerman—his dad was the well-known photographer Stephen Shugerman—was this tattooed Valley kid I'd known since the 1990s *Cobalt Café* days, back when I was booking shows there. For the Courtney Love gig, I hooked him up with drink tickets and VIP wristbands. That was my thing—I always gave my buddies free drink tickets so they wouldn't have to shell out for the ridiculous alcohol prices.

Well, let's just say Shug had more than his fair share of those drinks before we even made it upstairs. By the time we hit *On The Rox,* he was good and lit. We walked in just in time to see Courtney climbing up onto a table. She was soaking up every ounce of attention—twirling around, throwing her hands in the air, swinging that loose dress like she was still queen of the world.

It was equal parts entertaining and tragic, watching her move in this faded, past-her-prime glory. Shug leaned into my ear through the commotion and yelled,

"Dude, she kind of looks like a washed-up Skeletor."

We thought we were safe—too much noise for her to hear. But somehow, whether she read his lips or had some kind of freakish supersonic hearing, she zeroed in. Her eyes locked right on us. She pointed straight at Shug and growled, *"Come say that to my face, motherfucker. Right now, asshole—let's go."* Then she threw up her middle finger and started climbing down off the table like she was actually ready to throw fists.

I was in total shock. I looked at him like, *"Dude, let's get the fuck out of here—she's really gonna beat your ass."* Next thing I know, we're bolting for the back door, shoving past people, knocking drinks everywhere, laughing our asses off as we push through the crowd.

We finally spilled out into the night air, both of us doubled over, gasping for breath. Shug's face was red from laughing so hard. He yelled, *"Holy crap, we almost got our asses kicked by Courtney Love! She's fuckin' insane. No wonder people think she's batshit crazy."*

From then on, Shug and I kept a safe perimeter around her for the rest of the night, sticking to the shadows while we cracked jokes and swapped memories of our old San Fernando Valley days—and dreamed about the reckless Sunset Strip nights still ahead.

Years later, that night became one of my go-to stories. It always killed with friends and strangers alike. But sometimes when I look back, I kinda wish we hadn't run. Maybe we should've stood there and taken our deserved beating from Courtney Love. That would've been an even more legendary tale.

Oh well. Live and learn baby. Live and learn…

Dirty Money: The Road to Musical Stardom

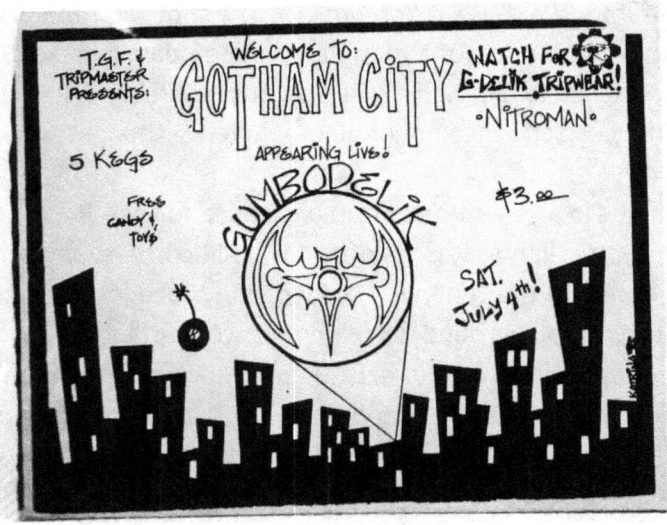

"You clowns don't know who threw this illegal party?"

After the Courtney and Paris debacle finally burned itself out, I figured I'd hit one of the pinnacles of insanity—pure musical chaos spliced with dark comedy.

But the truth? I'd already lived through a few others years earlier, back in the early '90s. At that point, I wasn't just working behind the scenes of music. I was hustling every angle I could think of. Illegal house parties with bands and kegs. Underground raves with DJs. Anything that scraped together enough dirty cash to keep the dream of stardom alive.

I had a tight crew: a few close friends and a band of brothers who lived high up in the Mulholland Highway mountains. They called themselves the Spring Boys. Together, we branded our little empire *True Gumbo Funksters*—T.G.F., aka *Gumbodelik*.

One night we decided to go all in: an outdoor rave in the Calabasas hills. Yeah, *that* Calabasas—land of mega-mansions, gated driveways, and movie stars. We called it *Gotham City.* The spot was unreal. Massive boulders stacked on top of a mountain, hidden past a locked gate. To get there, you had to hike half a mile up a busted fire road. Remote. Flat. Otherworldly. Exactly the kind of place where we thought, *Fuck it, let's throw a party.*

We hauled in a generator, portable sound, and kegs. Rigged fluorescent lamps, strip lights, stashes of candy, chill corners, and makeshift drinking dens. By the time we finished, the place looked like some post-apocalyptic playground, our own rave wonderland.

Promotion was old school back then: flyers scattered at Calabasas High and El Camino Real in Woodland Hills, plus word of mouth that spread like wildfire. By the night of the event, every party kid within twenty miles knew *Gotham City* was about to go off.

But here's the part we didn't know: that mountaintop wasn't just rocks and dirt. It was an ancient Native American burial ground. And to make matters worse, a teacher from Calabasas High snagged one of our flyers and handed it straight to the sheriff's office.

The night of the rave, everything clicked into motion. Some of the crew handled parking at the bottom of the hill. Others collected three bucks a head at the gate. A couple more worked the keg—two bucks a cup. The rest rotated shifts on music, crowd control, and the occasional brawl. Classic underground logistics.

Then me and one of my partners, T.S. Spring, realized we'd made a rookie mistake: no ice. Essential for the kegs. It was 8:30 p.m., about ninety minutes before doors. We jumped in his beat-up Suzuki Jeep, flew down Mulholland to Topanga, loaded up bags of ice, and started barreling back.

That's when the whole thing went sideways.

Traffic was backed up—over a hundred cars crawling toward our party. At first, we were stoked. Then we rounded a curve... flashing red and blue lights everywhere. Cops. Shutting the whole thing down. Redirecting traffic.

Panic mode. We pulled off, tried to blend in on foot like curious bystanders, but before we got far, cops jumped out of an unmarked vehicle:

"Freeze. Hands up."

"Where you headed?" one barked. My brain clicked into survival mode. *"Officer, my buddy T.S. here lives just down the road."* (Technically true, just not from that direction.) They turned to T.S. *"That true?"* *"Yes, sir."* I added, *"We heard about a party up the hill, figured we'd check it out."*

The big question came:

"You clowns don't know who threw this illegal party?" We shook our heads. *"No idea, sir."*

Somehow, they bought it. They sent us back. We strolled calm as hell to the Jeep, then looped around the backside of the mountain where we figured we'd go undetected.

T.S. hiked up on foot while I tried another route. In the pitch-black night, I off-roaded that Suzuki through gnarly terrain until I smashed the back tires into boulders and got stuck. No water. No way forward.

I climbed on foot, dodging searchlights from a police helicopter. At one point, a cop pretending to leave did a final sweep with his high-powered spotlight—the beam hit the exact spot I'd just dropped flat onto the ground. If I'd flinched, I'd have been nailed. Somehow, I slipped through.

By the time I got to the top, it was a ghost town. Silent. Just beer cans and candy wrappers scattered where *Gotham City* had been alive hours earlier.

I hiked back to Tom's, crashed on his couch. Around 3 a.m., he stumbled in—covered in dirt, twigs, out of breath. He'd been chased but evaded cops through steep cliffs. Dude was like a mountain goat.

Next morning, we freed the stuck Jeep and went straight to Eli's. He and my girlfriend had stayed behind when the cops swarmed. We banged on his window. He came out groggy, covered in dirt. *"You guys are NOT gonna believe what happened…"*

Turns out, the second we left for ice, a sheriff's Jeep launched over the ridge with more cars and a helicopter. Total ambush. The crew scattered, but most got caught. The whole setup—sound, kegs, lights—confiscated. They were cuffed, grilled, and threatened with jail if they didn't give us up.

But not one of them snitched. Eli said he didn't know. My girlfriend held her ground too. They all kept their mouths shut.

That kind of loyalty? Maybe dumb… but damn rare.

T.S. and the rest of us dodged all charges because of them. I was floored. I expected someone to fold the second *"jail"* came up. They didn't.

When Eli finally looked at us and said, *"So… when's the next party?"* we lost it. Laughing our asses off. Of course we were already planning it.

We were young. We were reckless. And we sure as hell weren't done yet.

We even had a Gotham City II at a different location…

What I realized years later was that the havoc around me wasn't just random noise. It was part of the fabric of music itself. Chaos was the undercurrent. And the truth? Most of us fed off it. I know I did.

There was something about the adrenaline, the endorphins, the constant edge. It became addictive. That tension, that unpredictability, kept everything electric. *It wasn't background static. It was the pulse.* Running through every set I played, every show I worked, even the ones I just walked into.

And The Roxy? It was never done dealing out its own brand of turmoil. A few months after the Paris and Courtney meltdown, a gnarly rock 'n' roll superstar and his barefoot movie-star girlfriend, who rolled up in a damn monster truck no less, proved just how sideways things could get. But this time it was in a totally different way.

Hope I don't get in trouble for this one.

Chapter 9

BEAUTY AND THE BEAST–Chris Robinson & Kate Hudson

"Can't a man get some fucking privacy around here?"

I was a big admirer of Chris Robinson's vocals and his work with *The Black Crowes,* but I can honestly say at the time I wasn't much of a fan of his wife, Kate Hudson. Not that I knew her or anything. I just wasn't into those fluffy, rom-com movies she starred in. Little did I know my whole perception of Chris and Kate was about to flip the day they showed up at the Roxy.

The booking office sent me a memo: Chris Robinson was scheduled to play an acoustic set with his brother Rich Robinson, *The Black Crowes'* guitarist. We knew it was going to be a packed, sold-out show.

Years back, *The Black Crowes* had played the Roxy, and the show was so oversold that one of the original, infamous owners of the Roxy and Whisky (I won't say which one—I'd like to keep my health intact) handed our head sound guy, "Dr. Evil aka Eddie O.," a fat bag of cash to secretly buy advance tickets from the box office. The plan? Flip them for $400 a pop on the day of the show. Ten tickets at $400 each... not bad for a few hours' work.

Unfortunately, two people standing in that long-ass line—who also happened to work with *The Black Crowes'* fan club—recognized "Dr. Evil" and reported the whole thing straight to the band's management. They went ballistic and threatened to pull the plug on the entire show unless someone was fired immediately. Translation: Dr. Evil had to take the fall.

And he did. Like a true soldier. He took the bullet for the bigwig and ate the blame without ever revealing who really orchestrated the whole thing. He was fired for a few months, but quietly rehired once the smoke cleared.

I couldn't help but laugh. It reminded me at the time of Oliver North falling on his sword for Reagan. That's how it goes sometimes. You take the hit to protect the boss—especially in Hollywood or Washington DC.

In my mind, anyone who plays real rock 'n' roll and can sing like a male Janis Joplin has to be *cool* in my book. Or so I thought. The picture in my head was Chris strolling into the Roxy with a huge smile, 1970s bell-bottom jeans, long hair, and an open shirt exposing his abs for all the ladies to swoon over. Why not? He was already world-famous, a millionaire, playing rock 'n' roll for a living, and married to Kate Hudson. How the hell could life get any better than that?

I greeted his tour manager, this calm, no-bullshit, Carole King–looking chick (let's call her Carole), who had that unmistakable *I've been in the game since the dawn of rock* energy. Like she probably knew what the hell was up back when Steven Tyler wrote *Sweet Emotion*. We clicked immediately, and she laid out the do's and don'ts of the backstage and Chris's rider.

Quick crash course for the uninitiated: a band rider is supposed to be a wishlist of what the band wants backstage before and after they play. Technically it's just a wishlist, since most clubs—including the Roxy—cross out half of it in the contract. But over time, thanks to rock star entitlement, it somehow became gospel. About 80% of bands throw a hissy fit when the rider isn't perfect. Marilyn Manson was the worst. Total nightmare. That's a whole other story in this book. The kicker? Most bands barely touch any of the food or booze anyway. They just leave it behind like it's trash. Complete waste of money, time, and effort. Classic rock star bullshit...

Come on, you rich-ass, limousine liberal musicians... people are starving out there!

I always let the bouncers and staff take whatever they wanted at the end of the night—it just never seemed right to throw it all away.

As soundcheck got closer, Chris was still running late. No sign of him, and we were five minutes away from the 3:30 p.m. call time. I was in the small backstage room with Carole when someone yelled up the stairs:

"Chris just got here—and he almost got into a fight with the parking attendant!"

Carole and I looked at each other, puzzled. A few minutes later, I heard Chris stomping down the hallway toward the backstage rooms.

When he entered, Carole noticed he had on a new paisley unbuttoned shirt. Trying to diffuse the tension, she said, "Hey Chris, nice to see you... wow, where'd you get that cool shirt?"

Chris shot her an angry glare and snapped,

"What the hell do you care!"

I thought, *Damn... better skip the whole hello. This dude needs some medication—or at least a crash course in meditation.*

Then he launched into it: apparently this "fucking asshole" parking attendant was asking him for money to park, and he almost threw down.

He said he left his car in the middle of the lot and told the guy to kiss his ass.

I told Carole we had already given the list of free parking for the night to our parking guy, so I wasn't sure what the hell went wrong. Chris should've parked for free.

(I only found out later that Chris had driven a different car and never bothered telling our Armenian parking guy, Vahe, that he was Chris Robinson and playing the show. Instead, when Vahe asked him for the $7 to park, Chris told him to "fuck off." That's when the near fistfight almost happened.)

Carole stepped in and told Chris that I was the production manager and I'd handle it. He muttered a quick "hey" in my direction and then bee-lined for the fridge. He opened it, took one look, and barked:

"What the fuck... this isn't even close to what I'm supposed to have... what kind of bullshit is this?"

Before I could open my mouth, Carole jumped in and explained that he was in the small dressing room, and that the one next door—the main room—had all his rider stuff, clothes, a better couch, the works.

Chris stormed out and flew into the bigger room. Seconds later, I heard him yell:

"This place is a shithole!"

I just laughed. Whatever cool-vibed rock 'n' roll attitude this guy once had had completely left him. Unbridled talent fused with drugs and money can do that. Carole just looked at me and said, "Yep, I don't know why I put up with this crap. I must be a glutton for punishment." I smiled and told her to let me know if she needed anything, and I'd tell my sound guys and crew to walk on eggshells.

To my surprise, the soundcheck went pretty smooth. My guys were on point. I'd already warned them to bring their A-game because Chris Robinson might rip them a new one, and under no circumstances were they to smoke pot or drink until the show was over.

Chris seemed to calm down once he started soundchecking with his brother—just the two of them—going over new and old songs. You could see it gave him some kind of inner peace. It definitely calmed his demons, at least for the moment.

As we got closer to showtime, I got a call from Carole to come up-stairs to the main backstage room. I went up, and Carole was on the phone. She told me to hold on a second, then hung up and said, "Ok, that was Kate. She drove the wrong way into the parking lot, and the parking guys didn't see her, but her truck is stuck in the middle of the driveway and she can't back up worth shit… so, can you go down and help her?"

I was like, "Hell yeah, no problem."

I ran down the stairs and went out the side door by the Roxy bar. As soon as I stepped outside, holy shit… Kate's truck was huge. This thing was like *BigFoot*—remember that monster truck back in the day? All black, lifted, massive tires.

I waved to Kate, and she opened the door and jumped down into my arms. She gave me a hug and said, "Thank you so much for helping, here's my keys."

I opened the side door for her and told her how to get back-stage—and to wear her beanie hat low so no one would bug her on the way in. She had on a little hippie getup: scarf and knitted beanie pulled low.

Somehow, I grabbed a handle and hauled myself up into her truck. As soon as I closed the door, the pungent aroma of weed smacked me in the face. The friggin' giant truck reeked of Sativa.

I turned the ignition key and suddenly *"Sugar Magnolia"* by the Grateful Dead blasted through the speakers. I looked around—Grateful Dead CDs and other classic rock discs scattered all over the floor, mixed in with random clothes and paraphernalia.

I was tempted to peek into the middle console—which I had a strong hunch was where the good green was stashed—but I do have a moral code I stick to, so I never looked inside.

Then I felt something under my ass. I pulled it out—it was her wallet. Again, I never opened it, but I had a good laugh. *Man, what a typical stoner move,* I thought.

I managed to swing her massive truck around to the other side of the lot, and Vahe and his Armenian crew just stared at me in confusion—like I was breaking some sacred parking lot code of conduct again, but this time in a giant monster truck. I laughed and rolled down the window. Vahe yelled in his accent, teasing me:

"Jay, what the fuck, did you buy a new truck?"

I told them it was Kate Hudson's truck and that I was parking it for her. They opened up a spot, and I slid that behemoth in and locked it up.

When I went back upstairs, I saw Kate sitting on a chair in the corner right by the stairs. I said, "Hey Kate! You left your wallet on the seat..." She looked up, all smiles: "Oops, thank you, thank you sweetie."

She gave me another hug, and as I pulled away, I got a good look at her face. Wow, she was even better looking in person—and she was so nice and down to earth. I said to myself: *how the hell did Chris Robinson snag Kate Hudson?*

I figured she loved rock and roll, and obviously the "bad boys" that came with it. It all made sense now, but I knew then it wasn't destined to last.

We were about 20 minutes from showtime, and the crowd was drunk and buzzing with anticipation. I was over by the soundboard talking to my guy and my main man Bolle, who'd been the faithful lighting director long before I joined the Roxy.

As we were going over protocol, I got a call from the main office upstairs to give a quick report on how everything was running. I ran toward the backstage entrance and saw Carole sitting in my usual spot next to the stage. The stairway lights were off.

As I approached, she goes,

"Hey JD, here, lemme turn the light back on for you."

She flipped the switch, and to both of our surprise—there was Chris, sitting at the bottom of the stairs with his zipper undone, and Kate Hudson sitting in his lap, clearly going at it.

The infamous backstage stairs...

He looked up like a madman and snapped, "Shut the fucking light off... are you fucking kidding me... can't a man get some fucking privacy around here?"

Carole instantly killed the light and muttered, "Sorry," while I jumped back out of the backstage, laughing my ass off. I thought, *Damn... I just walked in on Kate Hud-*

son going at it with Chris Robinson on the Roxy stairs. Oh man, it doesn't get funnier than this.

And yeah, I saw it for a second. Let's just say it hadn't seen the sun in ages, and it didn't exactly match the rock star image he projected on stage.

I guess if it doesn't work properly, that could make a man go mad. Hell, it would definitely make me run around pissed off at the world.

Well, after that little incident, Chris and his brother went onstage and absolutely rocked the house. His vocals were just as killer as the records, and he transformed into that cool, demon-free rock 'n' roller I had always pictured in my mind.

It was his world on stage, and he was the master.

I get now why some people say music saved them. If it weren't for music, Chris Robinson might have ended up locked away, far from society.

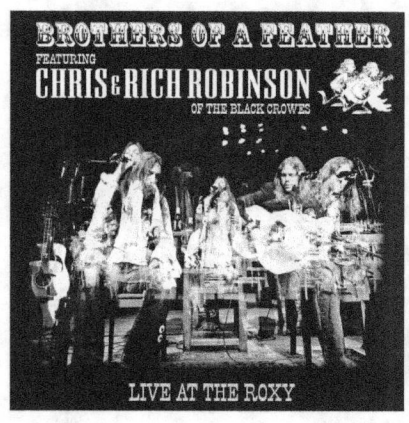

I never saw him again, but I did go back and watch all the Kate Hudson movies I'd never cared to see before. For the first time, I could see the great, positive energy in her acting. And I imagined that everywhere she went, another fan was probably born.

Maybe that's the power of art. It gives people second chances in ways life never could.

it all started with skateboarding in Brentwood, CA., 1979

The first time I heard of the Peppers was this poster hanging in my buddy sister's room... she was dating Flea, 1984

My band Ku De Tah sneered at all the popular glam rock that was still big in 1990

First time we paid to play the Whisky a Go Go, 1990 and sold 100 tickets to grace the stage

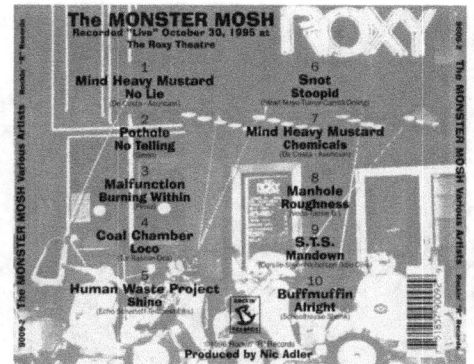

Mind Heavy Mustard alongside the most popular bands in Hollywood, 1995 for Nic Adler's Monster Mosh at the Roxy

I could've but I ended up not going to their video shoot for Smells Like Teen Spirit...Damn!

Helped load out Nirvana for their 1991 Roxy show... was paid cash

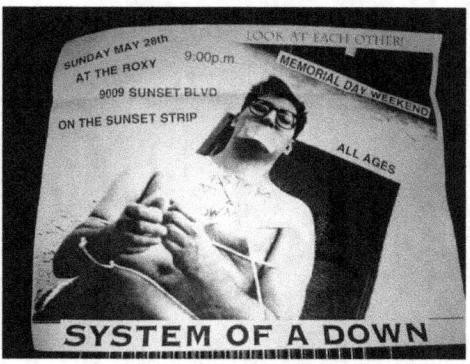

I helped SOAD land a few gigs when they were just starting out. At the time, my band Mind Heavy Mustard was actually bigger than them—though that didn't last long. LOL.

I booked Incubus at Mancinis, but this flyer that Brandon Boyd drew for the show got banned by the club

Booked this kick-ass show at the Cobalt Cafe

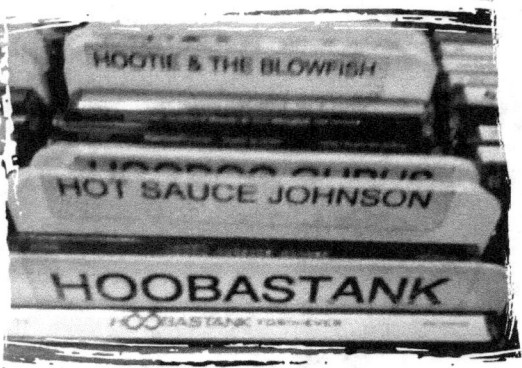

In between Hoobastank and Hootie & The Blowfish at Lou's Records, San Diego. It seemed like we were on our way

Rumblefish in our prime...we gave it
our damn best and came up a bit short
Photo: Kevin Estrada, 2001.

We booked all theses shows for M
Productions... see Rumblefish at the bottom

Hot Sauce Johnson in better times with Kevin Estrada, ReRun and The Roadrunner Records crew in NY.

I took a pic of our photographer Voake getting a close up of the action

A few of the Suicide Girls getting ready to hit the stage in lingerie

Not only did I book shows for the Whisky & Roxy but I also performed on some of them...double duty

Took this pic in our kitchen of Caveman, Mark McGrath and Chino from the Deftones, uniting in honor of kick ass times

Some of our waitresses had big time sass

Some of my favorite cousins hanging out backstage... Always had family come visit me

Mark McGrath was always a pleasure to have around... Easy going and positive energy. Seemed like all the ladies loved him

Me and one of my favorite assistants named Caveman...

My boss Nic Adler who was the son of legendary Roxy owner, Lou Adler

I was sponsored by Ibanez in 2001. See me in the 3rd picture down inbetween CKY and Six Feet Under.

Travis and DJ AM backstage at the Roxy for a photoshoot in my collage-covered hallway. Not long after I took this picture, they survived a plane crash—only for DJ AM to tragically pass away from a drug overdoes in his apartment.

Suicide Girl from the PETA I'd Rather be Naked than Wear Fur Event

Steve-O fooling around, seemingly wasted while rapping onstage

Chester and Duff having a quick laugh coming offstage after their performance with Camp Freddy

One of the pretty Camp Freddy girls

Decorated my Acoustic guitar like the Roxy backstage. Filled with autographs and a 1991 Cobain guitar pick

Party time w Cisco Adler and Whitestarr after their show

Yep! that's Cheech and Chong with yours truly...I looklike their son. ha!
Photo: Kevin Estrada

With *legendary guitarist Robbie Krieger from the Doors*

Onstage with Mickey Avalon... this shot ended up on the cover of LA Weekly—to my delight, I could finally say I made the cover. Lol.

Got this pic of Billy Gibbons ZZ Top without his glasses on

Backstage for a big benefit with Gene Simmons

Hanging out with Jerry Cantrell from Alice in Chains

Our smaller dressing room was always a mess but so many artists loved the gritty vibe and music history

One of my prized frames that I hung up backstage. There aren't many Bradley Nowell autographs out there since he passed before they really became big.

This wild gal hung from our ceiling by those two hook for the Janes Addiction show...ouch!

Tommy Lee always having a blast before his performance

Puddle of Mud in the house...we had the same manager as them, but the magic didn't seem to work for us

Even ex-boy band members would stop by and hang with all of us backstage

Russell Brand had a weekly residency with us... My guy Lee scrambling to fix sound problems mid-show. Russell still managed to hook up with one of our waitresses and an office staff girl. The man had mojo.

John 5 from Marilyn Manson having a good laugh backstage with Jerry Cantrell

Fred Durst giving me the devil horns,
posing for a quick photo backstage

I was a Battle of the Bands judge with Duff and Gilby from Guns &
Roses Duff told me a few stories about the Roxy that I promised not
to make public

Some actresses were total sweethearts...
Do you recognize her?

The official Roxy photographer and my buddy, Erik
Voake posing with Lemmy... Yep, we let him smoke
inside the Roxy

Steve Aoki ripping it up onstage for our DJ night

This girl had tattoos of autographs all over her body...
I let her backstage to get some more to add to her
collection

Always made artists and actors like Jack Black, sign their posters for us backstage

Travis Barker in our main Roxy dressing room

Tom Morello from Rage Against the Machine showing me his talented finger

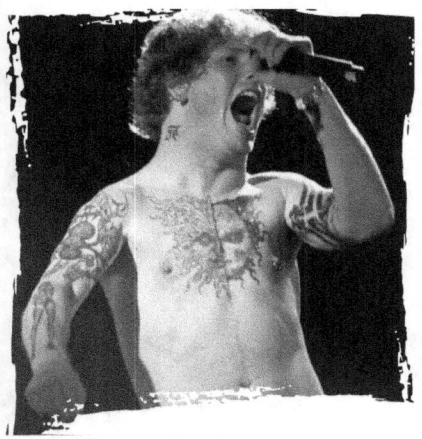

Cory from Slipknot kickin' ass as a guest performer

Caught The infamous Pauly Shore before stage time

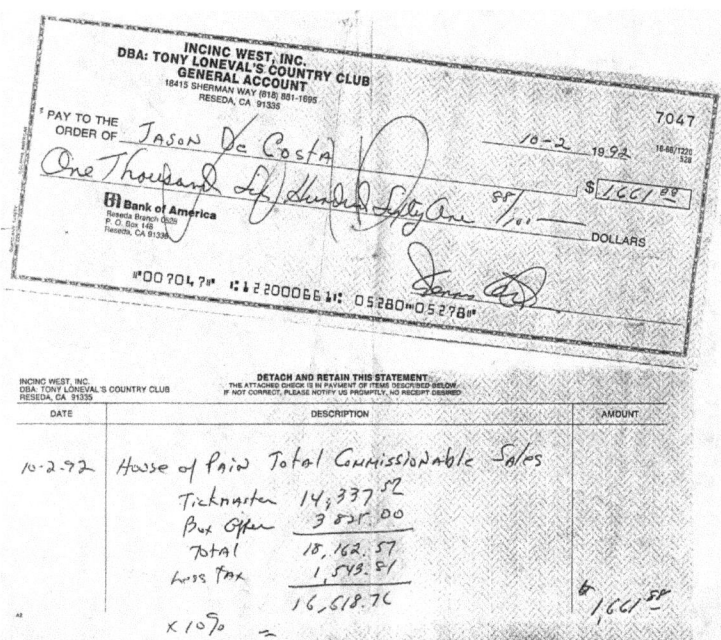

My first legitimate check that I received in the music biz for helping book and promote House of Pain at the Reseda Country Club in 1992

I always loved letting music students come and see how live music works in real time. These kids from Japan were hyped

A few years before I finally left the music biz

Damn man! I only took one vacation when I worked at the Roxy for over a decade... I have a lot to explore

2025 with family at the Shinedown concert

The Lifeline: Talent and Fame Only Buys Some Time

The flicker of pain, 2008 (Photo: Erik Voake)

"The stage can delay the inevitable, but when the lights go down, you're still left alone with yourself"

I get it now—why people say music saved them. Myself included. Without it, even the most successful artists—those with talent, fame, and fortune—can feel completely lost. It's heavy to realize how many of them were haunted by something they couldn't outrun. For some, it exploded outward as rage, self-destruction, or erratic behavior. For others, it was quieter but maybe even worse—a slow, crushing sadness they carried like a shadow they couldn't shake.

I still think about the artists who came through the Roxy, the huge names who looked like they had it all together from the outside. But up close—guys like Chris Cornell, Chester Bennington, and Scott Weiland—you could see it. Something troubling behind their eyes. A flicker of pain that never went away. You had to really pay attention to catch it, but once you did, you couldn't unsee it.

It was like music was the only thing holding the darkness back. *Their lifeline.* Onstage, they found a few hours of freedom, a place to turn pain into sound. But offstage, you could feel the weight pressing down, whatever was eating them alive from the inside. No amount of applause, money, or success could erase it. That void was always waiting in the silence.

What I learned standing side stage was this:
Talent and fame don't make you bulletproof. Sometimes they just buy you time. They give you distractions, they give you noise—but they don't cure the sickness underneath. Nietzsche once said, *"Without music, life would be a mistake."* He was right. Music doesn't erase the suffering. It gives it shape. It gives it rhythm. It makes it survivable, at least for a while.

That was one of the hardest truths I had to swallow in this business: music can be salvation, but it's not a shield against being human. The stage can delay the inevitable, but when the lights go down, you're still left alone with yourself. And sometimes, that's the hardest show of all.

Or as Shakespeare wrote:
"Give sorrow words; the grief that does not speak knits up the o'er-wrought heart and bids it break."

Chapter 10

WEILAND, CORNELL & BENNINGTON—Glimpses of Destiny

"Yeah, I do remember...I was so much happier back then"

As everyone knows, Scott Weiland, Chris Cornell, and Chester Bennington were all incredibly unique and insanely talented rock stars. Each of them reached the heights of greatness but, unfortunately, succumbed to tragedy in the end.

Working at the Roxy gave me the rare chance to meet and talk with them when no one else was around. Over the years, I had plenty of those behind-the-curtain conversations with famous artists (*and yeah, a bunch of them are in this book*). What I glimpsed in those quiet moments was something few ever get to see—a look into their aura, their psyche, and, though I didn't know it at the time, the shadow of their destiny. The conversations I had with each of them felt eerily similar, and I still remember them like it was yesterday.

People have always told me I have a certain charm. A warmth. A way of smiling or listening that makes people drop their guard and start talking. I guess I've always had that gift. I've never had trouble drawing out people's inner lives, even the ones with walls a mile high. Maybe it's because I was genuinely curious. I don't even know why I gave a shit, but I always asked the right questions, and they answered.

When I was very young, I thought I'd be a psychologist. But music pulled me in a different direction. Somehow that same curiosity, that same instinct to dig deeper, carried over into my relationships with famous artists. Maybe that's why they felt at ease opening up about personal things.

These three particular interactions made me realize something that's stuck with me: *happiness can be elusive.* Fame, wealth, success—none of it guarantees peace. In fact, sometimes it seemed to magnify the emptiness. Little did I know at the time that it would all end so catastrophically for each of them. The things they said to me... it was almost as if they were foretelling their own fate.

Alright. Let's start with my favorite: *Scott Weiland.*

I remember clearly back in the 1990s when hair metal dominated the Sunset Strip. I was playing in my non-glam, *Red Hot Chili Peppers*–inspired band *Ku De Tah.*

Since glam and hair rock was all the rage back then, we always got excited whenever we heard about another band with a vibe closer to ours. We were into bands that were basically the total opposite of the long-haired, lipstick-dude style dominating the Strip at the time. One of those bands was called *Clyde*[1]. They were cool and unique, and yeah—you could definitely hear some *Chili Peppers* influence in their sound too.

We found out they were headlining a show at the *Whisky A Go Go,* so my guitarist, Don C., and I decided we had to check them out live.

When we got to the Whisky, the place had been transformed into a neon-glowing jungle. It was packed wall-to-wall, and we were impressed as hell. But since *Clyde* wasn't going on until 11 p.m., we were stuck sitting through the opener, a band called *Mighty Joe Young.*

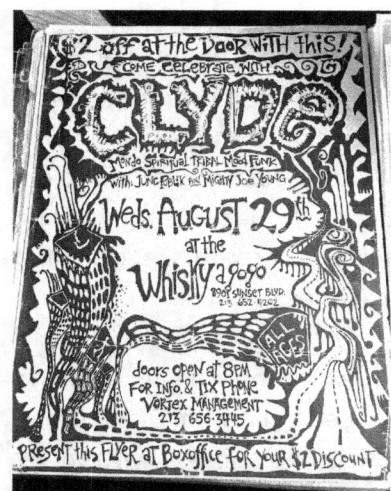

Clyde was dominating the Hollywood RHCP influenced funk scene—look closely and you'll see Mighty Joe Young.

We didn't know who the hell they were, and honestly, at that point, we didn't care. But the second *Mighty Joe Young* hit the stage and slammed into their first chords, we knew instantly—these guys were fucking beasts.

Their musicianship was off the hook, and the singer had the audience in his grip almost instantly. They came out dressed like 1920s paperboys but sounded like a pumped-up funk-rock four-piece with teeth. Three songs in, the bass player ripped a solo so nasty that Don and I just looked at each other with this frightened realization—*damn, we had a long way to go if we ever wanted to be in their league.*

The singer belted out tunes—half rapping, half singing—while topping it off with this cocky, frat-boy swagger that somehow worked. The crowd ate it up like candy.

---

1. Clyde was way ahead of their time. They had been playing for a few years, and other than the Chili Peppers, they were on a path and style of their own making. They faded into obscurity and I remember hearing the rumor that the singer had some major mental health issues and ended up hospitalized, forcing the band into hiatus...I'm still not sure if that is true or not.

I actually started to feel bad for *Clyde,* because I knew this unknown band was straight-up stealing their show. (*And sure enough, when Clyde finally came on, their set felt flat. All the energy had already been drained from the room.*)

By the time *Mighty Joe Young* wrapped, they had completely won over *Clyde's* crowd. Don and I just nodded to each other—*this band was the shit.* We both knew they were headed somewhere, some kind of stardom that we could only dream about. Deep down, we knew we didn't have the immense natural talent it would take—but these guys seemed to have it spilling out of them.

What we didn't know that night was that *Mighty Joe Young* would soon change their name and become *Stone Temple Pilots*[2]. Just as we predicted, they went on to become megastars, selling millions of records, adored and hated all at once.

Mighty Joe Young aka Stone Temple Pilots 1991.

Fast forward many years. Weiland had long been gone from *STP* but had carved out some success with *Velvet Revolver.* By then, he was a bit past his prime musically, but it looked like he was on a new kick—heading into the fashion world.

At one of our weekly Roxy meetings, the booking office told us that Weiland was coming in to do a fashion show. He'd perform a few solo songs, and then there'd be a runway show with models strutting around.

---

2. Mighty Joe Young had a completely different sound and look than Stone Temple Pilots. They were dressed like paperboys while rocking the white-boy funk with a frat-boy attitude. I remember when tons of other bands and Hollywood critics completely hated and criticized STP. People would call them "Stone Temple Pirates" and say they were fake and opportunistic. Honestly, I agreed that their style, attitude, and music felt completely manufactured. But I sure as hell couldn't say I wouldn't have done the same thing. As always, other bands and people were just jealous and envious of their quick success when they changed their style and became STP. Nothing wrong with their huge achievements—they could definitely write some amazing songs—and their success was well-earned, even if it was all manufactured.

When Weiland showed up that night, the first thing I noticed was how thin he looked. Still sharp in a full suit, but extra thin. I wanted to get him to sign my big Roxy poster—the one autographed by almost every major artist who'd come through the doors. I also had this itch to ask him about those old *Mighty Joe Young* days.

I hung the poster up in the backstage hallway, ready for him to sign when the moment was right, and went back to advancing shows and checking schedules in my office. As showtime crept closer, I peered out from the DJ balcony and saw the audience was decent—not a sell-out, but respectable.

Backstage had this weird, upbeat vibe—hottie models in various fashion pieces, some of them nearly half-naked, just floating through the halls. It felt more like a party than a rock show. When I stepped out of my office again (which was right next to the main backstage room), I literally bumped into Weiland. Not hard, just a little shoulder-to-shoulder.

"Hey Scott, dang, sorry man… I'm JD! I'm the GM here."

He looked at me, soft-voiced, almost timid, and asked, "Do you have another bathroom back here?"

The tone threw me off. It was so different from the super outgoing kid I'd seen at the Whisky back in the '90s—and definitely not the guy I'd watched command thousands with *STP* and *Velvet Revolver.*

Up close, he looked worn out. His thin, aging face didn't have that spark anymore. When I looked into his eyes, he couldn't hold eye contact. There was something unsettling in his expression—like he was trapped in a cage of his own making. That fire, that wild charisma that made him one of the greatest frontmen of his era—it seemed like it had flipped on him. He looked stuck, beaten down, like the drugs and the boredom had drained him dry.

I'd seen that same haunted look in a few other stars who came through the Roxy over the years.

I told him he could use the main office bathroom if he wanted priva-cy, then walked him down the hall, unlocked the door, and waited while he went inside.

When he came back out, I decided to go for it.

"Scott," I said, "do you remember the Whisky A Go Go show when you guys were *Mighty Joe Young* and you friggin' blew *Clyde* off the stage?"

He stood there for a few seconds, then opened his mouth, but noth-ing came out. It was like he was drifting back into some far-off place, a time from a completely different world. Finally, with a deep breath, he said,

"Oh damn, I do remember those days. That... yes, that was when it was all fun and new. I always had a feeling that we would do well. Yeah, yeah... I do remember... I was so much happier back then."

I nodded and smiled, telling him I totally got it. Then I reached out my hand. He shook it, thanked me again for letting him use the bath-room, and we talked a little more about the Roxy and music in general (He even remembered my old band *Ku De Tah*). When the conversation ended and I watched him walk back down the hallway, I felt this strange emptiness. I wasn't exactly sure why—but maybe his emptiness had rubbed off on me.

Then again, maybe that emptiness was also about me—and about a ton of other musicians I knew. We'd all grown up thinking that if we could just grab stardom, some magical level of fame and success like his, then we'd finally hold the Holy Grail: permanent happiness, permanent feelings of love around us.

But the brutal truth hit me again while standing there—like Scott, I was past my prime too. And I hadn't even come anywhere close to what he'd accomplished. The irony was, looking at him, I realized it probably wouldn't have mattered if I had. *Happiness isn't guaranteed at the top.*

That was a hard fucking realization to swallow.

The night went on as planned. Weiland's set was decent but low-en-ergy, and the fashion show actually went smoothly. I did get him to sign the Roxy poster[3], but even that felt strange. Watching him sign his name, I had this gnawing feeling in my gut—like something bad was destined to happen to him.

Leaving the Roxy, 2008 (Photo: Erik Voake)

I brushed it off at the time, told myself I was overthinking. But part of me already *knew.* And as I stood there wondering if he'd ever find that spark again—the same spark I'd seen in him as a kid onstage at the Whisky—I had this sinking suspicion that he never would.

Sadly, that suspicion turned out to be true. Six years later, in 2015, Scott Weiland passed away from an accidental drug overdose on his tour bus before a next-day performance in Minnesota. He was only *forty-eight years old.*

---

3. **This poster** is currently hanging on my office wall in St. Petersburg, Florida. I had so many artists and actors sign it whenever they came through the Roxy. Artists like Prince, Sting, Lemmy, Chris Cornell, Chester Bennington, Glen Frey, Dolly Parton, Brian Wilson, Perry Farrell, Slash, Tom Morello and more.

Chapter 11

CHRIS CORNELL—The Modern Day Richard Cory

"It always seems like life doesn't have any rhyme or reason for why things happen the way they do."

Chris Cornell decided to play the Roxy, and it just happened to fall on my birthday *(May 2nd)*. A second night was added on *May 3rd.* It was 2010, and by then, I was already the GM. At this point, Cornell was a full-blown grunge and rock-and-roll living legend. He was going to perform solo with his acoustic, then bring in a small group of musicians on some other songs. Both nights sold out.

When I saw Cornell at soundcheck, he looked tired and drained. I'd seen that look before, many times, with tour-weary artists who came through the Roxy. I'd even felt it myself after more than a few grueling tours.

He still sounded good, although it felt a little forced. Since it was just a run-through, I didn't pay much attention to the lack of energy. I figured it was the result of years of playing the same songs on repeat, combined with the monotony of relentless city-to-city touring.

Still, it felt good hearing *Soundgarden*, *Audioslave*, and Cornell's solo stuff echoing through the Roxy. So much raw power. Great guitar playing on top of that. And, of course, the guy had the looks of a Greek god—the kind of presence that must've drawn women his way for most of his life.

As I stood there watching, I thought: *Man, this dude is blessed.* Tall, dark, handsome, carrying a mountain of talent that had brought him wealth and fame. *What more could any man want?* I'll admit, I felt a twinge of envy mixed with admiration. With those gifts, it was no wonder millions of dudes probably envied him.

But little did I know, behind all of that, was a troubled, sad, lonely man. A real-life *Richard Cory.*

Richard Cory is a legendary poem by Edwin Arlington Robinson written in 1897 about a man adored by everyone, envied for his wealth, his status, and his grace. From the outside, he had everything anyone could possibly want. And then, without warning, he ended it all. The ending still shakes me, and yeah, it still brings some slight moist to my eyes almost every time:

Whenever Richard Cory went downtown
We people on the pavement looked at him
He was a gentleman from sole to crown
Clean favored, and imperially slim

And he was always quietly arrayed
And he was always human when he talked
But still he fluttered pulses when he said
"Good-morning," and he glittered when he walked

And he was rich—yes, richer than a king
And admirably schooled in every grace
In fine, we thought that he was everything
To make us wish that we were in his place

So on we worked, and waited for the light
And went without the meat, and cursed the bread
And Richard Cory, one calm summer night
Went home and put a bullet through his head

As Cornell came off stage, I approached his tour manager and asked if they needed anything. I was stunned, but not shocked, when he said, *"Yes, actually, there is something you may be able to help us with."*
He asked if I could get them some *Xanax* or *Ativan.*

This wasn't the first time someone had asked me for some type of illegal or legal drugs[1]. So, without blinking, I told him to give me a minute, and I'd check with a few of my crew. I knew my part-time night manager, *Wood,* dabbled in prescription meds. When he showed up, I told him about the request, and he nodded like it was no big deal. He said he'd take care of it. I walked him backstage and introduced him to the tour manager.

---

1. **Illegal and legal drugs** were done by many who worked at the Roxy *(management included)* and almost everyone drank. The audience would always smoke weed or do cocaine in the VIP section or upstairs at On The Rox.

I figured maybe Cornell needed it before the show—or maybe afterward, to come down from the adrenaline and actually fall asleep. I didn't think much of it at the time. But later, when I told my sound guy what had happened, he told me he'd heard Cornell had been sober for years.

I assumed maybe *sober* meant only from hard drugs and alcohol, not prescriptions. I wasn't sure, not until many years later... when I heard the news about his passing[2].

As my office at this point was next to the main backstage room, I ended up using the hallway bathroom, which was also for anyone who was in the second backstage room (which didn't have a bathroom). The main backstage room had a bathroom, but it was old and crappy. The toilet and/or sink were always getting clogged. Sometimes, while our guys *Chivo* or *Jose* would be fixing it, the headliners would be temporarily banished to the hallway bathroom with the rest of the opening bands.

On the second night of Cornell's performance, I was in that hallway bathroom washing my hands when, out of nowhere, Cornell walked in. His head was down, but when he noticed me at the sink, he said,

"Oh man, sorry... the backstage bathroom is messed up."

I told him, *"No worries, man, this bathroom's all yours—I'm done. My name's JD, I'm the GM here at the Roxy. Man, I've been following Soundgarden since the* Louder Than Love *days back in '89. You guys were one hell of an awesome and influential band, to say the least."*

He looked at me for a moment, almost like he was replaying those decades in his head. We ended up talking a little about random things—life on the road, the grind of touring, small stuff that just comes up in a quick backstage chat. Then, after a pause, I asked him what it was like to be at the beginning of that scene he helped create—the one that shaped music, culture, and kids like me when I was just eighteen.

---

2. **I heard the news** that Cornell had hung himself in the bathroom inside his hotel room. This was after performing a show earlier. He had traces of Ativan in his system. He was only 52 years old.

He said, *"Oh... that year was tough, lots of turmoil, and we were just getting started. I, um, was still pretty angry 'cause my buddy died[3] , but, uh, it's sad when anyone dies before their time. I guess overall I felt like that was a great album... we didn't even know how big the scene would get, and maybe it wasn't necessarily a good thing looking back."*

I wasn't sure how to respond. It came out disjointed, almost dazed, and I didn't even know who he meant until I later looked it up. I finally said something like, *"I hear ya. Bands are like family—you can love 'em and hate 'em at the same time. I'm sorry about your buddy. It always seems like life doesn't have any rhyme or reason for why things happen the way they do."* I extended my hand.

"Pleasure to meet you."

He looked at me with those deep hazel-grey-blue eyes and said softly, *"Nice to meet you too,"* before walking away.

Cornell went on to deliver incredible performances both nights. Both shows sold out[4] , ran smooth as hell, and he nailed song after song. On the first night, he even covered The Beatles' *Ticket to Ride,* and on the second, John Lennon's *Mother.* Afterward, I grabbed both setlists off the stage[5] . Looking over them later, I realized the truth had been laid out right there in his lyrics all along—dark, exposed, painful as hell. *Fell on Black Days. Black Hole Sun. Like Suicide. Roads We Choose. Disappearing One.* The puzzle pieces finally snapped together.

---

3. **Andrew Wood** was the singer of Mother Love Bone and the former roommate of Cornell. He sadly died of a heroin overdose at the young age of 24.

4. **The first show on May 2nd** was extra special because a bunch of my friends and cousins came out. My cousins Jared, Greg Jr., and Big John always rolled through whenever they could. I even snuck some of them in through the side door by the bathrooms. My cousins never had to worry though—the bouncers always let them in because they were family. I made sure to keep those guys happy anyway, usually by hooking them up with whatever snacks and food the artists left behind in the backstage rooms. At the Roxy, having those big Latin and Black security guys on your side was everything—they were like their own mafia.

5. **Setlists** of both shows are in my possession. For the May 2nd show, he performed songs Like Suicide, Carry On, Like A Stone and Ticket To Ride by The Beatles. On May 3rd, he performed songs Black Hole Sun, Fell On Black Days, Doesn't Remind Me, Mother by John Lennon and other songs.

Years later, I could still hear his voice in that bathroom hallway. I couldn't stop wondering how someone like him—a man with everything any of us could possibly want—could still be drowning in so much pain.

When I turned on the TV in 2017 and saw the news that Cornell had hung himself after a show, it hit like a punch. Not shocking. Not surprising. But deeply sad. It felt like the same sting I'd felt back in '96 when I heard Bradley Nowell of Sublime had died [6] Both in May. Both right around my birthday.

Moments like that make you stop and question your own life. I couldn't shake the thought: *if guys like Cornell, with all their talent, success, and love from fans, still couldn't find peace, what chance did the rest of us have at that elusive, steady happiness we're all chasing?*

To this day, I'm still searching for that answer.

So on we worked, and waited for the light,
And went without the meat, and cursed the bread;
And Richard Cory, one calm summer night,
Went home and put a bullet through his head.

---

6. **Bradley Nowell** of Sublime was one of my favorites in the mid-1990s. I had him autograph my acoustic guitar at a Long Beach BBQ in 1995 (I kept it in my Roxy office for years). But sadly, the next year he died from a drug overdose. He was only 27. I remember seeing his beloved "Lou Dog" at a BBQ in 1999. I pet and played with Lou while wondering if he understood what had happened to his owner—and why he was gone. It was kind of an existential crisis for me. Again, I felt that deep sense of loss and sadness when I heard that Lou passed away in 2001. It was strange... because I felt like I lost a family member, even though I had only met him once.

Chapter 12

CHESTER FROM LINKIN PARK—The Boy with the Thorn in His Side

"And then, in a shocking instant, they both disappeared from this
sometimes cruel and painful world"

I remember the days when *Linkin Park* was just starting to take off. It was 1999, and I was signed to *Outpost/Geffen Records* with *Hot Sauce Johnson.* We toured around the country, but whenever I was off the road, I was back in Hollywood running street promotion for the Roxy and other clubs.

I knew guerrilla marketing inside and out from all the years hustling for my own bands. I could always create a buzz by heading out with my drummer, *Possum,* and a few of my street team guys to plaster flyers and stickers all over town. On top of that, I was designing magazine ads for the Roxy, Whisky, Viper Room, and others—even while on tour—because I was one of the few people in the Hollywood scene who knew the early version of *Photoshop.* My buddy and future bandmate, *Jesse Goodman,* the original bassist in *Rumblefish,* was the one who first showed me how to use it.

When *Hot Sauce Johnson* finally broke up, I threw myself full-time into promo work for different clubs. One night stuck with me: handing out flyers for an upcoming *Linkin Park* show at the Roxy. I'd actually designed the flyer myself.

Designed this poster for the Roxy show...

By then, I'd already gotten my hands on one of their demo tapes and knew these guys had serious songwriting chops. I wanted to see how they'd hold up live, and since I could walk into any Roxy show for free, I wasn't about to miss it.

The venue was already jammed when I got there. Wall-to-wall kids, most of them from Agoura Hills—my old hometown for a few years in the '90s—where *Linkin Park* had been the local band. That night's performance proved what I already felt in my gut: this band's mix of *nu-metal, new wave,* and *rap* was going to blow up and take over the airwaves fast. Like I said earlier, my inner compass—*"DeCostradamus"*—was almost never wrong.

By the time *Linkin Park* was catching fire, I was already deep into my new band, *Rumblefish.* Funny enough, we ended up sharing the same lawyer, *Danny Hayes.* Even *Brad Delson's* dad, *Linkin Park's* guitarist, was printing our *Rumblefish* t-shirts. Their debut album *Hybrid Theory* shot straight to the top of the charts while *Rumblefish* was chasing major label deals with a buzz of our own.

I remember one meeting at Columbia Records with Tim Devine. He told us flat out that all we needed to do was "write a hit like Linkin Park" and "get rid of our side rapper and DJ."

That turned out to be a shitty decision. We eventually parted ways with our rapper and DJ, Dom Poniac and DJ Byrd, and went in a more commercial direction. Basically, we tried to sell out. And it bit us right in the ass.

CONTACT: **MIKE MAGLIERI**
310.652.4202 EXT. 11

Looking back, we probably would've had a better shot if we'd stuck with our original sound, our

The original Rumblefish, 2000.

original lineup, and that raw, stripped-down Slipknot-type style. Chasing someone else's formula only pulled us further away from what made us worth listening to in the first place.

When Rumblefish signed with Roadrunner/Island Def Jam in 2001[1], we went into the studio to record our album with Mudrock, the producer for Godsmack. At first, we were managed by Mikey Maglieri Jr., the grandson of Mario Maglieri—owner of the Whisky a Go Go and the Rainbow Bar & Grill, and part of the same family I'd worked for back at the Whisky before I eventually switched over to the Adler family and the Roxy.

Eventually, we parted ways with Mikey "Mags" and his partner Adrian Vallera—probably another mistake in hindsight—and ended up with a heavyweight manager, Bill McGathy, who also managed Puddle of Mudd among a ton of other big acts.

By that time, Linkin Park had already skyrocketed into mega-star status with *Hybrid Theory.* It was nuts to watch these local boys I'd seen grind on the Sunset Strip suddenly explode into one of the biggest bands in the world.

Meanwhile, our band got tangled in the usual record company politics and ended up shelved. Even though we recorded the album with a star-studded team—Andy Wallace mixed it (yeah, the same guy who mixed Nirvana, among countless others)—the so-called "powers that be" decided to kill it. No release. Dead in the water. We broke up in 2003.

During some of my time with Rumblefish, I was also hustling at the Whisky a Go Go as a part-time booker and hospitality guy for M

---

1. **Unfortunately, when we signed with** Roadrunner/Island Def Jam in 2001, we let the label push us into leaning more toward a Nickelback/Shinedown commercial style. Bad move. It backfired hard. Roadrunner poured their energy into Nickelback and their "hardcore" acts, while we got sidelined like a red-headed stepchild.We broke up in 2003, but in 2009 something crazy happened—I got a fat royalty check from ASCAP showing that our song "In My Head" was being played nonstop on Swiss radio stations. I later found out that somehow the track had landed in the hands of a programmer in Switzerland—even though our debut record was never officially released—and it ended up in the Top 5 rotation there... six years after we'd already split up.

Productions, the company Mikey "Mags" had started.[2] On top of that, I occasionally stage-managed a few shows at the Roxy.

By 2002, I left the Whisky completely and transitioned over to the Roxy full-time as the hospitality and stage manager.

By 2004, Linkin Park was slated to play a show at the Roxy with Jay-Z. That was how massive they'd gotten. Everyone in the world knew the name *"Linkin Park."* It was unreal.

Fast forward a few years, and I was firmly planted at the Roxy. I'd see Chester and some of the other Linkin Park guys come through for shows every now and then. Sometimes Chester would end up at our private upstairs club, On The Rox—the exclusive spot perched on top of the Roxy. He knew me by name.

I remember one time when he told me he'd seen us play back when Rumblefish opened for a headliner at the Roxy years earlier. He said he was impressed with our energy and stage show, then asked me what had happened to us. I gave him the whole story—the early success, the hype, and then the collapse that wasn't even in our control.

---

2. **M Productions was owned by Mikael Maglieri Jr.**—this giant kid, about 6'9" tall, with an incredible ear and real entrepreneurial chops. No doubt he inherited that from his grandpa Mario, the legendary owner of the Whisky and the Rainbow. Whenever I was off tour, I handled hospitality for M Productions and eventually worked my way up to one of the production managers and booking agents. Me, Luke Iblings, and Mikey "Mags" were booking all the big hardcore shows at the Whisky. At one point, we were also bringing in all the hottest hip hop acts—including Eminem, before he was even a household name—until Grandpa Mario pulled the plug. I still remember him flat-out telling Mikey Jr. there was to be "no more of that fucking rap music shit" at the Whisky. That was it. We had to shut down what had been one of the most lucrative scenes and shift our full focus to hardcore and emo shows instead. M Productions is still around today. Mikey now runs both the Whisky and the Rainbow—sadly, because his awesome dad (Mikael Maglieri) and Grandpa Mario have both passed away.

I laughed it off, tried to spin it like a joke, but when I finished, he looked genuinely sad. Like he actually felt that failure deep in his heart.

He didn't know me that well, but I could see real empathy in his eyes—like he felt a bit guilty for all his insane success. Maybe it was guilt because he knew how many other bands had failed or fallen short of their dreams while his band had exploded into one of the biggest in the world. He looked me dead in the eye and said,

"I'm sorry to hear that, man. It's tough being in music… so much is out of your hands."

I just nodded and replied, *"Thank you, man. I'm just grateful that I've been able to be on a music journey and still pay the bills."*

A few years passed before I spoke with Chester again. I remember the exact date, because it was right after my birthday—May 8, 2008. Chester was a special guest for the star-studded Camp Freddy performance. They had the weekly residency with us at that point.

By then, I had been promoted to General Manager, and my temporary office was out in the main area. I had my own room, but it was surrounded by desks where the Roxy office crew sat—the same people who always seemed to argue with me about what was "right" and "wrong" for the club. Let's just say I wasn't fond of being that close to them. They meant well, but they had zero idea about production logistics or what it actually took to run live music. I rarely saw eye to eye with them. At least I could close my door and shut them out when I had to.

I ventured out of my office after Camp Freddy kicked off and did my usual round: hit the kitchen, the sound booth, the light booth, and finally slid into the VIP section where I'd sometimes stand and watch the show. Not long after, I got a text from the box office: Chester had arrived, and they asked if I could walk him in through the side door. I grabbed my security guy, "Big Mario," and had him escort Chester in and lead him upstairs to the backstage area.

I kicked back and enjoyed the Camp Freddy set for a few minutes, but then I decided to head backstage to make sure everything was running smooth and nothing was getting destroyed. Whenever Camp Freddy played, backstage was absolute insanity. Fifty-plus people crammed into the room, half of them hot girls (young and old), the other half made up of current, has-been, or never-was rock star dudes. The booze was flowing, drugs were everywhere, and yeah, plenty of people were screwing in the bathrooms. On this night, the bathrooms were both locked, and I could tell from the noises and the groups of people waiting outside that some wild shit was definitely going down in there.

I spotted Chester waiting by the hallway bathroom door, looking irritated, so I pushed my way through the mob and walked up to him. I told him he could come use the main office bathroom instead.

He said, *"Oh man, thanks… people have been in the bathroom forever, and I gotta go."*

I cracked a joke: *"They're probably in there struggling to cut white lines on the bathroom counters, so yeah, they won't be out anytime soon. Here, follow me."*

I walked him down the hall into the office and pointed him to the bathroom. He went in, did his business, and when he came back out, I said, *"Chester, we've got your platinum album for Hybrid Theory hanging on my office wall. Do you think you can sign it?"*

He said, *"Oh wow, sure, no problem."* I handed him a marker, and he leaned over to write something. I couldn't see what he was writing, but it was more than just a quick scrawl of his name.

While he was finishing up, I said, *"Do you remember way back when you first played the Roxy, right before Hybrid came out and then you guys blew up and became huge? Isn't it fuckin' amazing how things sometimes work out for the best—like, here you are now, years later, signing your own multi-platinum album in the Roxy office and playing stadiums."*

He smiled, but there was this heaviness behind it, and he said something along the lines of, *"Yeah, we got so damn big. I always wanted to be a rock star, man, but shit, I'm still constantly trying to prove myself… I just try to numb myself to the pain, man."*

Then he gave this nervous laugh and added, *"I'm not sure why I'm telling you this, but ok. All good."*

With that, he forced out an awkward smile, thanked me again, and headed back out into the whirlwind of the backstage hallway.

Later, as he was getting ready to perform, I called out his name and snapped a quick photo of him before he walked down the stairs toward the stage. He looked right at me as I took it. When I saw that photo later, it damn near broke me—the sadness in his eyes told the whole story. The truth of rock stardom. The good, the bad, and the unbearable weight in between.

I went back into my office and finally looked at what he had written on the platinum album. It said:

"All love and thanks for letting me use the bathroom… Chester."

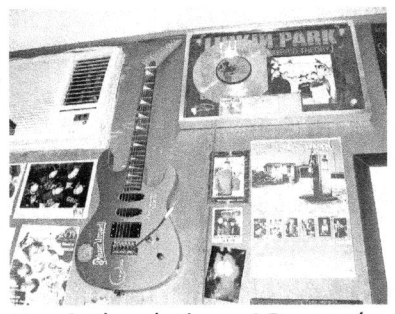

Here's the platinum LP record that hung in my office.

Sadly, Chester took his own life in 2017 at his home in Palos Verdes. He hanged himself just two months after Chris Cornell had done the same, and on July 17th—Cornell's birthday. They were close friends, bound not just by music but by a shared darkness.

To this day, I can't shake the question: *why didn't anyone—friends, family, somebody—step in and get him committed, or force the kind of help that might have saved him?*

Writing this part about Chester reminds me of the last photo of Robin Williams before he died. He had a tiny monkey perched on his shoulder, smiling[3], but you could still see the deep pain etched into the lines of his face. *He needed serious help, just like Chester did.* But somehow it never came. And then, in a shocking instant, both of them slipped out of this world—victims of its sometimes odd cruelty, and of the silence around their suffering.

Damn, man. Damn.

---

3. **I'll never forget the photo of Robin Williams** with that monkey on his shoulder, grinning and happy. Turns out it wasn't his monkey—it was Crystal the Monkey, the capuchin from Night at the Museum. Robin posted it on his 63rd birthday in July 2014, not long before he took his own life. That picture hit me hard. The monkey's smiling, Robin has a strained smile, but behind the eyes… you can see the weight. Same thing I noticed with Chester. Sometimes the magical ones are carrying the heaviest shit, and no one even knows until it's too late.

Even Legends Must Let Go...

"One day he told me, dead serious: I'm made of steel. I'll never die."

Having those experiences with artists like Weiland, and others who seemed destined for tragedy, always got me thinking about the people who never even reached any level of fame or satisfaction on the road we were all traveling. *Fame didn't save the big names, and it sure as hell didn't protect the ones who never made it past the underground.*

One of the hardest gut punches, of course, was losing my singer Sun Sannes, who jumped from a ten-story building in downtown LA, which I already talked about earlier. But he wasn't the only one. There were so many more along the way, each loss hitting me in its own fucked-up way, carving out scars that never really heal.

Throughout this book, I've mentioned my Roxy lighting guy, Bolle Gregmar. He'd been there long before I ever stepped foot inside the club. Over the years, he became my closest friend at the Roxy. I'd often retreat up to his bird's nest lighting booth above the soundboard to swap stories, vent, or just hang with someone who actually *got it.*

Bolle and I clicked because we were essentially cut from the same cloth. Both musicians, both still chasing the dream, even while grinding behind the scenes just to keep the lights on.

A young Bolle Gregmar with Ozzy and Eric Bloom of Blue Oyster Cult, 1975.

He was originally a badass drummer from Sweden who had been deep in the music world since the '70s. He had photos of himself as a teenage rock-and-roll Viking hanging backstage with *Freddie Mercury, David Bowie, Marc Bolan*—you name it. He even toured with *Blue Öyster Cult* as their lighting guy and eventually became an almost world-renowned historian and collector of BOC memorabilia. His Hollywood apartment basically doubled as a museum. *BOC* superfans from all over the world came just to see it.

But as fate would have it, Bolle ended up at the Roxy.

He was an artistically driven, well-educated lighting guy who took immense pride in his work at the club. At the same time, he never gave up playing music. Even into his fifties, he still believed his band might be the ticket out of the club-life grind and onto bigger stages.

Then the worst happened.

Bolle was struck with a brutal medical condition that left him paralyzed and unable to speak. He was taken to a hospital in Hollywood, and he's never left. Bedridden and still unable to communicate, a few of his close friends and family hold vigil and visit him when they can, holding out hope he might recover someday.

The part that burns me up the most is that Bolle wasn't a partier. He never touched drugs. I never even saw him drink, except for maybe a glass of wine here and there. *Nature just dealt him a cruel hand, the kind of fucked-up twist I've seen happen to too many people.* I still don't fully understand it.

And I still don't know who to be mad at. *Fate? God? The music business? Genetics? Just the sheer randomness of life?* It still messes with my head that Bolle's story took this turn and is basically over. *Maybe his redemption will come through the people who loved him and carry his memory forward.* That's what I hope, anyway.

And that makes me think about *Grandpa Mario Maglieri*, "Grumpy," one of the original legendary owners of the *Whisky* and the *Rainbow*. I worked for his grandson, *Mikey Jr. "Mags,"* at the Whisky before I made the jump to the Roxy. Grandpa Mario would swing by the office puffing on a cigar, checking the week's numbers. I'd yell out, "Hey, it's the legend himself!" and he'd grin like he owned the whole damn Strip.

One day he told me, dead serious: *"I'm made of steel. I'll never die."*

And I almost believed him. Even after he got cancer, I heard he had security cameras rigged up at the Rainbow so he could monitor things from his bed, making sure no one was ripping him off while he was laid up fighting for his life. *He really didn't think he was going to die,* just like he had told me years before. He stayed sharp, even as his body broke down and fate finally came calling.

Mario passed at 93, but he stayed the *defiant King of the Sunset Strip* till the very end. I figure by that point he finally realized he had to just let go.

Not long after Grandpa Mario, I got word that his son, *Mikael Maglieri Sr.*, had passed away from a sudden heart attack at just 73. Of everyone I knew on the Strip, nobody treated me better. I loved popping into the *Rainbow* just to hang with him. He was always laughing, drinking, and often posted up at the end of the bar chatting with *Lemmy from Motörhead.*

Back in the day, I used to see him at outrageous Hollywood house parties. But when the party moved to his small mansion up on Mulholland and Laurel Canyon, he became the full-blown *prince of Sunset debauchery.* Booze, weed, music blaring, everyone crammed in till sunrise. *He was like the Hugh Hefner of the music scene.* His death hit me harder than I expected. It was painful to hear how his journey on earth had ended. *I really thought he might live forever too.*

I also had a short but special moment with *Ozzy* at the Roxy when he and *Sharon* came to a *Camp Freddy* show because Ozzy was going to perform a few songs. I ended up escorting Ozzy and Sharon up to the backstage rooms, and when Sharon went ahead toward the room, I asked Ozzy if he could autograph the backstage sign I had made for him.

He said, *"For sure,"* and then proceeded to write: *"Fuck Everyone"* before signing his name.

When I saw what he wrote, I laughed and said, *"Ozzy, you're a living legend with an amazing sense of humor, man. You're never gonna die!"*

He looked at me and said, in his signature accent, *"Well, even if I do, I'll die a happy man."*

Then he yelled out for Sharon to come sign the paper, and she walked out and signed: *"Kisses, Sharon Osbourne"* with the date. When she saw what he wrote, she shook her head and said, *"Oh, Ozzy."*

We all laughed, and then went our separate ways.

It made an impact on me because when I was a young kid first learning guitar, *Crazy Train* was one of the songs I wanted to learn most. I had grown up listening to *Ozzy* and *Black Sabbath,* and he was a staple in life for so many decades. When the end finally came for him, I realized that even the most special people—the ones who change the world—still succumb to death in the end, and it was just a slow ticking of time till it happened.

Sometimes, I just couldn't stop thinking about how many people had been lost over the years. A few close friends from the Roxy staff had passed, too, including *Wood Fowler,* a part-time manager and a good friend. Wood had been around forever, originally working for *Sean Healy Productions* before the Roxy, and he was always chasing his own music dreams on the side. He was the guy in my *Cornell* story who could always "score" for the artists. *Wood died quietly in his sleep at just thirty-six years old from a lethal mix of alcohol and pills.*

I started counting. Band members I'd played with who died. Friends. Staff. At least a dozen. The music scene had chewed up a shocking number of people I cared about.

I could count on two hands the number of bandmates I'd lost to drugs, alcohol, or suicide. It was staggering. Half the people I'd once shared a stage with were just gone.

Dom Poniac Quant, the rapper for my band *Rumblefish,* was the only one whose death wasn't tied to addiction or bad health. He was this big-hearted, Samoan-looking bear of a guy, a true gentle giant. *He was shot and killed in cold blood after an argument with a neighbor spiraled out of control.* I still can't fucking believe it.

All of these people—bandmates, friends, mentors—some of them were definitely casualties of *Hollywood* and *Sunset.* I dedicated this book to them.

I know someday when my own time comes, I'll be thinking about this one particular quote. It's actually from the movie *Benjamin Button,* and somehow, it gives me a strange sense of peace:

Rumblefish with Dom Poniac with black shirt and our logo...

"You can be as mad as a mad dog at the way things went. You could swear, curse the fates... but when it comes to the end, you have to let go."

But not everyone got swallowed by tragedy. Some not only survived but thrived. Some couldn't be stopped. It was only a matter of time before millions knew their names. Were they always the humblest or best human beings to survive? Not always. But humility and kindness were never the requirements on the road to fame.

And speaking of arrogance and entitlement, one night at the Roxy truly stands out.

Let's leave the darkness behind and get on to that next chapter.

Chapter 13

ADAM LEVINE—Your Dressing Room Is Ready!

"I don't want more drinks—I want a dressing room. Damnit!"

This night blew up into a soon-to-be-legendary shitshow when *Michelle Branch* came to the *Roxy* in 2003, with *Maroon 5* as the opening band.

I knew Michelle. She'd played the Roxy plenty of times and always brought in a chill, good-vibes crowd that spent a ton of money at our overpriced bar—which always made management and the waitresses happy as hell. Her singer-songwriter vibe, paired with a cool attitude and that killer smile, made her one of the few artists we actually looked forward to having onstage. In this business, that was rare.

The office had been buzzing about the opening band. *Maroon 5* was floating around town for a while, and I remembered them from their *Kara's Flowers* days, playing a few small Roxy shows without much fanfare. Their debut album *Songs About Jane* had already dropped, but it wouldn't blow up until the following year. So in early 2003, they were still just another opener with some buzz. Since they were opening for Michelle, they'd get the standard support-band treatment, which also meant a short soundcheck.

Michelle rolled in for her soundcheck, and her tour manager pulled me aside with a request. She wanted both upstairs backstage rooms—the main one for her and the private bathroom, and the smaller one for her band and crew. I didn't know her booking agent had already called it in earlier in the week. Classic live music miscommunication. Upstairs Roxy management was always scrambling to wrangle chaos, so it never hit my radar. But the ask wasn't unusual. Plenty of bigger acts—*Red Hot Chili Peppers*, *Rage Against the Machine*, whoever—made the same request.

Both backstage rooms were small. The main room could hold maybe twelve people, while the smaller one fit around eight. Because of how inadequate the rooms were, it was always funny (and kinda insane) to see twenty-five to thirty-five people crammed into the main room, all standing shoulder to shoulder like a human sardine can. Sometimes it was so packed that the hallway leading to the rooms was clogged too. Imagine the entire upstairs bursting at the seams with people—and then the artist, who had invited all these folks plus their guests on the VIP list, standing there in the middle of it all, visibly uncomfortable and barely able to breathe.

So yeah—given that circus, it wasn't unreasonable for a headliner to request both rooms. It wasn't always about some infamous *"big ego"*—most of the time it was just about basic privacy and sanity. It was purely logistics, especially considering the Roxy was originally an old supermarket, of all things.

With all that in mind, I figured I'd let *Maroon 5* know we'd be putting them in the VIP section with their own table, plus drink and food tickets—just like we'd done for plenty of other openers in the same situation. No opening band had ever complained about this policy... but little did I know, it was about to turn into a thing. *LOL.*

After Michelle finished her soundcheck, she headed upstairs to her backstage room, her band trailing behind. As they got settled, I realized *Maroon 5* still hadn't shown up—it was well past their 5 p.m. soundcheck, and doors were supposed to open at 7. Finally, around 5:30, they rolled in and started loading through the big roll-up door on the side of the Roxy that led straight to the stage.

The band seemed relaxed as they greeted my sound guys, while my lighting guy Bolle helped them haul their gear. (The Roxy paid peanuts to the crew—including me—so I'd always hook Bolle up with the extra load-in work so he could make a little cash on top of his tiny paycheck.)

Once they were all loaded in, their thin-looking singer strolled in last. I remembered him from past shows at the Roxy and immediately clocked that same cocky strut—the kind that screamed he already thought he was a star. At that point, he looked like a clean-cut kid—not yet the tattooed, *"polite"* guy the public would later see once he became a household name.

After they wrapped soundcheck, I remember thinking, *Damn, this dude is super talented. Someday, he's going to be on the big stages.*

And I wasn't wrong.

Not long after this gig, *Dave Matthews* took them under his wing and had them open on his tour, blasting them straight into the fame-and-fortune stratosphere.

But at that moment, they were still just another opener supporting a headliner. What I didn't realize was they already thought they were world-famous.

Correction: Levine thought he and the band were already famous headliners.

After soundcheck, Levine disappeared. I hung with the rest of the band, handed them their wristbands, drink and food tickets, and explained the deal about Michelle needing both backstage rooms. I told them we had a VIP table set up for them. I assumed their booking agent had already clued in their manager, but I guess not. And clearly, the band didn't bother filling in Levine.

The rest of the guys seemed fine with the VIP table, nodding and thanking me for the wristbands and everything else.

We opened the doors right at 7 p.m., and a few people were already lined up, but it was far from a packed house. I checked in with our box office girl to make sure things were smooth, then headed upstairs backstage to where my production office was.

As I walked up the backstage stairs that led to the hallway (with the dressing rooms down the hall next to my office), I spotted Levine and a few others standing around, visibly annoyed.

As I got closer, Levine looked up and barked, *"Are you with the Roxy?"*

I said, *"Yes sir... what's going on? I'm JD."*

He fired back, pissed off: *"We don't have a damn dressing room... what the hell is up with that?"*

I explained that his manager or booking agent should've filled him in—that *Michelle Branch* had both dressing rooms, and it had all probably been worked out when the gig was booked.

He blurted, totally frustrated, *"Why the hell can't we have a backstage room!!"*

Then he looked down at the floor and muttered that he'd never played a gig without one, and that he wouldn't have done the show if he'd known he wasn't going to have a room.

I kept calm, smiled, and told him there wasn't much I could do about the dressing rooms. But I could give him extra drink tickets and let him use the DJ balcony, which was a narrow little spot backstage that overlooked the crowd and part of the main stage. Or, he could hang at the VIP table I'd already set up for the band. And lastly, if none of that worked, well, he could stand right there in the hallway where he was.

He looked up, shaking his head and muttering how it was total bull-shit they didn't even have a dressing room—and then came the kicker: *"The Roxy sucks."*

I let him vent while I reached into my pocket for extra drink tickets. But before I could hand them over, he snapped: *"I don't want more drinks—I want a dressing room. Damnit!"*

I couldn't help but laugh a little as he stared at me. I had never dealt with a support band that didn't understand we only had two small backstage rooms, and that who got them wasn't up to me once the deal was locked in. I found out later that it had all been worked out in advance, but no one had told the band—or Levine—which was entirely their team's fault. Not mine. Not the Roxy's. And definitely not *Michelle Branch's.*

Most bands, when told they didn't have a backstage room, were more than happy to take the extra drink tickets and a VIP table. They were cool and appreciative. (Hell, more than a few times, the opening bands didn't even get a table—they just got a couple drink tickets, some water, and had to hang out in the hallway or in the crowd.)

But let's just say... *Adam carried himself like someone who was used to getting his way.* And even though they weren't headlining yet, I guess he already believed they were famous—even if no one else had quite caught up to that idea yet.

Don't get me wrong—he was right about where they were headed. But in this moment, he was still just a local support act with a great album starting to pick up steam—not yet the massive big-dog success they were about to become.

I looked at him one more time, right into his upset, glassy eyes, and said, *"Dude, again, sorry... but unless you go talk to Michelle Branch and ask her for the second dressing room yourself, there's nothing I can do. You're welcome to stand here and drink, head up to the DJ balcony, or enjoy some nice drinks in the VIP area. It is what it is."*

As he walked away, he threw up his hands and shouted, *"Screw this place!"* Then stormed down the stairs, visibly pissed off and making a scene.

I ended up handing the drink tickets to the two people who fol-lowed him. They looked at me like, *Sorry about that—he's in a mood, but hey, we'll gladly take those drinks on his behalf.* And considering how mega-overpriced the Roxy's booze was, those tickets were like gold. I think his buddies realized that.

Maroon 5 finished their set to solid applause and loud claps from the crowd. They even came back out for an encore. I still remember some of the songs they played that night—great melodies and beats. I knew a few of those tracks would eventually land on Top 10 radio. Sure enough, about a year later, their songs were everywhere. They won a Grammy and went on to sell millions of records worldwide. *Songs About Jane* became an international smash.

I knew that night—opening for *Michelle Branch*—would be the last time they'd play the Roxy. They were about to get way too big for a room that size. Little did I—or the Roxy—know that almost a decade later, Levine would still be holding a grudge over that night.

I had already left the Roxy after 2011 because I was completely burned out from working in music—the vampire hours, the party atmosphere, and all the dark energy that eventually starts to take over your soul. I had moved on to the sports world, accepting a position as VP of a non-profit called *ACEing Autism,* which brought the sport of tennis to children on the spectrum. I still worked the SSMF (*Sunset Strip Music Festival*) once a year as the director of the backstage areas, and I gathered a few great stories from those experiences—but I was finally done with the Roxy.

I remember being at my condo in Sherman Oaks when I got a text from a tennis friend—someone who used to visit me back when I was at the Roxy. I glanced at my phone and saw: *"J, did you see what Adam Levine said about The Roxy on The Voice?"* And then, right after that, another one popped up: *"Dude, Adam Levine just obliterated The Roxy."*

A few more texts followed from old friends and random acquaintances. Some of them didn't even know I had left the Roxy the year before. (Keep in mind, it was now 2012—and I'd left in 2011.) Still, I knew what it had to be. I had a gut feeling that he was trashing the Roxy over that old backstage situation from a decade ago. But I couldn't help but wonder—why bring it up now, and what exactly did he say?

I shot back a few texts, and some friends replied that Levine had said he hated The Roxy because he couldn't even get a backstage room.

I straight-up started laughing out loud. I quickly texted back, *"I'm the one who broke that news to him! Michelle Branch had both dressing rooms that night!"*

Now I really wanted to see exactly what he said on *The Voice,* which at that time was one of the most-watched shows on television. After I finished dinner, I jumped on my computer—and boom—the clip was already online.

I cracked the biggest smile when I saw the banter between him and a girl who had just performed at The Roxy.

It went something like this: A *Voice* contestant named *Cassadee Pope* had just finished playing a cover of *Michelle Branch's "Are You Happy Now?"* When, right after the performance, Levine said verbatim:

"We used to open for Michelle Branch. I remember we opened for her at the Roxy, and they didn't even give us a dressing room. I hate the Roxy. I'll never play there again!"

After Levine blurted that out, Cassadee mentioned that she had a positive experience performing at the venue. Levine then doubled down, sneering:

"Oh, the Roxy is horrible. Don't ever go there. They screwed us over, and now they're paying for it."

I had a great laugh as I was reading this on Google, and it gave me a little bit of satisfaction to think that I had directly caused Adam Levine to not completely get his way—in a world where I'm sure he got his way most of the time. *How I wish I had secretly recorded that encounter with him backstage... I totally would have posted it on YouTube. It would've been massive.*

The very next day, after Levine trashed the Roxy on *The Voice*—and I'm guessing it was *Nic Adler* (the owner *Lou Adler's* oldest son) behind it—the giant Roxy marquee lit up, in big bold letters for everyone to see:

ADAM LEVINE, YOUR DRESSING ROOM IS READY!

Damn, I thought, wishing I was still at the Roxy to help put up those letters on the marquee. But I still felt a wave of satisfaction watching it get picked up by news outlets and music blogs. Levine definitely heard about it, though of course, he never commented.

I ended up sending Nic Adler a Facebook message that said:

"Hey Nic, if Adam Levine and Maroon 5 ever end up playing the Roxy again, I'll definitely come be the production manager for free… We can prank him and tell him the dressing rooms are under construction when he gets to the venue… LOL."

Nic sent back a big yellow smiley emoji. We both had a good laugh.

✦ AI Overview

Maroon 5's connection to The Roxy involves a negative experience in their early career, where Adam Levine stated the band didn't receive a dressing room when opening for Michelle Branch, leading him to criticize the club years later on The Voice. The club responded to Levine's comments with a sign on their marquee and defended their practices, with the owner explaining that headliners control dressing room assignments. While Maroon 5 has not recently played at The Roxy, the band's early days performing at the venue are a point of discussion due to this event.

Lessons Learned:

Looking back, this experience taught me a valuable lesson about *perception, entitlement,* and how miscommunication can snowball into lasting resentment. *Adam Levine's* frustration wasn't entirely unwarranted—he had expectations that weren't met—but the real issue was a breakdown in communication within his own team and with the *Roxy* staff. Everyone was always scrambling in this erratic, sometimes out-of-control world. (In the Roxy's defense, they booked over 330 shows a year, with so many intangibles and loose logistics that could fall apart on a dime.)

It cemented my belief that in the fast-paced world of live music and event production, things will almost never go as planned. It also reinforced the idea that *ego can shape how people remember events*—sometimes distorting reality to fit their own personal narrative. Levine saw the Roxy as the bad guy, but the truth is, the mix-up wasn't the venue's fault.

I walked away with a deeper understanding of how different people handle setbacks. And I learned that no matter how successful someone becomes, their reaction to small inconveniences can reveal a lot about their character. At the Roxy, all those peculiar characters—rock stars, divas, legends, and wannabes—always seemed to wear their colors on their sleeves. And *Adam Levine?* Well, he wore his loud and clear.

Drunk or High... Maybe Insecure

Adam Levine definitely seemed like a born diva—a superstar who already knew exactly where he was headed. The rest of us at that point—myself included—were just trying to catch up to what he already believed.

From meeting countless artists and seeing them unfiltered backstage, I realized more than a few were the opposite of humble or friendly. Some were flat-out arrogant. Others just plain weird. A few wanted nothing more than to escape the frenzy and the adoring fans as quickly as possible.

It always reminded me of that line from *Almost Famous:*

"They make you feel cool. And hey, I met you. You are not cool."

That summed up a ton of the artists I crossed paths with. The public sometimes saw gods. We saw flawed people like everyone else—drunk, high, insecure, raging, or broken.

Hemingway once wrote,

"There is nothing noble in being superior to your fellow man; true nobility is being superior to your former self."

Most of the artists I dealt with didn't live by that code. Their nobility was measured in dressing rooms, record sales, audience numbers, and whose name was lit up on the marquee.

And yet, sometimes the arrogance wasn't really ego at all. Sometimes it was *defense.* Fame warps people. It twists them into what they swore they'd never become... or maybe just strips them down to who they really were all along. Which brings me to *Adele.*

Chapter 14

ADELE—Tale of the Shit-Show Monitors

"I can't bloody hear myself, and until I do, I am not performing!"

Everyone always seemed to ask me which artists were cool and down-to-earth and which ones were a total pain in the ass and hard to please. People were often surprised by my answers, and to this day, I'd put the *Adele* show near the top five of diva-type craziness and chaos.

Over the years, I somehow found a way to deal with narcissistic, arrogant, type-A personalities that sometimes passed through the Roxy. It was definitely an art form I developed over time. Sometimes I'd find a way to soothe their egos and shift their attitude, but other times, there was nothing we could do to calm their craziness—at which point, I'd have to set them straight and drop the hammer, letting them know exactly what the Roxy could and couldn't do. In some instances, I actually enjoyed dropping the hammer and bringing them back down to earth while telling them *no*—there are quite a few stories in this memoir where I did just that.

Adele hadn't reached superstardom yet at the beginning of 2008, but there was a ton of buzz around her as an artist. She decided to do an *"An Evening with Adele"* tour, marking her debut in North America. This was promoted by *Live Nation*, one of the largest event promoters in the world (in 2010, *Live Nation* merged with *Ticketmaster*).

Everyone was hyped for the show, and since I'd heard a few of her songs playing in the booking office, I was pretty amped to see her perform live. Her voice on the tracks was incredible, and I wanted to see if she could pull it off in person.

The day of the show, *Adele* had her own sound guy, but we supplied the monitor guy, stage manager, and the loading crew. I had tried to get one of my trusted guys—Brandon "Bizzy B," Nacho Libre, or Wild Eyed Lee—to handle the monitors, but Nic Adler decided to bring in a Scottish, hard-partying swashbuckler of a soundman named *Frankie Fingers* to handle the show, much to my chagrin.

I had often fought Nic tooth and nail about hiring Frankie because, while he was amazing at sound and got the Roxy to sound absolutely killer (as I understood it at the time, he had been let go from the Viper Room, though no one ever complained about his sound skills), everything else he did always seemed to jeopardize Roxy shows. He'd always show up late, sometimes be high as a kite, disappear between sets, and generally create a ruckus by talking to the bands onstage while we were trying to keep things on time.

All the bands knew him and mostly liked him—I definitely liked him as a dude with massive problems—but suffice it to say, he always brought chaos whenever he worked. I knew we might be in big trouble with *Frankie* on monitors, especially since this particular show needed to be tight and on point—not a late-running shitshow like we sometimes had when Frankie was at the helm.

In fact, I received an anonymous poem about Frankie that I never figured out who wrote. We had several sound and monitor guys, loaders, lighting staff, promoters, and photographers who all dealt with Frankie. I had my suspicions, and even though it was rude, crude, and definitely not politically correct, I ended up keeping it in my office and sharing it with people who could relate and not be offended. Even Frankie got a good laugh out of it—but there were definitely more than a few people, especially in the main office, who would've been highly offended by it. (Looking back now, I guess I wouldn't blame them.)

The person who wrote it might've even been fired, so I never let on who I thought it was. But I had to stay tough, because eventually, Nic Adler got wind of it and demanded to know who wrote it. I told him I had no idea and stuck to that story until I was blue in the face. For clarity: we all treated it as an inside, satirical roast—not a statement of literal fact.

Here's the poem in its full glory:

> Lil Frankie Fingerz,
> he can't keep his money straight,
> spendin' it on cocaine,
> hookers & weed...
> chocolate cake.
>
> His pants and shirts are dirty,
> he smokes and drinks the cheapest wine.
> They say he smells like an old Persian carpet,

picked it up at the five and dime.

No one will let him borrow money,
'cause his finances are such a mess.
Just yesterday at the Roxy
he told me his car
couldn't pass the smog test.

His computer was stolen,
he dropped his cell in a puddle.
He ripped his cheap velour pants,
we call him "boy in a bubble."

So this is the story
of poor lil' Frankie,
who told his tall tales—
no one could reach such heights.

That's why early this afternoon
Lee, Brandon & Nacho say:
"Please tell me, Jay…
Frankie ain't workin' tonight."

So, with that, you can see why Nic was pretty pissed when he saw the poem. Could've been a lawsuit or liability. It was straight-up bullying gone wild, but it captured the backstage perception at the time. I told Nic it was obviously a joke—definitely offensive, but a definite roast of the legend people told about Frankie, not a factual dossier on his life.

So, I took a deep breath and made sure to stay on Frankie's ass the whole night. If he ended up fucking up, I for sure would be in trouble, even though I was the one who didn't want him on the show. I told *Frankie*, "Dude, you can't go outside and disappear for smoke breaks right before the show starts—and not until *Adele* walks off stage."

He agreed and then said something like, *"I hear ya, mate, don't worry, I got it all under control."*

I said, "Sure you do," then raised my eyebrows and made the two fingers to my eyes, then pointed them right at him, basically saying,

"I got my eyes on you."

Adele's crew arrived, and they started loading in all the equipment. My guys got them all up on stage, and we were ready to start sound-checking. Their sound guy got the band dialed in, and Frankie was work-ing on the monitors, seeming to get everything sorted.

When we thought everything was good to go, Adele's tour manager went backstage, where Adele was doing vocal exercises, and told her we were ready for her to soundcheck.

As she entered from the backstage area, to my eye she didn't have the label gloss yet and was heavier than the pop-star mold of that era. I figured she hadn't quite gotten the makeover that potential stars get from the labels when they're presented to the masses. But then, I also thought that at this point in 2008, when everything was all about the well-polished gloss given to major-label female singers like *Beyoncé*, *Rihanna*, *Katy Perry*, *Shakira*, and others... they all looked thin and in shape and could sing and dance.

I began to think maybe Adele was going to be a whole different approach to what a woman music star could be—like, maybe the exact opposite of what was popular at the time: a plain-looking, mumu-wear-ing, full-figured English girl with an amazing, soulful voice and more serious, authentic songs and approach.

I realized that maybe this was a genius move—going the exact op-posite of what was pervading the mainstream at the time.

As she began singing the first song, she stopped halfway through and said, in a thick English accent,

"I can't hear my voice clearly in the monitors."

With that, she started the song again, but about a third of the way through, she stopped again and said more forcefully, *"I can't really hear myself. Can we get our act together on the monitors?"*

At this point, I walked up to her sound guy and asked, "Why isn't she using in-ear monitors?"

He looked at me and said, "She didn't want 'em," then scrunched his shoulders up as if to say, "Nothing I can do!"

I looked back at the stage and saw Frankie coming out, switching up the monitor cables. They probably needed to be switched out, but they definitely should've been tested before Adele got to the venue. But in true Frankie fashion, he showed up late, and they were never checked.

He switched them out and then yelled out in his Irish accent, *"Let's give it another go!"*

Adele looked at Frankie with a weird glare that seemed like she didn't like him even though she didn't know him, and then she started the song again and immediately stopped, blurting out, *"This is bloody ridiculous. Can we get the monitors so I can hear them?"*

I climbed up on the stage, and Frankie met me there. I said, *"Frankie, what the hell is going on? Turn the friggin' monitors up so she can hear herself!"*

Frankie then says, *"Look, mate, I have them cranked up, and if I go any higher, there will be feedback. It's our monitors—they're old and crappy."*

I told him to go back in, and then I stood by Adele, ready to hear what she wasn't hearing and see for myself what was going on.

As her band kicked into "Chasing Pavements" again, I stood next to her, and so far, so good with the monitors. She started to sing, and I could hear her voice pretty well through the monitors, but then she stopped again and said,

"Can you bloody hear me? I sure can't, and it's making it impossible to sing."

I told her that her band was pretty loud and that she needed to remember our monitors were pretty crappy in general and probably not used to the higher quality she was used to. She then looked me dead in the eyes and said,

"I don't give a shite about how old they are, just fix them or rent other ones."

I checked my phone, and we were about twenty minutes from doors opening. I told her that there was no way we could rent monitors at this point because the rental place was closed, and it would have needed to be arranged ahead of time—at least a day before or the early afternoon of the event.

She then proceeded to say, *"We aren't opening doors until I can hear myself."*

I said, "Okay, hold on a second. I'm gonna try and get this solved."

I went over to Frankie and said,

"Dude, you're killing us. What the fuck is going on? This never usually happens. What can we do to fix it?"

Frankie blurts out, "As I recall, she's a fuckin' diva, and there's nothing wrong with the monitors. I switched out the cables, the mics, and the board is fine."

Frankie tried several other things, but nothing was working. I had to run up and tell the office that we were having severe sound issues and that Adele wouldn't let the doors open until she was happy with the monitors.

I got a call from Nic asking what was going on. I explained that Frankie might be screwing up, but at the same time, it could be that Adele wasn't used to smaller monitors like we had, and that she didn't have an in-ear system, which would've solved everything.

Nic told me to figure it out, make it work, and get doors open as soon as possible.

At this point, we were almost an hour late for doors. I then told Frankie to stand with me next to Adele and listen again to confirm the monitors were loud enough and that she should be able to hear herself. I asked Adele nicely to start the song from the middle, and she told the band.

They counted off—*one, two, three, four*—and kicked into the song.

Adele started singing, and Frankie and I looked at each other—the monitors actually sounded decent. Not amazing, but her vocals were definitely audible, although the band was still loud and they hadn't turned down at all.

We were both shaking our heads because we weren't sure what she was talking about, saying she couldn't hear herself.

Then she stopped the song again and said, *"Fuck! This isn't going to work. I can't bloody hear myself, and until I do, I am not performing!"*

I thought, Oh shit, we're in trouble now...

I could already imagine the powers that be over at *Live Nation* calling up the Roxy in the morning, ripping them a new one, and then Nic calling me into the office for my verbal beating that would last for weeks.

I told *Frankie* to keep working on the monitors and maybe try taking some of the band's monitors and putting them in front of her, or come up with some off-the-wall solution to make her happy. Meanwhile, I started calling other clubs to see if we could borrow any extra monitors.

Another forty minutes passed as I was frantically calling the Key Club, Whisky, and Viper Room, seeing if they had any extra monitors we could quickly grab—and unfortunately, none were available.

I came back, and Frankie was still working on the monitors, while Adele's sound guy and others were on stage trying to figure out what Adele wanted and needed.

We were now ninety minutes late to opening doors, and our box office crew, waitresses, and kitchen staff were all wandering around asking me what the hell was going on.

I tried to explain, but all I could tell them was that Adele had a specific way she needed the monitors to sound. The problem was, she wasn't really giving us clear direction—just that she couldn't hear herself and wouldn't let us open the doors until she was happy.

The Adele crowd stuck outside waiting for our doors to open....

With chaos swirling inside the Roxy and the sold-out, restless crowd outside, Adele finally stopped the soundcheck again and barked, "Well, I guess it'll have to do. You can open the bloody doors now." I walked over to Frankie, frustrated, and said, "What the hell happened with all this crap?" I knew Frankie was a great sound engineer, even though he was irresponsible. He was in his forties and had tons of experience. Looking all frazzled, he adjusted his glasses and said, "J, I'm telling you, as I remember it, she's a fukin' cunt, spoiled diva, and there was nothing really wrong with the monitors. I did everything I could, and she still wasn't happy." I looked at him, and he seemed totally honest. I had to agree with him on this one—maybe Adele was just causing confusion and acting like a diva for some bigger reason we didn't get.

I didn't understand it, and Frankie didn't get it, but she was definitely over the top. No other artist in the decade I'd been at the Roxy had complained so much about our monitors. Even Kool & The Gang, with their 9 members on stage, were good with our old-school monitor system. We were perplexed. It made no sense.

With the semi-blessing from Adele to open the doors, we were now about 2 hours late, and the crowd was pissed—they had been waiting outside the whole time. I gave the OK to the box office and staff to open immediately and get the people in. As we opened the doors, I could hear the gripes from the fans about waiting so long. Also, there was no opening act, so there was no one to warm up the audience and cool them down. Our waitresses were complaining that people were rude and off-putting, making remarks about how long it took to open the doors. A few people even posted on Twitter that the Roxy made them wait in line for two hours in 55+ degree weather and then followed up with complaints about drink prices. It definitely wasn't a good start to the night.

Doors were supposed to open at 7 PM, but now it looked like Adele wasn't going to start performing until 9:30 PM, even though she was originally slated to start at 8 PM. *Oh well,* I thought—at least she didn't cancel the whole friggin' show. I get a call to go backstage and talk to her tour manager. I head backstage, and they let me know that Adele will be starting in 15 minutes and that she would explain to the audience that there were technical difficulties as to why everything was running late. With that said, I went down to get my guys set. Bolle was good to go in his booth, and my guy Nacho was ready to help the FOH engineer.

However, I look in the monitor booth, and there's no sign of Frankie. I'm like, "Oh shit, no way has he disappeared again... I'm gonna friggin' kill him."

I set off on the prowl outside after checking the whole inside of the Roxy, asking staff and others if they'd seen Frankie—no one had. I jet over to the Rainbow Bar & Grill, right next door (we share the same small parking lot), rush into the patio, looking at all the tables, and asking the waitresses if they'd seen Frankie. No one had. I decide to head to the back bar at the back of the Rainbow, which is outside, and damn, there he was, smoking a cigarette and laughing, talking to Lemmy from Motörhead. I walk right up, say *"Excuse me, Lemmy,"* and turn to Frankie and say, *"What the fuck are you doing over here, Frankie? We're starting now in 10 minutes, and it's been a complete shit-show, and you're out here smoking with Lemmy. Are you trying to get us both fired, or are you just a fool—or both?"*

With that, Frankie put out his cigarette, drank his last sip from his glass, and then followed me as I was telling him, "You know she's acting like a high-maintenance diva, and yes, the monitors are fine as we both know, but truth doesn't matter in this instance. She has some really powerful people behind her, and we're gonna look like incompetent fools if she complains to them."

He started to say that she was delusional, the monitors were fine, blah, blah, blah, and I told him to *shut it* as we opened the side roll-up door to head into the monitor booth.

Luckily, just as we were closing the roll-up door, Adele steps from backstage to the stage, and her band is already waiting. Now, mind you, the big Roxy curtain is down, and no one knows yet that the show is about to start. She gives the nod to us, and then I flash Bolle in the lighting booth the signal that the stage is ready. He lets Adele's FOH know everything is good to go. Bolle shuts off the bright stage lights, and the crowd stops chatting, starting to roar. Her audience is electric with anticipation, and as the curtain goes up, people are cheering, clapping, and yelling. Adele seems relaxed and flashes a big smile as she kicks into her set.

Everything seems fine at first, but then all of a sudden, as the first song is finishing, she looks over at the monitor booth and points, signaling that the monitors need to come up more. She still looks peeved, like she did at the soundcheck, and I turn to Frankie and say, "Turn it up... do something!" He tries to turn it up, but as she's talking into the mic and getting ready to go into her second song, she points again that the monitors need to come down. I'm with Frankie on this one, and I'm like, "Dude, I think she's gone crazy or something." Frankie turns it down a bit, but she keeps making hand signals that we don't quite understand, all while she's singing. The hand signals are all over the place.

She finally gets into the song, and although she's acting like she can't hear herself, well, she sounds amazing coming out of the house speakers—the band sounds great too. She goes into her third song, and after that one, she says on the mic, "Ya know, I'm dealing with toddlers here at the Roxy with their sound." The crowd laughs and screams while she makes gestures that basically say the Roxy are idiots. There was nothing we could do but hope to make it through her set and then send her on her way. *I think I was praying for that at this point.*

After her fifth song, the crowd erupts in applause, and she starts laughing and bantering with the audience. I thought everything was all good now. I took a big sigh of relief, but little did I know, she saved her biggest verbal whipping for last. Right before she started her next song, she turned and looked at the monitor booth, then said to the audience, *"I just want you to know that... the reason all of you had to wait two bloody hours was because of the Roxy. They just couldn't get their act together, and they still can't."*

With that, the crowd started booing, and she was loving it.

Right at that point, Frankie was like, "I don't care if I get fired, I'm outta here... that fukin' bitch is out of her mind, mate. This is ridiculous. You heard the damn monitors, they're fine..."

I talked Frankie off the edge and got him to calm down and take a breath. I said, "Look, I won't say anything about you off smoking cigs with Lemmy right before the show, but I will back you up on the monitor fiasco. Yes, she seems to be a total nut, and the monitors were fine after you fine-tuned them. I think she just had a stick up her butt and wouldn't let up. Maybe it became like some weird game for her." He then stuck it out and said, as long as I had his back, he would finish out the show.

Adele proceeded to finish her set to thunderous applause, and she actually sounded amazing. I could definitely see that, even without her polished look and branding, she was still going to be a mega star because of her voice and the songs she sang. I knew this was going to change the pop atmosphere because she was definitely one of the most authentic artists to emerge in a long time.

As we finished, Frankie went outside to have a cigarette, and I let him have some space, as this was probably one of the hardest gigs he'd done in years. I so much wanted to use this against him and get Nic to fire him, but I knew that whatever he tried wasn't working for her. It might have started as a problem with the monitors, but it definitely wasn't the monitors.

The only thing I could think of—and this was a total assumption—was that Frankie was Irish with a big-time Irish accent, and Adele was English. Maybe there was something there, but I wasn't sure. And I'm still not sure.

I got called into the main office the next day, and Nic was like, "What the hell happened last night?" I stuck to my guns and said that it wasn't Frankie and the monitors, but that it was something with Adele, and that I heard the monitors standing right next to her, and they were good and pretty clear. Not amazing, but as good as they could be. I pointed out that she sounded amazing and the show went without a hitch, other than the monitors. I also stuck to my word and didn't mention the Lemmy incident. I'm definitely a man of my word. That's all you really have in the music business—your word is gold, and if you mess that up, no one will ever trust you again. Like I've said before, the music biz is like a giant mafia, and everything spreads real fast—especially amongst the clubs.

The next day, I got an email from my friend Jennifer at Live Nation, whom I'd dealt with concerning any show that they brought to the Roxy. I had to laugh as I read it:

Can I request Lee and Nacho for any future shows? Frankie causes too much drama. Especially the Adele show… Lee and Nacho have been great! Thanks! You guys are awesome!

And with that, I had actually won on both fronts. I kept my promise to Frankie not to throw him under the bus, but at the same time, I knew I didn't have to put him on any major *Live Nation* shows, and Nic wouldn't be arguing with me about it anymore. My own brand became even stronger with the whole Roxy, as things like this confirmed that I was completely in reality, and the things I said were truthful, not political. All I cared about was doing a great job and letting people know the truth about the good and bad at the Roxy.

In fact, I had this policy that totally worked for me all the time—until Frankie arrived. It went like this: I told my whole crew, "You can drink, do drugs, and even have sex at the Roxy, but—this is a big BUT—you can only do it after the show is done." I didn't care about what they did on the job, but they had to deliver an almost flawless performance on their part (unless it was truly out of their hands), and then I would be the most lenient boss they ever had. However, if they didn't deliver, and if I found out they were drunk or on drugs or something else that made me and the Roxy look bad, well, they'd be fired on the spot. For the record, I wasn't endorsing illegal activity; my rule was *zero tolerance during the show*. What people did off the clock and out of public areas was their business—not the venue's.

For some reason, this approach totally worked. All my crew was always on point until the show was in the books. Then, they'd go wild. I suspect a few of them drank or did drugs while they were working, but they still delivered and made themselves and me look good. I think I was one of the best bosses a person could have—no judgment, just do a great job, and I'd give you the world. It definitely worked with all my crew over the years, who were basically just disgruntled musicians who never quite reached the musical Holy Grail... just like me. So I guess I had a soft spot in my heart for them.

Now, Adele, as we all know now, became mega famous with hit after hit and millions of records sold. However, her personal brand was carefully crafted to make her appear so nice, gracious, and modest. I laughed when people I knew would say that she was a totally down-to-earth, anti-diva, and was so kind and humble. I wouldn't even tell them about her rants at the Roxy, but I would always say, *"Yeah, that's what her marketing and brand want you to think, but appearance isn't always the truth."*

Years later, I was surprised that she was finally portrayed by a few news articles as a diva, due to her newer polished, high-maintenance style that I always knew lurked under the down-to-earth schtick. *The Guardian* article called her one of the last traditional divas, like Whitney Houston or Mariah Carey, and her Las Vegas residency cancellation sparked "diva" accusations, as fans felt the last-minute announcement was unprofessional, despite her emotional explanation. A *Spectator* piece criticized her "relentlessly miserable" emotional output as self-indulgent, suggesting a Marie Antoinette–like disconnect given her wealth and Beverly Hills lifestyle. And finally, her *Carpool Karaoke* appearance gave birth to the "glimmering diva" look with expert makeup and dramatic gowns, contrasting her earlier "relatable Tottenham girl" vibe.

Frankie and I definitely got the brunt of her earlier, hidden-from-public diva personality, but in the end, it all didn't matter. She was a superstar who was launched into orbit from the Roxy Theatre stage. I was there right next to her at soundcheck as her amazing voice came through our shitty monitors… *clear as day.* Lol.

Begin forwarded message:

> **From:** ▮▮ Jennifer" <Jennifer▮▮@LiveNation.com>
> **Date:** May 23, 2008 12:51:37 AM
> **To:** decostarox@mac.com, nicrox@mac.com, "▮▮, Greg" <Greg▮▮@LiveNation.com>
> **Subject: Live nation shows**
>
> Can I request Lee and nacho for all future shows? Frankie causes too much drama.. Especially for the Adele show…
> Lee and nacho have been great!
> Thanks! You guys are awesome!

In some strange way, after the Adele debacle, I ended up getting my wish…

In Through the Out Door...

At the Roxy, we had this big, heavy metal roll-up stage door that opened straight out to the east-side parking lot that wrapped around the club.

Every band and performer loaded their gear through that grimy alley door. And whenever a major artist needed a quick getaway from the madness, that was the way out. Slip through the door, straight into a waiting car.

No meet and greets. No autographs. Just gone.

But that door wasn't only about quick escapes. It was its own strange kind of stage—a threshold between the turmoil inside and the darkness outside—but it also held dreams on the inside, and sometimes energetic hope waiting just beyond it.

Behind that metal frame lived a whole other cast of characters. People the audience, the execs, and the screaming fans would never see.

One of them is burned into my memory. We called him *"Newspapers."*

He showed up almost every night, shuffling around with stacks of old papers stuffed under his arms.

He couldn't talk much, not in any way that made sense. Always in the same filthy layers, hands black with dirt, greasy blond hair tangled to his shoulders.

He'd press his ear against that cold, dirty metal door and just listen—listening harder than half the people inside ever did.

Sometimes we'd toss him a beer. He'd grunt, take it, and slam it down. The kitchen guys gave him food now and then.

I used to wonder who he was before all this—before the grime, before the broken words. Maybe in the early '80s he was young, tall, chasing his dream on the Strip. Maybe he had the look. Maybe even the talent.

But the Sunset machine chewed him up. Drugs, booze, rejection. Instead of being the one on stage behind the roll-up door, he ended up on the other side of it.

Samuel Beckett once wrote: *"I can't go on, I'll go on."*

And in some twisted way, that's exactly what *"Newspapers"* did. He was barely surviving, but he kept coming back week after week, year after year. Still pressing his ear to the metal. Still clinging to the only thing that maybe made him feel alive.

He was one of Hollywood's many ghosts, except he wasn't gone yet. Just another broken man holding on through sound waves and steel. It reminded me of T.S. Eliot's line from *The Hollow Men:*

"This is the way the world ends / Not with a bang but a whimper."

"Newspapers" didn't have a bang left in him. He was all whimper. But he was still there, listening, like he refused to fully disappear.

That door had stories.

Some sad like his, others wild, surreal, even magical.

It was the Roxy's secret portal—spitting out disarray, swallowing lost souls, and sometimes ushering in legends.

And that's where the story of Sheila E.'s after-hours birthday party begins—a night when *Prince himself* rolled up through that same door.

Not to escape, but to blow the roof off the place.

Chapter 15

PRINCE, SHEILA E., & THE BLIZZARD OF OZ

"You earned that one—as the only person to probably ever play *Eruption* on Prince's guitar."

Early on when I started working at the Roxy, I realized that the load-in roll-up door wasn't just another slab of metal—it was something more. A passageway. A symbol. For some, it led to their destiny of greatness. For others, it was a path that never guaranteed success. And for a few, like I told you a few pages back, it was the only escape hatch for an artist who wanted to leave quickly without being noticed.

That roll-up door had seen everything since 1973, and once again, it would open wide—first before sunrise for Ozzy Osbourne's crew, and then later for Prince himself, ending with a party that bled into the dark of the next morning.

It hits differently now knowing Ozzy has passed on. The man who defined an entire era of rock—the Prince of Darkness himself—walked through that same roll-up door countless times. At the Roxy that day, he was still larger than life. Nobody thought of endings. Nobody thought about mortality. But now, looking back, it feels heavier knowing he's gone. *The blizzard eventually clears for all of us.*

So here's what happened: Sheila E. decided to throw her late-night birthday bash at the Roxy, with the one and only Prince coming as the special guest performer. The plan was for the party to start at 1:30 a.m. and rage until sunrise (we got the permits to stay open after-hours). Meanwhile, earlier that same day, Ozzy was scheduled to film a private shoot for his show *Battle for Ozzfest*. Bands would compete over a series of gigs at different venues for a slot on his tour.

Ozzy and Sharon had two massive throne chairs brought in, plus a ton of gear—and they needed to load in at 5 a.m. Which meant I had to be there at 4:30 a.m. to open everything up. I was already calculating the hours and realizing the obvious: I was about to work a straight 24+ hour shift. *No breaks. No extra pay.* Just the usual under-the-table envelope from the Roxy, half my salary in cash wrapped in plain paper with no name, secretly left on top of the safe locked behind a door in the main office.

That was the deal at the Roxy—*always hustle, never complain.* The ones who complained didn't last long.

So I showed up at 4:30 a.m., still half-asleep. Westbrook, my sound guy, met me with coffee, and together we rolled up that big door to let in the Osbourne crew. Within minutes, gear was flooding in. But then one of their guys slipped going up the small steps to the stage and slammed face-first into the wood. Nose broken. Blood on the stairs. Blood on the stage. Just like that, the day was off to a bloody start.

This wasn't the first time something like that had happened loading heavy equipment up those shitty little stairs. Hell, I hurt my back badly carrying in an amp for another show—the guy holding the other side slipped, all the weight crashed on me, and I was stuck on the second stair taking it full-force. I was out a week on painkillers, and my lower back still bothers me to this day.

I grabbed a towel and tried to mop up the mess, but the blood had already seeped into the grain of the wood. That stain was going to be there for a while. *I laughed to myself, thinking about how that damn roll-up door never just meant one thing. It played by its own rules and had a life of its own.*

By 9 a.m., the inside of the Roxy looked like a gothic rock castle. The thrones glowed under perfect lights. The stage was stacked. In the VIP section, judges like Chester Bennington from Linkin Park were prepping to critique the hopefuls. It actually looked… fuckin' amazing.

Ozzy and Sharon arrived, and I hung with them backstage for a bit. We laughed about Jack sneaking into *On the Rox* even though he was underage. I assured them he was always safe with us keeping an eye on him. They signed a few things for the Roxy, and then it was time to roll. The filming went smoother than expected—solid energy, big laughs, no drama.

By the time Ozzy's crew was loading out, Sheila E.'s crew was already pulling up. Perfect handoff. One of Prince's guys—subbing for his main guitar tech—came through the roll-up door with a few of Prince's guitars and his rig. I waved him in. *That famous white Cloud guitar practically glowed under the daytime stage lights* as he tuned it and set it up for soundcheck.

Sheila E. showed up around 3:30 p.m. and immediately started her own run. Total pro. She bounced between drums and percussion like it was child's play. You could feel the electricity already.

Still no Prince.

Finally, the text came through: *Prince is outside.*

I walked to the stage, down to the roll-up door, and started raising it. And there he was.

Pink polka-dot shirt—half unbuttoned—gold chains draped over a lightly hairy chest. White pants. White high-heeled boots with glittery trim. The man looked like a walking enigma, and kinda like a sharply dressed Liberace Jr—regal and strange. And short—maybe 5'2", but at least four inches taller with those heels.

He stood still. Didn't look at me. Didn't flinch.

I broke the silence. "Hey Prince, I'm the production manager here. If you need anything, just let me know."

Nothing.

Then slowly, he turned his head. Eyes locked onto mine. And in this deep, deliberate voice, he said, *"I'm all good."*

Then he turned forward again and walked straight to the stage. Didn't acknowledge anyone. Walked past his band. Past the crew. Straight to his mic. My tech buddy strapped him with the Cloud guitar without a word. Prince raised his hand. Counted off—*one, two, three.*

Raspberry Beret.

The band exploded behind him like they'd rehearsed for weeks. But they hadn't. That's just what playing with Prince meant. *You were ready. Period.*

I watched from the side stage, completely mesmerized. This guy was a living rock and funk god. And I couldn't help but flash back to being sixteen, hanging in my girlfriend's bedroom, staring at her Prince posters, practicing guitar, trying to copy solos from Prince and Jimmy Page and Van Halen. And now here I was—watching him blaze through three songs on my stage.

After the last note, he handed the guitar back to the tech and walked right back toward me. People were calling out—"Bye Prince!"—but he kept his eyes straight ahead.

I rolled up the door again. He stopped in front of me. Then, like a scene out of a movie, he turned his head and quietly said, *"Thanks."*

And then he disappeared into the waiting car.

Back inside, the tech was tuning the Cloud guitar. I walked over.

"Dude, Prince is kinda strange, man. He didn't even say a word to anyone—not even you!"

He laughed. "That's just his thing. Keeps the mystique. Behind the scenes? He's chill."

Then he looked at the guitar. "Wanna try it?"

I was like, "You serious?"

"Yeah. We got backups. Curtain's down. Rip it up, man."

He handed me the Cloud guitar. I threw the strap over my shoulder and launched into *Eruption.* All of it. My fingers flying on Prince's fretboard, my buddy throwing up the horns. *For a moment, I felt like that sixteen-year-old version of me had finally caught up.*

This wasn't just another music gig. It was one of those rare moments where everything I'd been chasing felt real. All the late nights, the shitty load-ins, the busted gear, the endless grind of scraping by—it somehow all led to me standing there, playing *Eruption* on Prince's Cloud guitar inside the Roxy. *I wasn't thinking about making it. I wasn't thinking about tomorrow. Just that, right then, I had ended up exactly where I was supposed to be.*

When I handed it back, I tried to give him the Prince guitar pick I was using—the very one Prince had used during soundcheck.

He waved me off. "Keep it. You earned that one—as the only person to probably ever play *Eruption* on Prince's guitar."

We both laughed, and I thanked him.

I still have that white and purple pick today. *Prince* embossed across it like a badge of honor.

After Prince left, we put covers over Sheila's drums and percussion gear, and moved the band's equipment toward the back of the stage. The local bands waiting outside were eager to load in. We opened the roll-up door and started bringing them through one at a time. It helped that booking had set it all up with a common backline of amps and drums—smart move given how tight the night's schedule was.

As the first band loaded in, one of the younger guys came up to me, clearly nervous and excited. "Man, this is such an honor. It's our first time playing the Roxy... I can't believe we're gonna be on this stage where so many great bands have played."

I asked how old he was. "Sixteen."

And in that second, I was pulled back to my own teenage years. *Back when I thought playing the Roxy or Whisky meant you were on a straight path to salvation.* I didn't realize then how long and winding the road really was, or how fast time would pass. I was in my mid-thirties now—still grinding—and to the world, that was already old if you hadn't made it yet.

I looked at that kid and saw myself. All that energy. All that hope. Even if the odds were stacked a mile high, he was just starting his journey. And for a young band, walking through that Roxy roll-up door? That was a milestone. For bands from LA, from the U.S., from anywhere in the world.

I'd seen thousands of them come through that door over the years. All with the same dream—not just for fame, but for a chance to make music, pay the bills, and maybe find a little meaning along the way. The thing they all shared? Ambition. Passion. That hunger for what it felt like to stand on stage under real lights with the crowd in front of them.

The Roxy stage had a magic to it. And that roll-up door—it was the way in.

Once everyone was loaded in, doors opened, and we kicked off the show. The younger bands tore through their sets, one after the other, and by midnight it was all done. We cleared them out and started prepping for Sheila E.'s 1 a.m. party.

She and her crew rolled back in through the roll-up. We sent them backstage while we opened the front for guests. The crowd came in hot—friends, family, industry folks. There was still booze to pour until 2 a.m., and the room lit up fast.

Around 1:30 a.m., Sheila hit the stage. People lost it. She started jamming, and guest musicians kept rotating in and out. Two hours into the set, I got another text: *Prince was returning.*

I headed straight to the roll-up door. When I got the next ping, I opened it, and there he was again—this time in a crisp white suit, another pair of outlandish heels, and his same unreadable expression. He had a small entourage behind him.

"Hey Prince... welcome back. If you need anything, just let me know."

Same head turn. Same eyes. Same deep voice. *"I'm good."*

It was like a glitch in the matrix. Like Prince was programmed to say it the exact same way. *I half-joked to myself—this guy might be a damn Prince android or clone.*

Sheila spotted him from the stage. The crowd hadn't seen him yet. She turned to them, hyped and glowing:

"Hey family, I got a special friend that's gonna play a few songs with us."

She pointed our way—and boom. Prince stepped into the lights, crowd screaming.

He hugged Sheila, strapped on his guitar, and they jumped straight into *Let's Go Crazy,* followed by *Raspberry Beret,* and then a full-on jam that went deep into the morning. Sheila destroyed the drums. Prince shredded solos. The band just rode the wave.

By around 4:30 a.m., they wrapped it up. Prince waved to the crowd and headed straight toward me.

I rolled up the door again.

As he walked by, I said, "Incredible, man. You killed it."

Without missing a beat, and without turning to look, he replied, *"You know it."*

Then he stepped into the back of the car. I stood there, door still up, watching it roll off into the dark... Just soaking in the cool moment and laughing to myself about the fact that Prince would never have any idea that I completely shredded *Eruption* on his famous Cloud guitar. Man, what a night.

That roll-up door had witnessed it all—and had been the silent witness to everything that had happened on the Roxy stage since 1973. *If only he could talk, the stories he could tell.*

So I gave him a name. ***Rolly.***

From Glitter to Grime...

There's a strange kind of whiplash when you go from royalty to pure debauchery in the span of a few nights at the Roxy—but that's exactly what made the place so incredible.

One night, you're in the presence of *Prince* and *Sheila E.*—two absolute masters of their craft, exuding this otherworldly control over the room. When Prince stepped through *Rolly* the roll-up door to the stage, it was like gravity shifted. Everything got still, like the world was paying attention. He barely said a word, but you *felt* him. And Sheila, man, she had the kind of talent and energy that didn't just light up the stage—it *rewired* it. It was one of those rare nights when the glamour wasn't fake, and the magic was real.

But the thing about magic is, it doesn't hang around forever. It comes, it stuns, and then it vanishes back into the smoke.

As Shakespeare said, "All that glisters is not gold." The shine can rot fast. A good thing, stretched or twisted the wrong way, can collapse into something uglier than the junk you thought you'd risen above.

And then there were nights that didn't just fall from that high—they *nosedived* straight into absurdity. Nights when the glitter turned to grime.

Which brings us to *Ron Jeremy.*

If Prince was the embodiment of mystery, Jeremy was the embodiment of *too much information.* And I don't even mean that as an insult—just a fact. No elegance, no mystique. Just greasiness, body hair, and a Santa Claus suit. And somehow, it still fit inside the Roxy's ongoing circus.

That's the thing about this business, and maybe life in general—there's a razor-thin line between *sacred and profane.* Between *art and spectacle.* And you don't always realize you've crossed it until you're standing in the dressing room, listening to moans echo from the bathroom while Santa gets dirty.

So yeah, buckle up. We're leaving *Paisley Park* and heading straight into the *XXX files.*

Next stop: *Ron Jeremy, red velvet, and my holiday trauma.*

Chapter 16

SANTA CLAUS RON JEREMY—And His Little Horny Elves

"Don't stop, don't stop, I'm almost there!...you're doing great"

They called Ron Jeremy *The Hedgehog,* but every time I saw him waddling around—stringy, greasy hair clinging to his scalp, obese belly stretching out those way-too-tight shirts, and sweat exploding from every pore—I didn't think hedgehog. I thought *wild pig.* Straight-up, filthy, human grossness.

I tried to avoid him every chance I got. If he spoke to me, I'd fake a call, duck out for a fake meeting, or suddenly have somewhere I needed to be. He creeped me out on a deep, instinctual level—like he was the embodiment of everything rotten about Hollywood. I never liked when he showed up at Roxy shows, and I sure as hell stayed away from him anytime I was at the *Rainbow Bar & Grill.*

Sometimes I'd catch him across the patio, shoving slices of the famous *Rainbow* pizza into his mouth, washing it down with soda or wine. Bits of crust stuck to his shirt, grease stains layered with splashes of red from whatever he was drinking. He looked like a walking trash can. I'd be grossed out, but then he'd say something kind of mellow or polite, and I'd second-guess myself for a second. *Maybe he was just a weird, harmless guy.*

But that couldn't have been further from the truth, as I'd come to find out.

What always blew my mind was how many people—fans, tourists, even young women—flocked to him. On the patio at the *Rainbow,* he was like a magnet for bad taste. People wanted autographs, selfies, hugs. Even girls who looked fresh out of high school would wrap themselves around him like he was some kind of rock star, while their friends giggled and snapped pics. It kinda turned my stomach.

And I wasn't naive. I'd seen it all. I'd been around the adult film scene in Hollywood. I'd known more than a few porn girls personally—partied with them, hung with them, even had my own backstage romps at the Roxy and untamed nights on the road. But something about him always made my skin crawl.

He'd roll up with two or three younger girls in tow, and all I could think was: *Those poor, fucked-up girls.*

It was weird, too, because I loved the band *Sublime*—and they used to name-drop him in their lyrics like he was some kind of legend. I was even there, 1995, Cal State Dominguez Hills, when they brought him onstage and let him speak into the mic. The crowd ate it up.

To certain kinds of dudes, Ron Jeremy was a hero. He was fat, gross, hairy, yet still slept with hot porn stars for a living. That gave hope to every creepy guy who thought if Ron could do it, maybe they had a shot too. That if a guy like that could become a legend in porn, anything was possible.

I used to laugh about it. But deep down, I knew: *Ron was the patron saint of incels and weirdos long before that was a thing.*

Then came the memo from the booking office: some company had rented out the Roxy for their Christmas party and hired Ron Jeremy to host it—dressed as Santa Claus, no less. There'd be a DJ, booze flowing, and then Ron would take the stage to hand out bonuses and gifts to the company's employees. I figured he'd show up lit or on something, and I'd be the one stuck wrangling him onto the stage.

I wasn't wrong.

He rolled into the venue right as the party was getting into full swing—around 9:45 p.m.—with two women in tow. One was a younger porn chick I didn't recognize. The other was *Penny Porsche,* an older adult actress I'd seen floating around the Roxy and *Rainbow* plenty of times. I'd caught her back in our kitchen more than once, chatting up the waitresses. She wasn't bad-looking for her forties, but her massive fake boobs were cartoon-level ridiculous.

As soon as I spotted Ron, I called out to him, told him he could head backstage and change into the Santa suit. I reminded him he had about thirty minutes to get ready—he was supposed to emcee and hand out the goods by 10:30. He nodded and said, "Okay, got it, boss," and disappeared backstage with the two girls.

The crowd was already going—about 150 people packing the floor, dancing hard to the DJ while Bolle ran a killer light show. Everyone was loose, drunk, and riding the high. I figured as long as Ron made it onstage at some point to hand out the presents and bonus checks, we were good. So I went to talk to a couple friends who'd dropped by to say hi.

Time slipped.

At 10:30, Ron still hadn't surfaced. But no one seemed to no-tice—everyone was partying too hard to care. I assumed he'd show up any minute now in full Santa gear, maybe stoned, maybe staggering, but at least ready to play the part.

Another thirty minutes passed. *Nothing.*

Then one of the company's employees came running over to me near VIP, slightly panicked.

"Hey, we can't find Ron. Can you help us look for him? He's supposed to be onstage handing out gifts."

I told her I'd track him down and get him onstage pronto.

My first guess? He was backstage somewhere, either drunk, passed out, or balls-deep in distraction. But there was also a decent chance he'd snuck across to the *Rainbow* to harass some girls and stir shit, like he always did.

I figured I'd start with the backstage.

I made my way up the stairs. I already knew the office staff had cleared out early, and the only ones left in the building were all down-stairs—the waitresses, kitchen crew, my sound guy, and Bolle running lights.

As I hit the top of the stairs, I heard it—muffled moaning. I figured Ron was getting busy with the girls he'd brought and I'd have to break it up to get him onstage. But as I walked down the hallway toward the backstage rooms, the moaning got louder... and it wasn't coming from backstage. It was coming from the hallway bathroom—the same one where I once saw Paris Hilton dancing and blowing kisses to herself in the mirror.

I stopped and listened, waiting for a pause. As soon as things quieted down, I tried the door. Locked. Then, just as quickly, the noise ramped up again—Ron's voice echoing through the crack.

"Come on baby, just a bit more, just a bit more. I'm not there yet..."

I bent down and looked through the slim gap by the door han-dle—and started laughing.

There was Ron, his Santa shirt wide open, fat and hairy belly spilling out, pants around his ankles, fake white beard still strapped on. He was leaning back against the tiny bathroom sink while Penny was kneeling on the disgusting floor, trying her best to force Ron's limp junk into her mouth. He was sweating bullets, head thrown back, mumbling,

"Don't stop, don't stop, I just need to get there... you're doing great..."

Ron was leaning hard against our tiny hallway bathroom sink...

All I could think was—*he can't even get hard.* She's yanking it, trying to suck it, doing everything short of CPR, and nothing's happening. It was sad. I was grossed out. And honestly, I knew if I didn't interrupt, it could go on all night.

I stood up and pounded on the door. "Ron! Save it for after the show. You're an hour late—they need you onstage now."

From inside, I heard, "Just a minute! Trying to finish up something!"

I yelled again. "Now, Ron. Now."

A pause. Then: "Listen, baby... let's try again after the show. I wanna finish."

A few seconds later, the door creaked open. Ron stood there, sweaty, disheveled, beard hanging crooked. He looked like he'd just survived a flash flood of saliva and shame.

I pointed toward the stage.

He sighed. "Okay, okay, I know—I'm being paid to be fuckin' Santa Claus tonight."

And just like that, he waddled down the hallway toward his Santa throne and fake snow.

I followed him down the stairs toward the stage. Penny trailed behind me, and just as we were descending, I felt a pinch on my ass. I turned around and there she was, smirking, mouthing the words, *Let's go back.*

Didn't shock me. She was an adult film actress, and every porn girl I'd met in Hollywood seemed down for whatever. I just shook my head, mouthed back, *Can't. Sorry,* and kept following Ron.

I chuckled to myself. Surrounded by adult film actors with that same vacant stare Penny had—that mix of sleaze, burnout, and moral rot that Hollywood seemed to normalize. It was insane sometimes. And yeah, I wasn't exactly a saint, but I couldn't destroy my own moral compass just to swim in that kind of filth. *I lived in the den of debauchery—I just chose not to drink too deep from it.*

To his credit, Ron actually did alright once he hit the stage. He was drunk, sloppy, but kind of funny. He handed out the presents and bonus checks while the crowd howled and ate it up.

The weirdest part? They'd set up this throne-like chair center stage, and people lined up to sit on his lap for raunchy photos. Grown-ass men and women, cracking up, hamming it up, loving it.

When it was all over, Ron headed backstage again—this time with the younger porn girl on his arm. Penny had vanished. Probably wandered off back to the *Rainbow.*

Time passed, and by midnight the DJ was still going, but the kitchen crew was ready to start shutting it down. Our longtime cook—everyone just called her *Mama*—was this tough, no-bullshit Hispanic lady who'd been working at the Roxy since the place first opened in 1973. She was now in her early seventies, barely spoke English, but still had a ton of grit. Every night, like clockwork, she'd grab a broom and bucket and head backstage to start cleaning.

I'd forgotten Ron was even still in the building.

About five minutes later, I see Mama running out from the backstage hallway looking completely stunned—eyes wide, shaking her head.

She waves me over fast and mutters, "No good. No good. Dirty fat man and girl. No good."

I burst out laughing. "I got it, Mama. I'll take care of it."

She shook her head again, but cracked a smile as I headed back.

This time, the hallway bathroom was quiet. But the main back-stage room? Not so much. I could hear full-on sex sounds echoing out. I pushed open the door.

And there it was.

The bathroom door inside the room was wide open, and Ron had the younger girl bent over, bracing herself against the toilet—hands gripping the seat, some of her long brown hair actually dipping into the bowl. Ron's Santa pants were around his ankles, his suit bunched around his gut, and his hairy ass was on full display as he went at it from behind.

I almost puked.

Honestly, it looked like some rejected scene from a low-budget 1980s holiday porno—like if someone had slapped the title *Santa and His Horny Elves at the Roxy* on a VHS tape you'd find in a bargain bin.

I shook my head, half laughing, half nauseated. "Ron, dude—you're relentless! You've got twenty more minutes and then Mama's coming back to clean. Wrap it up, man!"

Thirty minutes later—of course—closer to 12:30, Ron and the girl finally stumbled out from backstage, sweaty, makeup smeared, clothes twisted. They looked like they'd just been through a full-on sexual hur-ricane—smeared makeup, twisted clothes, the works.

I watched as they slipped out the side door and started walking toward the *Rainbow*.

Back to the depravity. Back to the *Rainbow Bar & Grill* debauchery.

I just stood there, shaking my head, laughing to myself as they dis-appeared out through the side door.

In the end, Ron Jeremy's story unraveled the same way so many Hollywood myths do. The larger-than-life persona collapsed under the weight of who he really was. Dozens of women came forward with dev-astating accusations, and today he sits behind bars. News outlets have reported on his declining health and alleged dementia. It's tragic in one sense, but also inevitable—the kind of downfall that reminds you how thin the line is between legend and disgrace. At the Roxy, I'd already seen glimpses of that line, where the glitter turned to grime.

His fate just proved what I already knew: no mask of fame or notoriety can hide the truth forever.

Young, Beautiful, and Tragic: The Porn Road to Nowhere

"That damn porn stuff? It lives on the internet forever. But you can move on from it."

Dealing with porn actors like Ron Jeremy always made me think about the *sexual decay* and nonstop *debauchery* that surrounded me for years—how at some point, it all started to feel almost normal. But deep down, I knew it wasn't healthy. And from what I saw, it sure as hell didn't lead to happiness.

I'd known plenty of girls who ended up in porn. A lot of them didn't start out that way. They were just cute girls who loved music and bands and being around the scene in Hollywood. In the early 2000s, you'd see them at shows—wide-eyed, excited, dressed to impress—and eventually, many of them drifted into porn. It was a way to pay bills, sure, but it also gave them access to the clubs, the bands, the lifestyle. I even dated a few of them before they crossed into the adult world. What always shocked me was how many of them started out wholesome—reserved, even. Then Hollywood did what it always does: it flipped the script.

The most devastating story was Megan. She went by the stage name *Naughtia Childs.*

I was still working at the Whisky at the time—under Mikey Maglieri J r.—while playing in my band, *Rumblefish.* I'd met Megan back in the '90s. She was super cute, sweet, from San Diego. She'd drive up to Hollywood to catch concerts and hang around the scene. We met at the *Rainbow* after one of the Whisky shows. She came up to me and said, *Hey, I think I just saw you at the Whisky. I'm Megan.*

We clicked right away—talked about music, her dream of working in the industry. I gave her my number and she came out to one of my shows soon after. We became friends. We only hooked up once, but we didn't sleep together—she actually came off kind of conservative. Not a groupie. She really wanted to get out of San Diego and break into the music business.

We lost touch for a bit. Then one day I got a text from her. She said she was modeling now and moving to Hollywood. We never ended up reconnecting in person.

But I found out what kind of *modeling* she was doing completely by accident.

One night, a band that had played the Whisky left behind a couple of porn mags—I still don't know why. Our office was right across from the second backstage room, and the Whisky rooms didn't have doors. I walked in, grabbed the mags, figured I'd toss them onto our big table in the office next to all the other random music rags.

But then I opened one up... and did a double take.

There she was. Megan. Full-page spread. Naked. Smiling. Gleaming, with another girl wrapped around her.

I stood there for a second, stunned.

Then I pulled out my phone and dialed her number.

When she picked up, I told her what I saw. She didn't deny it. She came clean. Said yeah, she was doing nude modeling—and now, she was an actress too.

I had questions. A lot of them. She explained how it all started back in San Diego. Some guy approached her, said she could earn a thousand bucks doing a nude photo shoot. She needed the money, thought it sounded easy enough. *(I guess she wasn't quite as conservative as I thought.)*

She ended up doing a few shoots, each time getting paid, but had no idea where the photos were ending up. Next thing she knew, she was popping up in different magazines. I knew how it worked—those sleazy porn guys were probably selling her photos left and right, raking in real money while tossing her a couple grand here and there. Peanuts.

After a few months, they offered her two grand for a girl-on-girl shoot. She wasn't into women, but she did it anyway. Then came more money, more shoots. Still just photos. Until some big producer offered her a place to stay—and suddenly, she was living with him and doing movies.

I was like, *Wait... what?*

She told me she'd love to see me. Said I should come by and we could talk more about everything. I told her my buddy Eddie—yes, that Eddie, aka *Dr. Evil,* the Roxy soundman—was with me, and asked if it was cool to bring him along.

She said, *Of course,* and gave me the address.

On the drive over, I showed Eddie a few pictures of her. His eyes damn near popped out of his head. *"She's so pretty,"* he said. *"Why's she doing porno shit?"*

I shook my head, shrugged. *"I have no idea, man. Maybe we'll find out."*

We finally pulled up to the townhouse—it was in a surprisingly nice neighborhood in the Valley. Megan opened the front door, standing there in a short skirt, tight tank top, full makeup, bright smile, and those big, wide eyes.

Jason! she beamed, then jumped into a big hug and kissed my cheek. I introduced Eddie, and she gave him a hug too.

The moment we stepped inside, it hit me. Just past the entry-way was this weird fountain built into the front glass—bubbles rising through glowing pink liquid like a stripper's fish tank. The whole place screamed *porn den.* Shag rugs everywhere. Leopard print, zebra print, tiger stripes—it was like walking into *Boogie Nights* in 3D.

We followed Megan up the stairs, and that's when it got even more ridiculous. The staircase was long and winding, with framed photos covering every wall on the way up. In every single one, the producer guy—older, slick, looked like he thought he owned the world. His walls were plastered with framed shots of him with rappers, porn stars, and rock musicians. At the top, the prize: him grinning next to an Ice-cold famous rapper.

I didn't say a word. Just shot Eddie a look, raised my eyebrows. He smirked and shook his head. We kept climbing.

As Megan stepped onto the landing, I caught a glimpse under her skirt—no underwear. I just shook my head again.

Her room was just as over-the-top. All pink walls, fuzzy pillows, cartoonish details—it looked like Barbie's playhouse. She sat cross-legged on the bed. Eddie and I took the little couch in the corner.

I asked her a few questions, just trying to make sense of the whole thing.

She explained that after moving up from San Diego, the producer offered her free rent and solid pay to do movies. I was still wrapping my head around it when she casually said she'd already filmed ten—and had more lined up.

I asked if she was happy with the decision—if she regretted leaving her dream of working in music behind.

She told us she'd tried. Tried to intern, tried to get in the door, but the pay was nonexistent. Everyone wanted her to work for free. So when the nude photo shoots started bringing in real money, and then the movie offers came next, she said she couldn't pass it up.

It's just acting, she said. *And the money's great. It's not a big deal.* Except... her family didn't know.

I said, *Hopefully they don't find out.*
She laughed nervously, then started to tell us about some of the scenes she'd done—but someone from downstairs interrupted, yelling for her to come meet a new director.
She got up, walked to her dresser, pulled out a folder, and handed it to us. *Check out my new promo shots—I'll be right back.*
And just like that, she was gone.
Eddie and I opened the folder. Inside were stacks of glossy color shots—nude stills from magazine shoots, porn sets, and warehouse locations out in Chatsworth.
As I pulled a handful of photos out, something slipped and fluttered to the ground. A large-format negative strip. Eddie picked it up, held it to the light—and both of our jaws dropped.
There was Megan. Naked. In a hardcore group scene—hands and mouth occupied, surrounded by guys. It hit me like a punch to the gut.

Oh shit, we both said at the same time. *Shit just got real.*
We shoved the strip back in the folder like a couple of kids who found something hidden in their parents' closet. Then we sat there on the couch, wide-eyed and quiet.
A moment later, Megan came back in and smiled.
Sorry about that—what'd you think of the photos?
Eddie jumped in first. *You look great. You're gonna be famous for sure.*
I nodded. *Yeah. Just curious... how long do you plan on doing this?*
Without missing a beat, she said, *"Indefinitely, I hope."*

We shifted the conversation back to music, bands, life outside the Valley porno bubble. But then Megan leaned back on her bed, legs slightly spread, still no underwear—and I couldn't tell if she was inviting something or just craving attention.

She wagged her finger, motioning us closer with a teasing grin.

Then Eddie—definitely not in rock star mode—blurts out, *"Oh man, I have a girlfriend… but if I was single? Damn."*

He looked at me. I shrugged and said, *Megan, we never hooked up, and honestly… I'm kinda sorry we didn't. But yeah, like Eddie—I've got a serious girlfriend now.*

She didn't flinch. Just smiled, stood up, and said, *"No worries. Let's go downstairs and grab something to drink."*

As we passed the main bedroom, the door was wide open. The producer was lying on a king-sized bed draped in a leopard-print blanket. In front of it—no joke—was an actual lion skin rug, full head still attached. He was surrounded by a few sketchy-looking dudes, all gathered around the TV watching what looked like a casting tape. Girls walked in front of the camera while a few guys tossed out commentary—like some creepy casting-room vibe straight out of *Boogie Nights.*

He glanced up and said, *"Hey Megan—don't forget we've got an early shoot tomorrow. Don't stay up too late, alright?"*

"Okie dokie," she called back as we headed into the kitchen.

Inside was this stunning girl—dark hair, piercing blue eyes—eating fast food with a sleazy older guy who had producer vibes all over him.

Oh hey, Megan, she said. *What are you up to?*

Megan introduced us. The girl leaned in and gave us hugs. *"I'm Kara,"* she said.

Turns out, a few years later, she'd end up dating my bass player—and blow up in the adult scene as *Kristina Black.*

Small world.

We made some small talk, but then Kara casually dropped, *"Man, anal is so hard."*

The older dude nodded and added, *"Yeah, you looked like you were in pain earlier today."*

Kara laughed and said, *"I've decided I'm not doing anal again, but I'm open to everything else."*

That pretty much wrapped the night.

We said our goodbyes. Megan gave us long hugs at the door and told us to keep in touch.

Once Eddie and I got in the car, we just sat in silence for a moment.

"Dude… what the hell did we just walk into?"

Neither of us had an answer. These were sweet, smart, pretty girls. And yet here they were—neck deep in something that felt way darker than it looked on the surface.

We both felt it. Something was off. Something foreboding.

I had this sinking feeling that Megan was heading toward some kind of wreck. *I hoped I was wrong. But it didn't feel that way.*

I lost touch with Megan for a while. Between working more shifts at the Whisky and hitting the road with my new band, *Rumblefish*—still chasing another major label deal—our paths just didn't cross.

Then, at the tail end of 2001, I found myself at this party in the Hollywood Hills. Loud, crowded, and smoky. At some point in the night, a group of people strolled in, and I instantly recognized one of them—Mikey Maglieri Jr.'s dad, Mikeal, leading the crew in a badass trench coat.

Right behind him… was Megan.

After greeting Mikeal with a hug, I turned and said, *Megan!* She wrapped me up in a big bear hug—but when she pulled back, something was different. Her spark was gone. She looked tired. Older. Weary.

She didn't have that same glow I remembered from the last time I'd seen her.

I asked how she was doing. She told me she'd left the adult film world and was trying to get work behind the scenes in music again.

"Why'd you leave the industry?" I asked.

She hesitated. Then said, quietly, *"Because I was embarrassed. People I didn't want to know… found out. I felt ashamed."*

I always assumed her family had found out—but she never said for sure.

I told her that if anything opened up at the Whisky or through M Productions, I'd do what I could to help her get a foot in the door.

She looked like she really needed a win. Her energy was low. Like something had broken inside.

We talked more, and she admitted she regretted getting into porn at all.

Said she hoped it wasn't too late to start over.

And that's when I said something I still regret. Sometimes my mouth moves faster than my mind.

I said, *Megan, you're only 22. You made a mistake—but you can still turn things around. Just know... that damn porn stuff? It lives on the internet forever. But you can move on from it.*

Her face changed. It was like the words I said physically hit her. I saw her eyes well up—but she held it together.

"You're right," she said. "It's not too late. Please... if you hear about anything at the Whisky, let me know. I'm living near Sunset now with two other girls."

I hugged her again.

For sure, I told her. "Let's get through New Year's, and I'll reach out next week—or the week after."

And that was that. For the moment.

I said goodbye, and she disappeared back into the party. I left to hit another one.

After New Year's, I got back to the office and asked the main Whisky team if they were looking to hire anyone. The in-house booking agent said they were actually considering bringing on a booking assistant.

I told them I had someone perfect in mind—*Megan.* Said she might be a great fit. I'd have her call.

I tried calling her. No answer. Left a few voicemails. By the end of the week, I figured maybe she found something else or was out of town.

I wasn't expecting the news that came next.

I was at the *Rainbow* when one of the waitresses I knew pulled me aside, her face somber. "Did you hear what happened with Megan... Naughtia?"

Immediately, my stomach dropped. I asked quietly, "Please don't tell me she died?"

She nodded, eyes full of pity. *"It's so sad. She killed herself a few days ago... jumped off the balcony of her apartment."*

Somehow, I already knew. Even before the words came out, *I felt it.*
Another tragic ending on the long, brutal road of chasing dreams.

Back at the office, I jumped on the computer and looked it up. *January 7, 2002.* Megan had taken her own life—leapt from the fourth-story balcony of the place she rented with two other girls.

A few people who knew her said she'd been drinking that night—and had taken a half tab of LSD.

Devastating doesn't even begin to cover it.

It reminded me how many forks there are on the road of life—and how easy it is, when you're young and chasing something, to take a wrong turn that leads somewhere dark. Somewhere final.

I thought about *Kurt Cobain.* About my old singer, *Sun Sannes.* About all the others who made that same decision to leave this world.

I hope they found some peace, wherever the road after life has taken them.

It brings to mind a quote I saw as a kid... or maybe I made it up. I'm still not sure.

Death is not the end... It's just a door, opening to a new beginning.

I really hope that's true.

Chapter 17

MARILYN MANSON—Legend of the Backstage Vulture

"Manson says if he doesn't get the pizza and everything else, he won't have the energy to perform."

The Roxy was directly involved with the short-lived but ground-breaking *Sunset Strip Music Festival (SSMF).* By 2011, I'd already hung up my hat as the GM of the Roxy, but my old boss—*Nic Adler*—recommended me to take charge of backstage production for the festival.

My job? Running backstage with a small crew I'd handpick myself.

Sunset Boulevard was going to be completely shut down for the festival. From the moment you hit the *Rainbow Bar & Grill* and the *Roxy,* there was going to be a massive stage set up right in the middle of the street. The festival stretched for blocks, all the way down to the *Whisky a Go Go,* where the second stage would be. All the major clubs—*Roxy, Whisky, Key Club, Viper Room,* and *Cat Club*—would be open, with bands tearing it up inside while the big acts blazed away outside.

The west side main stage was set to feature *The Offspring* and *Marilyn Manson. Steve Aoki* and *Far East Movement* were holding it down on the east side stage.

Now, I had never worked with either of those acts, but I quickly found out one of them was going to be a shitshow—hard to handle, completely out of control.

As usual with my festival duties, I handled all the shopping for the headliner riders[1]. I'd toss the smaller bands' riders to various crew mem-

---

1. **In another story, I explain the full concept of a band or artist's "rider."** Over the years, I came up with new protocols and procedures regarding these riders and ended up sending them out to other production managers I knew. See, most of the good booking agents would cross out the rider and stamp each page with "TBD at discretion of hospitality," but there were always some clubs that would end up bending over backwards, fulfilling every little whim from an entitled artist. It was ridiculous. The problem was, these clubs would hurt all the other venues by catering to every last detail on these ridiculous riders. Most of these clubs would go out of business eventually because live music venues were always struggling to stay afloat. They'd barely scrape by, relying on overpriced drinks just to keep the doors open. The smart clubs? They knew how to pinch every damn penny they could.

bers to deal with the day before. Altogether, we had about ten bands to manage, which meant fulfilling ten riders with a budget that barely scraped the surface.

I decided *Marilyn Manson* was going to get the top priority, with *The Offspring* right behind him. We weren't going to fulfill every single request—no festival ever does—but we'd knock out the big ones. The opening acts? They'd get the basic shit: water, beer, a bottle of booze, and a couple of random throw-ins.

Most of the time, opening bands were cool and knew what the deal was—be grateful for whatever you get, even if it's just water, beer, and some food vouchers. But once in a while, a band with a massive ego would show up, demanding to know why their rider wasn't 100% ful-filled[2].

My answer was always the same:

"Look, I hear ya, man. But we've got a tight budget. The headliner made some unexpected demands that ate up most of it. Not much left for the peasants… oops, I mean openers. But hey, if you ever headline, I'll make sure you get most, if not all, of your shit. You'll be the big shots then. You bring the people, you get the gold."

So with a bigger budget for *Manson* and *The Offspring*, I downloaded their riders and printed them out. *The Offspring's* rider was pretty stan-

---

2. **I always had a long-standing** argument with the Roxy staff about the natural hierarchies when it came to bands playing at the club. Nic and the upstairs office just didn't get the concept that if we tried to please every band equally, we'd end up pissing off the headliner. Why? Because we'd be pulling from the headliner's budget to make the openers happy—and that always went sideways. It was a goddamn conundrum.The "powers that be" at the Roxy were always on my ass, telling me to save money and cut corners because we were barely scraping by to keep the doors open. But since the office leaned "left" philosophically and wanted this equal, almost socialist approach to everything, the two instructions just didn't mix. If we actually applied socialist principles to our production policies, we'd have been out of business faster than you could blink.In the weekly meetings, I'd try to break it down using simple analogies to explain the importance of hierarchy when it came to band requests. I'd use the gold, silver, and bronze medal analogy—headliner gets gold, direct support gets silver, and all the other opening bands get bronze. Everyone's requests should be fulfilled in that order. The headliner was my main concern, and everyone else came second. Eventually, when the other bands (through their hard work) became headliners, we'd treat them accordingly—no bias, no bullshit. It might never happen, but if it did, we'd cross that bridge. It took about a year for them to get what I was saying.

dard for a headliner[3] —fairly reasonable. But *Manson's?* That shit was twenty pages long and included at least four grand worth of stuff. The amount of food he requested? I figured he must have an army rolling with him.

With a budget of only $800 for Manson, I had to get creative. He was going to have to deal with what we could scrape together.

Then came Manson's bizarre request. He didn't want to be in the usual backstage building—the one right next to the main stage. This was a strange ask, considering that same building had worked fine for bands like *Korn, Mötley Crüe, Smashing Pumpkins, Ozzy, Fergie,* and *Slash* in the past.

But Manson? He wanted three trailers set up outside, with two of them just for his personal use. The festival organizers scrambled to get them delivered the morning of the show.

I rolled up to *Sunset Blvd* around 5 a.m., had my crew help unload all the riders, and got started setting up the rooms. The stages were under construction, and I gotta say—it was a surreal feeling to see *Sunset* completely shut down. No traffic, just massive stages rising in the middle of the street.

I told the crew to cram all of Manson's food and drinks into his main trailer. *The Offspring* got the two big main rooms inside the building, and the openers were shoved into the smaller dressing rooms scattered throughout.

As we got closer to wrapping up the setup, Manson's crew started trickling in. Let me tell you, these guys looked like they'd just been through hell—tired, bitter, and worn out.

---

3. **The Offspring** were easy to work with. They had a massive entourage—about forty people—and it seemed like their main crew had brought along family members too. There were so many people in their camp they decided to set up shop right outside the building that housed all the backstage rooms. They rolled out foldable tables and chairs, creating a little command center on the sidewalk, with cables snaking back into the building to power everything. Their crew looked like a bunch of old-school surf/skate punks—the kind of guys who, even in their forties and fifties, were still "keeping it real." Ball caps, full sleeve tattoos, gear that screamed teenage rebellion... even though they were decades past the age of pulling it off. But hey, at least they were still living the life, right?

I remember thinking, *Damn, these people probably hate their jobs... and they probably hate working for Manson too.*

I made this assumption because every time I saw a gnarly, over-the-top rider, it usually meant the artist was a huge pain in the ass—or at least damn near impossible to please.

By this point, the trailers were all set up, packed with food and booze. And then, out of nowhere, Manson's hospitality manager runs up to me like she's on fire. She's in full panic mode, telling me,

"Manson won't step foot in his trailer unless it's completely black inside."

I was like, *"Wait... what? You mean he wants the whole thing painted black, windows blacked out?"*

She fires back, *"No, no, we can use cloth, but everything—including the ceiling and floor—needs to be black. Even the appliances."*

I just stood there. *"Holy shit, are you serious right now?"*

Apparently, she wasn't kidding. Manson was supposed to roll in about forty minutes.

I quickly called up my assistants, Molly and Jess, and told them to run to the craft store and buy up as much black fabric and tape as they could. Then, I told the rest of the crew to get ready to turn the trailers into a damn black hole. They all looked at me like I was messing with them.

Somehow, we managed to get those trailers completely blacked out, and they ended up looking like some creepy-ass gothic cave buried deep beneath the earth. I couldn't help but laugh—those trailers looked like a horror movie set, but I guess that was the vibe Manson was going for. We pulled it off in about thirty minutes, and luckily, Manson was running a little behind. Later on, I found out that on the last page of his rider, he had a specific request to have all his backstage areas "blacked out."

Manson finally showed up, and for the first thirty minutes, every-thing was calm. It was peaceful, like the calm before the storm. And then... I was right. I started hearing screaming coming from Manson's trailer. His assistant came storming out, frantic, running straight toward me and my crew. She blurts out, *"Manson's starving. He wants a huge order of sushi—and more strawberries."*

I told her, *"No problem,"* handed some cash to my crew girl Eva, and sent her off to grab the order.

Eva comes back a while later and tells me she needs more money than the $75 I gave her. I'm like, *What the hell? Isn't this order just for Manson?* She nods, but says the order was massive—$150.

I just stared at her. *Is he feeding an army or what?*

She tells me Manson gave her a very specific, very large order. I sighed and said, *"Fine, just get the sushi."* But in my head, I was thinking, *This guy must be starving—or maybe he just had an endless appetite.* Little did I know, it was on another level.

Even though the festival had already started letting people in, we were still a ways off from *The Offspring* and *Manson's* sets. It was still daylight, and as I was walking outside, checking on everything, my girl Molly runs up to me, completely out of breath.

She says, *"Manson needs more strawberries."*

I looked at her like, *"What the hell? We already got him two baskets!"*

She tells me his tour manager said Manson had been tossing them around whenever he was pissed off about something they did—or didn't—do.

I couldn't stop laughing. I told Molly, *"Go tell his tour manager to come talk to me."*

A few minutes later, the tour manager, a really friendly gal, walks up and tells me Manson had already gone through both baskets and had been pelting her and the crew with strawberries.

I just stood there shaking my head, telling her that was the funniest shit I'd ever heard. I asked her why they took that kind of abuse. She laughed it off, but there was this sheepish look in her eyes, like she knew it was fucked up but couldn't admit it. She thanked me for agreeing to get more strawberries.

I told her flat out, *"I don't want to hear about this strawberry bullshit again."* Then I called up Nandor and told him to go buy four baskets and bring them straight to her. And to hurry—because I could already picture Manson losing his shit if it took too long.

It was funny—Nandor brought the baskets to the tour manager, and as she was walking into Manson's trailer, all of a sudden the door flies open and out come strawberries, flying through the air. Manson's screaming, *"What the fuck took so fukin' long?"* She's zig-zagging like a ninja, ducking and dodging flying strawberries, and I yell, "Watch out—friendly strawberry fire incoming!"

She cracked a laugh, but you could tell she wasn't amused. As she got closer, I said, *"Well, you guys must be getting paid pretty well to take that kind of abuse."* She shot me a look that said: *We don't get paid shit, and I still don't know why I put up with this crap.*

I actually felt for her and her crew, because I knew exactly what it was like to work for tyrants. Hell, in the music biz there was always some Mussolini-type dickhead running around, flexing their power and torturing everyone in reach.

Oh well, I thought, *nothing I can do about it.*

An hour passed, and *Sunset Blvd* was packed with people. It was one hell of a sight—booths lined up down the middle of the street, businesses open, clubs rocking, and opening acts tearing it up on both the east and west stages. Everything was running smooth, all the bands seemed happy with their backstage setups and the limited hospitality we could throw together. I even came in right on budget, which was a big relief. No more requests. Or so I thought.

I was enjoying *Bad Religion* crushing the main stage when Nandor comes running up again, looking stressed out. He blurts, *"Manson wants two pizzas, chicken wings, and french fries."*

I looked at him like, *"How the hell can he want more food?"* I told him, *"Go grab the tour manager."*

She shows up, and I laid it out: *"We've already filled Manson's trailer with most of the shit from his rider—snacks, fruit, dips, desserts, sodas, beer, alcohol, all of it. And we just dropped $150 on sushi two hours ago.*

My view from the SSMF office...

I'm tapped out. Tell him we can't do
anymore."

About fifteen minutes later, she comes back with, *"Manson says if he doesn't get the pizza and everything else, he won't have the energy to perform."*

I knew it was just some power-trip bullshit, but I called the higher-ups and got the extra money approved. Once I had the green light, I sent Nandor to grab everything from *The Rainbow Bar & Grill.* I told him to haul ass because we had a pissed-off rockstar eating like a damn animal. Thirty minutes later, we had the food.

I gathered the crew and told them the whole strawberry and food saga. We all cracked up. I told them to take a break, do whatever the hell they wanted for a bit. We were already twelve hours deep.

As we finally got closer to Manson's set, guess what? Another fucking request for more strawberries. At that point, I'd had it. I told his tour manager flat out, *"No more. No money left in the budget, no more strawberries. If you guys want more, walk down to the grocery store and buy them yourselves."*

She looked like she was about to cry but finally relented. With a defeated look, she muttered that she'd figure it out.

Now it was finally time for Manson's headlining set. I saw him crawl out of his dark hole of a trailer, and it was clear this wasn't the same *Marilyn Manson* from years past. This was an out-of-his-prime dude, still caked in makeup, still rocking the long hair, but now carrying extra weight his tight vest could barely contain. The buttons looked ready to blow.

I couldn't help but imagine everything inside him—sushi, pizza, chicken wings, drinks, snacks, fries, strawberries—all trying to find their way out, held hostage for now by his massive gut. A gluttonous gothic cavern of a gut. My crew and I traded looks of shock and amusement.

Manson was only about a hundred feet from the stage, but of course, he requested one of our guys drive him there in a golf cart. His crew just walked, but not Manson. Nope. There he was, sitting alone in the back of a golf cart while everyone else hoofed it. He had a top hat on, his thinning hair flapping in the wind as he rolled past. He had the cart drop him right at the stairs leading to the stage.

The street was absolutely slammed, thousands of people buzzing for Manson's set. *The Offspring* had just wrapped about thirty minutes earlier, and man, they fucking killed it. They ripped through all their hits, and the crowd ate up every second. They might've been a little past their prime, but the energy didn't lie. The place was electric—people moving, screaming, singing along to every word Dexter belted out.

Now it was dark, and *Manson* finally stepped onto the stage. The lights exploded into an insane spectacle: a twisted mashup of cabaret, goth, and burlesque, with dancers, props, and a band that was tight as hell. They played to pre-recorded tracks, and honestly, that was probably the only thing saving him. It felt like the backing tracks were doing most of the heavy lifting.

But the crowd didn't care. They were eating it up, roaring after every song like they were witnessing some dark messiah. *Manson* leaned into it, launching into his trademark rants about life, religion, and every controversial topic he could spit out. You could feel the tension, the shock value, the vibe he built his whole career on.

It was a spectacle, no doubt about it. But standing there, watching from the side, I could see what most of the crowd couldn't. The edge wasn't sharp anymore. The chaos felt forced. It was more theater than danger now.

I was standing on the side of the stage with my crew, watching Manson give it his best shot. But halfway through the set, it became obvious: he was sweating like a beast and gasping for air. Then, all of a sudden, the vocal backing tracks started overpowering his *"live"* vocals. It was like watching someone's tank run dry. You could see the buttons on his vest straining, barely hold-ing on. I honestly couldn't understand why the hell he hadn't taken the vest off already. Those buttons were seconds away from snapping, and I couldn't help but imagine how embarrassing it would be if they did—exposing his big, pale gut for the world to see. A midsection that would finally escape, claiming its freedom once and for all. I cringed and laughed at the thought.

Somehow, Manson made it through the set, and with the audience screaming for more, he came stumbling off the stage, down the stairs, screaming for the golf cart. Luckily, two of the guys with the cart were just a few feet away, and they pulled up fast. Manson headed straight for the backseat, and when he collapsed into it, his friggin' buttons finally snapped and flew off, shooting out of the golf cart like they were on a mission[4] . His sweaty white shirt was exposed underneath, and his now liberated beer belly poked out for all to see. My crew and I looked at each other, desperately holding our mouths so we wouldn't burst out laughing in front of him.

As the golf cart guys drove him away, Manson had somehow lost his top hat. His balding head was now visible, with stringy, badly dyed hair flapping in the wind, like some old, dark, and weathered caricature riding off into the sunset. It was one of those images that sticks with you, and I still laugh every time I think about it.

When he finally disappeared into the trailer in the distance, the floodgates opened. We all started cracking up, swapping stories about the insanity of the day. Everyone was exhausted, and now we were all slap-happy from fatigue. We were done with the festival, and I told my crew they could have any of the leftover food or alcohol from the artists. I told them to indulge, that they had earned it. The crew was happy as hell, and I was grateful for all their hard work and discipline.

I let everyone head home, but I didn't leave the *Sunset Strip* until a few hours later at midnight, after everything was checked off and

---

4. **There were 3 buttons that popped**, and two of them went flying. After Manson left, I went looking for them and found one. I still have that button today, sitting in my home office memorabilia box. Every time I look at it, I get a good memory and a laugh. It's a tiny piece of history that always brings me back to that moment.

wrapped up. I'd been on my feet for about 18 hours straight and was only getting a flat fee of $750 for the entire day. My crew got $300 each. Seems like crumbs when you factor in what should've been overtime (which, of course, never came). But what really got to me—and what most people didn't realize, and the bigwigs in the music industry never addressed—was that all the people working behind the scenes, making sure the artists looked and felt amazing, *we got paid peanuts.*

Me and my handpicked crew waiting for our peanuts...

You've gotta love the hell out of working in music to accept that kind of pay. But, to be totally honest, and in defense of those who justify the low pay for the crews, the damn *Sunset Strip Music Festival* never made a profit in its five years before they pulled the plug. In fact, it always lost money, and the only people who actually made anything were the artists. Don't get me wrong, the artists definitely earned it after all their years of grinding, but I always noticed there wasn't any real trickle-down effect. In the end, we were just a bunch of monkeys doing the dirty work. While the artists and venue owners like the *Roxy* lived it up in places like Malibu with millions in the bank, the rest of us were fighting over the crumbs that fell out of their pockets.

I thought to myself again, *No wonder most of the crews I encountered looked so bitter and crabby. They never got fairly compensated for what they did, and the drinking and drugs they mostly did? Well, that just soothed the pain of it all.*

Wrapping it all up after a 21 hour day at SSMF...

NOTE: *In 2013, when I was backstage again for the* Sunset Strip Music Festival, *I saw the new Roxy production manager—the guy who had taken my place—standing outside the Roxy. I went up to talk to him. He was one of the guys who originally didn't understand my concepts, since he worked in the office and wasn't really in the trenches like I was. At the end of our conversation, he looked me straight in the eye and said,* "JD, man… I gotta admit something. You were right about everything you said years ago concerning production and protocol. I'm sorry we fought against you… we were totally wrong."

I smiled, shook his hand, and said, "Thank you, brother." *As I walked away, it felt damn good to finally be vindicated after all the years.*

Chapter 18

The Thin Line Between Confidence and Cruelty

There's something that stays with you after a night like that Manson show.

I'd worked with intense artists before—big egos, high needs, wild expectations. But this was different. Manson didn't just push limits; it felt like he enjoyed watching people fail to reach them. He came down hard on his crew in a way that, to me, felt personal. I saw seasoned pros—people who'd been in the trenches for years—tense up like scared kids backstage. It wasn't just darkly comedic. It was demoralizing. And it didn't feel like an act.

That night taught me a big lesson about power. *When you surround yourself with people too scared to push back, it's easy to start believing you're untouchable.* But that kind of control doesn't elevate you—it burns everything around you down. What I saw that night stuck with me. It reminded me exactly the kind of person I never wanted to become.

I wasn't working at the Roxy anymore by then, but I'd lived a decade inside those walls. I'd seen how fame could twist people, how fast things could slip, how thin the line was between confidence and cruelty. *The music industry doesn't teach you to be kind. It teaches you to survive.* But if you lose your decency in the process, what the hell are you surviving for?

I used to have keys to the upstairs—On The Rox. That place was never clean or safe, but it had its own kind of truth. Away from the stage lights, where the masks came off. Sometimes for the better. Sometimes not. That little upstairs club was my escape hatch, my backstage to the backstage. I laughed there. Partied there. Fell in love there. And I watched people fall apart there too.

Looking back, I know I lasted in this business because I knew when to lean in and when to walk away. I wasn't perfect—far from it. I took my share of hits. But I watched, I listened, and I learned.

The Manson night wasn't part of my Roxy era, but it brought that era into sharper focus. It reminded me why I'd made it out. Why I'd stayed steady when others didn't. And why I never forgot what it looked like when someone let the darkness win.

Because the truth is, it's not just the music biz that can break people. It's the silence in between—when the show ends and you're left alone with your own thoughts. That moment when you ask yourself: *Am I happy with who I really am? Not just who I think I'm supposed to be.*

As Joseph Conrad wrote in *Heart of Darkness:* "The mind of man is capable of anything—because everything is in it, all the past as well as all the future."

Only time will tell what's real.

What came next wasn't louder. It wasn't bigger. It was upstairs. And it was very, very real.

Welcome to On The Rox.

Chapter 19

ON THE ROX—We're on a Highway to Hell

"Some people make the choice to live fast and die young."

On The Rox, tucked upstairs above the Roxy, was almost more magical than the main room where the shows went down. Not quite, but close. It definitely had a vibe of its own.

Even in the 2000s, it still felt like an exclusive secret. You couldn't get in without a wristband or a backstage pass, and taking pictures was strictly forbidden. A few times, security caught people trying to sneak photos and would snatch their phone or camera and make them delete the evidence right then and there.

I actually managed to take quite a few pics up there, mainly because I was one of the bosses and also threw club nights for extra cash. I got *10% of the bar* when I ran those parties, and that was some solid side money (always paid in cash). I had my birthday up there more than once and would book the room for friends who wanted private parties or birthday blowouts. Drinks were always free for me, though I wasn't much of a drinker—*luckily.*

My 39th Bday party, 2009.

One time, early on when I was still stage manager at the Roxy, I gave an interview while also playing a gig with my band *Rumblefish.* In that interview, I casually mentioned how I was always upstairs at *On The Rox* after shows, getting free drinks and more. That didn't go over well. The manager of *On The Rox* lost it. He claimed Nic Adler had a strict policy that no one got free drinks up there. Because of my comment, he looked like a liar and a fool, and he marched straight to Nic.

When I had a sit-down with Nic, I just shrugged and said, "Well, too late—the interview's out. I didn't know about the policy." Nic just gave me this look, like I was *Bruce Willis in Die Hard*—always causing chaos, always somehow getting away with it. I knew I had that protective bubble around me. I was too good at my job to get canned, but I also knew exactly how far to push things. I'd get scolded, sure, but never seriously punished.

I actually met my first wife right outside *On The Rox.* She was an au pair from the Czech Republic, and I was out front hosting one of my club nights. She and her friend, also an au pair, were walking by with two dudes who looked completely out of their league. The girls looked like Russian catalogue models—blonde, blue-eyed—and I stopped them and said,

"Hey, all of you wanna come upstairs, dance, grab a drink?"

They said yes, and I followed up with, *"Are you gals like Russian models or something?"*

They both looked instantly pissed. *"We're not fucking Russian—we're Czech!"* they snapped. I laughed and said I meant it as a compliment, and their looks reminded me of pretty Russians. They relaxed and started laughing. I waved them in.

Later that night, I found out they worked in Hermosa Beach. They were new to California and had never been to Hollywood. The guys they were with? My ex told me one of them was a *DirecTV* tech who invited them out for the night. I laughed and said those guys were way out of their league. They cracked up and admitted they thought the same thing, but no one else had asked them out, so they rolled with it.

I ended up getting both their numbers and invited them to see my band play at the *Whisky.* Our after-party was, of course, upstairs at *On The Rox.* They came with a whole crew of Czech friends—all gorgeous, all au pairs. My ex and I hit it off that night, and yeah, the rest is history.

Back in the day—the real-deal 1970s—the place was another level of exclusive. The upstairs was a private den for Hollywood's elite: *Jack Nicholson, Warren Beatty, Bowie, Elton John, Keith Moon.* Every major band from the era passed through there to drink, party, and disappear behind closed doors.

There was a small, hidden office near the bathrooms with a short, wide door. Everyone called it *The Nicholson Room.* Legend had it Jack used that little cave as his personal spot to do coke, drink, and hook up. I can confirm: the room was real. It had this dark, moody glow from deep blue lights, a couch that folded into a bed, a small upright piano, and just enough chairs to get shady. I know for a fact a lot of people got wild in there. *We'll get into that part later.*

One of the most infamous stories tied to *On The Rox* was the night *John Belushi* partied there before his death. He had been at *The Roxy* for a show and then went upstairs to *On The Rox,* partying until about 1:30 a.m. He was with *Cathy Smith,* who years later admitted she fed him drugs and gave him the fatal injection back at the *Chateau Marmont.*

Witnesses later said they saw Belushi doing cocaine and heroin—speedballing—and that he looked sweaty and out of control. One witness, who confided in me during my time working there (and who'll stay anonymous), said Belushi actually started to overdose in the club. A couple of people carried him out of the bathroom and down the stairs into Cathy's Mercedes. From there, they drove to the Chateau. The valet helped him into his bungalow, where Cathy gave him the final, fatal hit. She ended up serving about fifteen months for involuntary manslaughter.

I remember one of the Adlers (not Lou, but another family member) once joked it was too bad Belushi hadn't died at *On The Rox*—because then it would've been *legendary,* like *River Phoenix* at *The Viper Room.* I always thought, *maybe.* But if that had happened, the place would probably be overrun with tourists trying to snap selfies where Belushi died. So maybe it's for the best it happened at the Chateau.

The '80s brought full-on craziness with the glam and hair metal scene. Stories I heard from old staff painted a picture of people openly doing coke on tables, cutting lines right on the bar. People had sex in the bathrooms all the time. Security tossed folks out constantly for being too wasted, too loud, or too wild.

I also heard *Guns N' Roses* used to sneak booze up from *The Rainbow* and get hammered in the booths till 2 a.m.—sometimes even until 3. *Axl* reportedly got kicked out once for threatening a Roxy security guard.

There were plenty of drug deals in the *Nicholson Room*. Producers lured girls in under the promise of introductions or access—sometimes in exchange for "favors."

I had a key to that room but didn't like people seeing me go in there with a girl. One time, after a brutal fourteen-hour shift, I used the room to crash for a quick nap. I moved a big piece of furniture and noticed a tiny door behind it—low and narrow, like something out of a fantasy film.

Out of curiosity, I opened it. It led straight into the attic of *The Roxy*. I crawled through into darkness—broken furniture, random junk, old memorabilia scattered everywhere. I used my phone as a flashlight and eventually found a hidden switch. When I flipped it, the attic lit up. I found all kinds of old stuff and used a lot of it to decorate the backstage.

From then on, that attic route became my *secret passage*. This was before my first wife—when I was still dating different girls. I'd invite one to a show, and if things went well, we'd sneak up through the DJ booth, into the attic, and across to the Willow door. I kept it unlocked from then on. We'd crawl through and end up in the *Nicholson Room*. Perfect hookup spot.

I only got caught once.

One night, I was in the room with a girl I was seeing. We were getting frisky. She was on top of me when, out of nowhere, I heard a key slide into the lock. The door flew open.

The *On The Rox* manager, Rizzle, had shown up forty-five minutes earlier than expected.

He froze in the doorway and said, *"Oh shit—what are you doing, man? This isn't a brothel."* Then he cracked up and slammed the door shut.

My girl didn't even flinch. She just kept going—probably tipsy enough to think the whole thing was part of the sex, drugs, and rock 'n' roll lifestyle.

Yeah, I was a little embarrassed. Word got around. A few waitresses started teasing me, saying things like, *"Hey, I heard you were honoring the spirit of the Nicholson Room,"* then doing the naughty finger wiggle as they laughed and mock-scolded me.

All in the name of some dark fun.

One time, during my *Highway to Hell* club night, we had a totally packed house, and *Jack Osbourne* showed up—as he often did. *On The Rox* was strictly twenty-one and up, but Jack was a regular. We all knew him, and he was always a cool kid. He'd sneak drinks sometimes, but the waitresses never served him.

I never really understood why *Ozzy and Sharon* let him roam around there on his own, but they lived close to *The Roxy* and we always made sure he was safe and stayed out of serious trouble.

He usually came to my night, and on this one occasion, we closed late—around 3 a.m. Eventually, we cleared everyone out. But *Jack,* who had just turned eighteen, the *On The Rox* manager *DT,* and a girl named *Angelina* stayed behind.

I'd gone downstairs to grab a few things and realized I'd left my jacket upstairs. Around 3:30 a.m., I headed back up. As I crept up the stairs, I heard kissing and moaning. I slowed my steps, rounded the corner, and peeked up where I could see the bar, dance floor, and stage. The DJ booth had a big plexiglass window that overlooked the room.

To my total shock—there they were, in the DJ booth. From my angle, it looked like Jack and DT were both going at it with Angelina. Her pants were down while standing; Jack, who had just barely turned eighteen, was on his knees going down on her. Angelina, who was twenty-six, stood flushed and laughing, while DT, who was thirty, was behind her, sucking on her boob. She was moaning like she didn't care who heard.

I froze in disbelief. This was the same girl who played the *good-girl act*—the one who didn't do drugs, who worked retail, who told me she didn't *"go there."* What I was watching looked straight out of a porno.

None of it fit the image I had of her—or of them. Maybe I was even a little envious. But I kept it to myself, walked back down quietly, and never told them what I saw.

It cracked me up later, because she kept that wholesome image—even on *The Osbournes.* Luckily for her, *Sharon* never found out, or that storyline could've gone nuclear. I stayed loyal and kept my mouth shut.

Side note: Angelina once told me that *Kevin Costner* hit on her. She said she went to his house, thinking he'd be interested in helping her acting career, but instead he poured her a drink and said, *"So what do kids your age do to get crazy? We can definitely make any crazy stuff happen here."* She told me she was offended and bailed.

I only know her side of it, but she even showed me a selfie of the two of them at what looked like his house.

She definitely had me fooled with that whole *"good girl"* act.

Now, an even crazier night happened on a late Saturday up at *On The Rox.* We had a huge show, packed downstairs, and some cute girls rolled in—one in particular was this little blonde who was already buzzed when she arrived. She came backstage where I was posted up near the stage and said, *"Hey there, my name is Daria and I want to have a great time tonight. Will you let me backstage?"*

I looked over at my security guy, and we both told her no one was allowed back there yet since the band was still playing. She sighed and said she'd be back.

An hour later, she returned—now clearly drunk. She threw her arms around me and even tried to kiss me. When I pulled away, she turned and grabbed my security guy's junk and said, *"I'm horny."* I told her to come back at the end of the set and I'd let her check out backstage. I was sure there'd be some appreciative people back there.

The band wrapped up, she came back, and I let her in—telling her to have fun but don't go too nuts. About forty-five minutes later, she came back down slurring, saying everyone up there was boring and didn't know how to party. I laughed and told her to head to the afterparty at *On The Rox*—it'd be more her scene.

She was cute, so I figured she'd be fine with her friends. I walked her and her two girlfriends to the inside entrance of *On The Rox* and let them go up. Around 2 a.m., after finishing up my work, I went upstairs to check things out. She was hanging with some of our security guards. I asked where her friends went, and she said they ditched her. *Jose,* one of my security guys, was giving her a ride home. Cool. Sounded safe enough.

But something didn't sit right. Around 2:30 a.m., I went back up to check again. *On The Rox* was officially closed at that point.

As I reached the top of the stairs, I saw something straight out of a porno. There she was, surrounded by three of my security guards. One was getting oral while the other two were in her hands. I burst out laughing.

"What the hell are you doing?" I said.

The guys just looked at me and shrugged. *"She insisted,"* one of them said.

I asked her, *"You really want to be doing this?"*

She pulled back, slurring, *"This is exactly what I was looking for… just having fun."*

Joey, one of the guards, grinned and said, *"Dude, come join the fun."*

I shook my head. *"Nah, not my thing… too weird. You guys do your thing."*

I asked who was taking her home. My guy *Jose* raised his hand. *"Me."* I told them to lock up when they were done and went back downstairs.

I never told a soul. Not the office staff, not anyone. They probably all would've been fired.

I've seen some shit. Staff hooking up, drinking, doing drugs—I never snitched. Don't know why exactly. Maybe I just didn't want to be that guy. It was rock and roll, and I figured I'd gain more respect by staying quiet.

And I did. The security crew trusted me. I always wondered if I should've been stricter, but I knew *loose lips sink ships.* Keeping my mouth shut helped me survive in the music biz for decades.

I guess I was just playing a long game of *Survivor.* And I never got voted off the island.

For quite a few years, *On The Rox* was one of my favorite playgrounds. I met and dated women there. I met my first wife there. I threw birthday parties, hosted club nights for extra cash, honed my skills as a DJ. I did interviews, band photoshoots, meetings. It was like a second home.

Having the keys felt like access to a *secret kingdom.* And yeah, I took full advantage of it.

But I was lucky. I didn't drink much, and I never got into drugs. That might've been the one thing that kept me sane around all the chaos. That's probably why I lasted so long—because I never fully surrendered to the dark energy that came with the fun.

There was a manager after DT named *Jeff,* who took over for a while. He wasn't so lucky. I saw him living fast and loud, and one day he was just… gone. Overdose. Just like that.

And he wasn't the only one. Plenty of people got swallowed up by the lifestyle. I'm sure more than a few alcoholics were made upstairs at *On The Rox.* Because the thing about those good times—they don't last forever.

Some people make the choice to *live fast and die young.* Others don't make a choice at all—they just get caught in the current. For some, it's a brief explosion of energy. For others, like me, survival means adapting—riding it out, learning what to take in and what to leave behind, and eventually finding the door out.

On The Rox was part of that wild ride. A place where I lived, created, and sometimes barely dodged the fallout.

If there's any lesson in it, it's this:

Sometimes just surviving is its own form of rebellion.

And I guess I always had my own brand of rebellion—that stubborn streak that kept me alive.

As Hemingway wrote in *A Farewell to Arms*: *"The world breaks everyone, and afterward, some are strong at the broken places."*

Chapter 20

The End of the Road...

My final show with my last band, Sound of the Struggle...

Remember when I told you back in the intro that we'd circle back to the long road and see where it all really ended? Well, you made it through the madness, the chaos, the laughs, and the heartbreak. Now the wait's over. Here it is—raw truth, no filter, reality in all its messed-up glory.

After the collapse of Rumblefish, me, Possum, and a new bassist named JMac decided to drag an old project out of the shadows—a band we'd once started but never fully launched. I gave it the name it deserved: *Sound of the Struggle.*

This time there was no gimmick, no filler. No DJs. No rappers. Just stripped-down, straight-ahead rock and roll. Full-on riffs, pounding grooves, and raw energy. *Imagine AC/DC colliding head-on with that early-2000s heaviness—you could feel it in your chest.*

We pulled *Rob A.* from *Hot Sauce Johnson* back on guitar and added a wild card: *Sheldon T.* A high-octane frontman who'd fronted *Quiet Riot* for a minute and tore it up with *Adler's Appetite* from *G&R.* The guy had the look, the pipes, and the stage command to back it up. He was almost a decade younger than the rest of us, but that just meant he brought the reckless energy we were missing. He was a live wire—and exactly what we needed.

Our first show? Opening for *Metal Skool (Steel Panther)* at *The Roxy.*

It was wall-to-wall, shoulder-to-shoulder insanity. The crowd was lit—girls flashing, dudes howling, beer flying everywhere—and we fucking delivered. Tight. Loud. Fast. No gimmicks, no fluff. Just raw rock and sweat.

After the set, *Cisco Adler* (my boss *Nic's* brother, a successful producer at the time with *Shwayze* and *Mickey Avalon,* and the guy who'd once run through half of Hollywood's socialite royalty—*Paris Hilton, Mischa*

Barton, Rod Stewart's daughter Kimberly) comes up to us hyped as hell. He kept saying,

"You guys are my favorite band right now. When can I produce you guys?"

We believed him. Hell, we *wanted* to believe him.

We started opening for *Steel Panther* on a few different Mondays during their infamous *Roxy* residency. My longtime friend and booking icon, *Dayle Gloria,* was running the shows, and she knew how to stack a bill. She always gave us the sweet spot—the slot that set the fuse for the night and got the party lit.

It felt like the dream was back—even though it was 2010 and I was forty years old, long past my so-called prime. *But fuck it—we were playing to packed houses again.* That old surge was back in my veins. For a moment, I thought *maybe this was it.* The redemption arc. *Maybe Sound of the Struggle was the band that would finally shatter my twenty-plus-year glass ceiling.*

And then came the night.

We were booked again to open for *Steel Panther* at the *Key Club*—their big launch show at that venue after they'd bailed on the *Roxy* over money disputes. The energy was through the roof. I invited everyone I knew. And when we hit the stage, the place blew up. Lights out, intro roll, and then *BOOM*—we exploded into our opening track.

It felt incredible. I was moving, strutting, pretending I was still twenty-five. Sweating, yelling, leaning into the crowd, ripping through solos like I still had the fire. And afterward? One of the girls I was dating after my divorce, *Elizabetha,* dragged me out to her car and… let's just say the rockstar fantasy carried on. I thought to myself, *Hell yeah. I still got it.*

The next day, I called *Possum* to see if he had the video recording of the show. He said, *"Dude… yeah. You need to see this."*

I popped in the DVD, ready to relive the glory.

And then—*boom.* Gut punch. Reality check.

There I was on screen… bloated, red-faced, my guitar playing sloppy, my backup vocals flat. I didn't look like a rockstar. I looked like a chubby, burned-out *Jerry Garcia* impersonator at some dive bar, trying to relive a dream that wasn't mine anymore.

The crowd? Yeah, they were screaming—but they would've screamed for anything. They were drunk. They were there to party. *I wasn't killing it. I was clinging to it.*

Right then and there, I knew: *this was my last show.*

I called *Possum.* Told him I was done performing live. Told the band it wasn't them—it was me. And I meant it.

And that was it—the last shot, the final chord. The dream I'd been chasing since I was eleven finally flatlined.

After that final *Sound of the Struggle* show at the *Key Club*—after seeing the footage and facing the truth—I realized it wasn't just the stage I was finished with. I was burned out on the whole damn grind. The late nights, the endless hustle, the constant fight for scraps.

I wasn't just closing the curtain on being a front-line player. *I was done with the shadows backstage too.*

The last show...Time to hang it up.

Months after that night, *Nic* called me into his office. He had a serious look in his eyes, the kind that told me this wasn't just another routine conversation. Then he said something I'll never forget:

"You're way too smart for this job now. I can see you're burnt out. Do you think you've been here too long?"

I looked him straight in the eye and said, *"Yes. I'm ready for the next chapter of my life."*

And I was right. I'd been on that stage and behind it—promoting, producing, trudging, and trying to survive in a business that could lift you up one day and chew you up the next.

Out of respect and gratitude to *Nic* and his dad *Lou,* I stayed for a few more months to help with the transition—trained the new staff, passed along what I knew, and made sure the place didn't collapse the second I walked out. I didn't want to just vanish. I had too much respect for that room. For what it meant to me.

When I finally stepped away, it felt surreal. *Like closing a chapter in a book I didn't think would ever end.*

But my book wasn't done yet.

A few months later, *Nic* called me again. He wanted me back—for one last gig. Not as a performer, but as the guy who knew how to run shit when everything was on fire.

He asked me to take charge of backstage for the *Sunset Strip Music Festival—SSMF.*

I had already worked *SSMF* in 2008, 2009, and 2010, running the entire backstage. It was a beast of a job—long hours, managing egos, making sure everything ran smooth while everything around me tried to fall apart. But I loved it in a strange way. It reminded me of the same chaotic energy that first pulled me into this world.

So when *Nic Adler* called in 2011, asking me to come back one more time, I couldn't say no.

That festival reminded me *why I stayed in the business for so long.* But it also showed me *the burnout. The years lost. The toll.* Yet at the same time—*the love. The glory. The insane, unforgettable ride.*

And as it all finally came to an end, I realized something: *it's better to regret something you have done than to regret something you haven't.* That mindset gave me some peace. But deep down, I still couldn't shake the sadness—the weight of knowing I gave it everything I had to make it in music, and still fell short. Mistakes and all.

But for some reason—and I'm still not sure why—that damn *Benjamin Button* quote came flooding back:

"You can be as mad as a mad dog at the way things went, you can swear and curse the fates, but in the end, you have to let go."

And maybe that was the final lesson. *Letting go doesn't mean you quit. It means you survived. It means you lived.*

Acknowledgments

To my family: My mom, Becky Crystal — may my love be the brush-stroke that follows you on your eternal journey. Love never dies...You'll forever be the original *Lost Picasso.* My dad, Rick DeCosta (RIP), who loved me without condition and shared his wisdom even when I hadn't earned it. My little brother, David Crystal. My stepdad, Artie (RIP), who always championed me. My stepbrother, Ryan Crystal and my niece Katie, and all the other Crystal family members. My cousins Jared and Darin, my sister Jody and her husband Big Adam, cousin Helena, Stacie and Dana, Uncle Ed, Aunt Elyn, Randy & Gavin, and all the Milmeister's/Weinstein's/Miller's—my blood till the end. My uncle and aunt, Greg Sr. and Grace Olmeda; Big John and Dana; and Greggie Jr. (RIP... you are missed). Cousin Andy Olmeda and Jonathan. My stepbrother Mickey Kopanski. The Deportos/Doportos, the DeCostas, and the Acostas (Justin & family)—and to all the family no longer with us, like my stepmom Cathy and my stepsister Christie (RIP). My birth mom, Rosie Rendon (RIP), and my birth dad, Dennis Milmeister (RIP). My great-uncle Nate Milmeister and Grandpa Milt (RIP). To Laura and Mark Chenelia for their love of Steven (Lil' Stevie) Chenelia and Erin Chenelia.

To my beautiful Jersey Dragon, Stacy—who cured me with her beauty, love, empathy, and amazing healthy food—and to her family: Antonio "Skatonio" Kaplan, who gave me the idea to make this book more personal; Elise; Abi (Abs); Kallister "Kahlan" Grumby & Joey Thunders; Tyler & Darcy; and Aunt Donna & Joe.

To my brothers, bandmates, crew and management in *Hot Sauce Johnson, Rumblefish, Ku De Tah, Mind Heavy Mustard, Sound of the Struggle,* and all my other bands and musicians I played with growing up—Possum Hill, Rob Asuncion, Gino & Nick Garofalo, Don Calhoun, Ireesh Lal, DJ None Carrillo, Noah Lerner (thx for the "red" idea), Gary

Giss, Davi Rivas, Aaron Abelt, Sun Sannes (RIP), Jorgen Gilcrease, Sean Zaghi, Robert Kavian, Mark Ruvelson, Rob Pehrson (RIP), Chris Cano, Tim Baca, Christian Oronoz (RIP), Tim Geigis, Greg Priest (RIP), Todd Beattie, Mike Ryan, Dom Poniac (RIP), DJ Jay Byrd, Dungis (MIA), Sheldon Tarsha, JMAC John McLaughlin, Tarver Marsh, Tony Henderson (RIP), Jonathan Brightman, Mike Magaña, Mike Crowley, Jason Cruanus, and too many others to name.

To Kevin Estrada and his family, a real living legend—thank you for signing my band, going to bat for us, and writing my foreword.

To Jeff "Uncle Jeff" Rogers and his most wonderful wife, Cathy, who always inspire me to stay positive in life.

To my old and new friends: Wilfred "Wilfeis" Williams (*Dr. Wilfred's Space Cookies* at the Escobar Mansion), Stefan "French Pickler," Raudel Barba (*Coach Don Quixote*), John Feehan, Skip Sorich, Mike Fusek, Todd Nagler tha Bagler, Ashley Fickel (counsel), Brett & Tiffany Blumstein, Rick "Likky" Bruner, Brett & Alyssa Trebil, Tom Spring, Wes Heim, Monica Wiesener, Andy Tibbits, Rusty Rayburn, Lisa Gauff, and old friends from Brentwood, Malibu, the San Fernando Valley, and San Diego... too many to list but you know who you are.

To all my Pickleball and Tennis buddies everywhere—you know who you are...too many to name here. Thanks to Steve "Ultimate Tennis" Oliver, Adam Young, Shawn Walker & The Pickleball Club of Carlsbad, Nancy "Nucky" and Brian Blasquez, Scott Mortensen, Scotty Maga Lyman, Adriana Tomazelli, Lion Mane Alex Meier†, Pip Parker Webster, Lobmed, Buddy Falor, Jimbo Watkins (St. Pete League Champ), Easton & Dylan, Stephen E. (*XRP Baby*) & Zballer. Plus, Loague, The Goot & the whole Bardy Party Crew.

Thanks to Leslie Simon for hiring me at Mancini's, and Dave Politti for giving me a job at the Cobalt. Also, Keith Durr, for bringing me into the live music scene and club promotion.

To all the people who spent time with me and/or helped me on my musical and/or life journey—Heather Oblon & Flubba Martinez, Suzy Geers, Jill Augusto, Adrian Vallera, Tina & Jimmy Truxal, Tom Spring, Susie Capetillo, Kelly Alires, Jen & Damian Rinaldi, Jamie Tate,

Lisa Strum-Sweetingham, Erin Duffy (up near Salinas), Carolynne Jones, Gina Bell, Dr. Lucy Turek (thx for the guitar idea!), Mike Wilson, Leah Di-Bonaventura, Jennifer Fong, Jennifer Powers (Lil Sis), Heather Morales, Jacqueline Lavian, Kirsty Lingman, Susan V. Hill, Dr. Nancy Hornstein, Connie Polentz-Klein, Dr. Renato Monaco, Dr. Bejamin DeVries, Michael "Commander" Haupt, Stephanie & Wolf (Rock n Roll) and many more.

Thank you to those who helped me in one way or another: Mirka P., Julie Ward aka Julez Bryant and her team and family—Gia, Myles "Doey," Brian and Ghostrider(RIP) + Jen & Michael Limber(I learned a lot from you) Thank you for being a part of my life. Big Erik Voake. Noah and Angie Newman. Philippe Rodrigue (my YouTube video). Lauren Plutsky. Kirsty Lingman. Laura Glick Meyer. Chris Echevarria. Josh Lambert. Rich Heyn & Dave Aguilera.

To the *Roxy* crew from 2001–2010, and especially Nic and Lou Adler. To the *Whisky* and Mikey Jr. of *M Productions,* who gave me a job in the beginning—along with his great dad, Mikael Maglieri, and his grandpa Mario (RIP). And to everyone backstage who lived this circus with me.

To the music business that gave me a shot at the grail: *Outpost/Geffen, Noise Records,* and *Roadrunner/Island Def Jam.*

To everyone who helped me on the music road: Carla Cummings, Cynthia Brotman & Vicki Blake, Dan "Pothole" Canamar, Dayle Gloria the Icon, Dr. Evil aka Eddie Oertell, Eric Talledo the OG street teamer (Yo Kid!), Kathie Merritt, Luke Iblings (*M Prod.*), Maggie Wang, Maria Gonzales, Michelle Abriem, Mike Taft (Ibanez), Mikey Doling & Sonny Kronix (Down Pick), Monte Conner, Nancy Byron, Pam "Spam" Allen, Ro Kohli, Robert Hayes, Shelly Brown, Tairrie B., Vinny Kostiw, Nikki Sweet, Scott Reifman, and all the others in Hollywood who helped me on the bumpy road to stardom.

To the *Roxy* crew—the bartenders, stagehands, security, ticket girls, and every poor bastard stuck in the fire with me—you know who you are. We lived ten lifetimes in that building. But let's not forget all my crews: Bolle Gregmar (RIP), Darren "Jenk" Jenkins, TJ McDonnell, Frankie O'Reilly, Lee Mayoux, Nacho, Jason Westbrook, Kenny Crayton, Ryan "Rizzle" Stuber, Molly Gibney, Lizzy Sherman, Molly Sims, Eva & Nandor Izing, Julio Maldonado, Leonard Contreras, and Erin Funk Brenner.

To the artists who gave me their best and their worst when I tried to stage or production manage them—and to all the hundreds of hard-working bands I shared the stage with over a 25-year period.

And finally, to all the artists and musicians who never quite reached the holy grail of their journey—you are not alone.

About the Author

Jason "JD" DeCosta grew up in Malibu and Brentwood, California, and spent nearly two decades at the heart of Hollywood's music scene. From 1993 to 2011, he worked every angle of Sunset Strip nightlife, rising from hospitality manager to general manager at the world-famous Roxy Theatre, Whisky a Go Go, and the Viper Room. He also lived the other side of the dream, signing major-label deals with his bands Hot Sauce Johnson (Outpost/Geffen, 1999) and Rumblefish (Island/Def Jam, 2002). That dual perspective—artist on stage and manager behind the curtain—gave him a rare insider's view of rock and roll's chaos, glory, and heartbreak.

After Hollywood, JD reinvented himself. He launched a marketing company called Jack Brando Media, served as Director of Marketing for the famed jewelry brand Julez Bryant, built a tennis coaching business, and helped expand the reach of Aceing Autism, bringing tennis to children on the spectrum. He later found success as a real estate investor, while also competing as a senior pro pickleball player.

Today, JD is semi-retired, traveling the world and calling St. Petersburg, Florida home with his wife and their two black lab hounds, Romeo and Figaro.